Build Your Own Wi-Fi Network

About the Author

Shelly Brisbin is the author of nine books, including two editions of *Mac Answers: Certified Tech Support* (McGraw-Hill/Osborne) and *Adobe GoLive 6 Visual QuickStart Guide for Windows and Macintosh* (Peachpit Press). She has written about technology for 15 years, specializing in networking, the Internet, and the Macintosh. The hundreds of magazine articles she has written have appeared in *Macworld*, *MacWeek*, *The Net*, *New Media*, *Sun World*, *WebTechniques*, and many others. She served as Networking Editor at *MacUser Magazine* and has held editorial positions with technology-related publications and companies. Shelly did her time in the dotcom bubble, successfully extricating herself before it burst. She has also worked as a system administrator and a consultant. Her worst job, at the age of 16, was handing out brochures in a grocery store for the Texas Department of Agriculture. Shelly lives in Austin, Texas, with her husband and several animals. In her spare time, she runs a music-related mailing list and Web site.

About the Contributing Author/Tech Reviewer

Glen Carty, CCIE and author of *Broadband Networking*, McGraw Hill/Osborne (Glen wrote Chapter 10, "Security" and provided a technical review of this book), has been designing and building local and wide area networking solutions since the early 1980s. He is also a contributing author to the book *Troubleshooting, Maintaining, and Repairing Networks* (McGraw-Hill/Osborne) by Stephen Bigelow. As a senior manager with IBM, he was responsible for global design and design standards for the networking solutions offered by IBM Global Network.

Build Your Own Wi-Fi Network

Shelly Brisbin
with Glen Carty

McGraw-Hill/Osborne

New York   Chicago   San Francisco   Lisbon   London   Madrid   Mexico City
Milan   New Delhi   San Juan   Seoul   Singapore   Sydney   Toronto

The McGraw·Hill Companies

McGraw-Hill/Osborne
2600 Tenth Street
Berkeley, California 94710
U.S.A.

To arrange bulk purchase discounts for sales promotions, premiums, or fund-raisers, please contact **McGraw-Hill/Osborne** at the above address. For information on translations or book distributors outside the U.S.A., please see the International Contact Information page immediately following the index of this book.

Build Your Own Wi-Fi Network

1234567890 QPD QPD 0198765432

ISBN 0-07-222624-2

Publisher
Brandon A. Nordin

Vice President & Associate Publisher
Scott Rogers

Editorial Director
Tracy Dunkelberger

Associate Acquisitions Editor
Lisa McClain

Project Editor
Jenn Tust

Technical Editor
Glen Carty

Copy Editor
Marcia Baker

Proofreader
Marian Selig

Indexer
Jack Lewis

Computer Designer
Michelle Galicia

Illustrators
Michael Mueller
Melinda Moore Lytle

This book was composed with Corel VENTURA™ Publisher.

*This book is dedicated to the memory of Bill Peete (1951–2002).
Those who were fortunate enough to know Bill will always
remember his enthusiasm and the spirit of joy and
adventure with which he lived his life.
I miss you, Bill.*

Contents at a Glance

Contents

Acknowledgments

I would like to thank the many people who helped make this book possible:

The team at Osborne, including Lisa McClain, Tracy Dunkelberger, and Jenn Tust, has made this project a pleasure. They're a talented group of folks who shared my desire to make this a successful project.

Several wi-fi equipment vendors helped enormously with technical information and equipment loans. Special thanks go to Diana Ying of Linksys, who provided several access points and network adapters, along with product images. Thanks also to Mark Shapiro of Agere Systems. I also worked with equipment from NetGear, D-Link, and Zoom.

Thanks to Jennifer Berger and Jill Roter at *Macworld Magazine*, who have assigned me to write several wi-fi articles, giving me access to a whole lot of equipment even before this book project began.

Thanks to my friends Chris Breen, Bert Hayes, and George Wyche, who answered random questions for me whenever I asked.

Several enlightened businesses in Austin, Texas, where I live, provide free access to a wireless network and to the Internet. The best of these is Flightpath Café, where a substantial portion of this book was written.

Thanks to everyone there who kept the coffee brewing and chose cool music for the stereo.

My husband, Frank lent his usual quiet support during the frenetic development of this book. He also helped with equipment and network testing, as well as general inspiration. It was Frank who sparked my interest in wireless technology when he brought home an access point a couple of years ago. Thanks, sweetie.

Introduction

Welcome to *Build Your Own Wi-Fi Network*, a guide for anyone who wants to use wireless technology to share Internet access, exchange files, or establish a cable-free computing environment. This book introduces you to today's most popular and affordable wireless technology, IEEE 802.11, also known as wi-fi. The goal of this book is to teach you how to buy, build, and maintain a wireless network. What you learn will enable you to create a new wi-fi network for your home or office or to expand an existing wired network to support wireless access. Through straightforward explanations of the technical aspects of wi-fi, step-by-step instructions for installing and configuring equipment, and practical advice on setting up and using your network, the book takes you from wi-fi novice to free-roaming mobile computer user in 13 chapters.

The first step in working with wi-fi is learning a basic understanding of the technology behind it. In Chapter 1, I explain wireless networking in general and how wi-fi compares to other technologies. Next, Chapter 2 explores the nitty-gritty details of how wi-fi works and how knowing these details will help you build a network that takes advantage of the technology. Chapters 3 through 6 concentrate on wi-fi equipment and services, showing you how to buy the right access point, network adapter, antenna, software, and Internet service for your needs. You'll learn about product features and how to determine which ones you need and which ones you can do without.

Chapters 7, 8, and 9 show you how to set up wi-fi equipment and networks, using popular devices as examples. You go step-by-step through the process of setting up an access point, network adapters, and ad-hoc wi-fi networks. You'll learn to set up wi-fi devices under Windows, Mac OS, and Linux operating systems, giving you a breadth of information that's usually missing from wi-fi equipment documentation.

Chapter 10 takes on the hot topic of wi-fi security. Because wireless communication occurs in the air, it's more susceptible to eavesdropping than other types of network transmission. In addition, security problems associated with wi-fi's built-in security features have caused many to fear for the integrity of their networks. In this chapter, you learn to evaluate and plug security loopholes in wi-fi.

When you're ready to use the wi-fi network you've built, Chapter 11 will introduce you to some applications that are used on all kinds of networks as well as to the implications of going wireless.

Finally, take an advanced course in building your own wi-fi network. Chapters 12 and 13 deal with issues faced by those who want to plan and build large networks, including access point placement, radio interference characteristics, the use of multiple access points, and wi-fi network analysis.

For your reference, I've added two appendices—a glossary of terms and a whole lot of links to wireless resources on the Internet.

Chapter 1

The Wireless Revolution

Rarely does a new technology sweep both the consumer and business markets as quickly as wireless networking has in the past few years. Families, coffee shop owners, small businesspeople, airport operators, and large companies have all gone wireless. This gives web surfers, telecommuters, and travelers unprecedented freedom to stay connected, even beyond the boundaries of conventional wired networks that tie people to their desks as they exchange information with colleagues or surf the Internet. Because you're reading this book, I assume you're eager to build your own wireless network or, at least, you're curious about how to do it. In this chapter, I begin the journey by introducing you to the benefits and applications of wireless networking, as well as to some of the leading wireless technologies in use today. Although the rest of this book focuses on one wireless technology called wireless fidelity (wi-fi) or IEEE 802.11, it's important for you to understand where wi-fi fits into the overall landscape of wireless communication.

Let's be clear about what the term "wireless network" means. At its most basic, a *wireless network* is one in which you can communicate with other computers from your own computer without being connected to anything with wires. This means you don't need a modem, an Ethernet cable, or any of the other tethers that normally prevent you from taking your laptop into the back yard, the retail floor, or the middle of a classroom. This book is about unplugging the wires without losing your connection to the outside world.

Why Wireless Networks Are Cool

Wireless networks are cool both because of the characteristics of the networks themselves and the ways these networks can be used to bring a new type of communication to places where it didn't exist before. The benefits of wireless are available to both home users and folks who want to use them as part of a business. Either way, wireless becomes most compelling in situations where building or adding to a wired network would be difficult or extremely expensive.

In many homes, a wireless network will be the first network ever installed. Although many of you have two or more computers, the idea of linking them might never have occurred to you because the benefits of a network might not be obvious. All the benefits of a wired network are available from a wireless one, and setting up a network without cables is often simpler.

Mobility

The most obvious benefit of a wireless network is the freedom of movement it provides. With a laptop or handheld device, family members can surf the Web from the patio or workshop. Team members can refer to files on their desktop computers during a meeting in the conference room. Traveling employees can easily join the office network without having to find an available Ethernet port or even a desk. Workers who move around the office or other work facilities as part of their jobs can take a laptop or handheld device with them, maintaining access to e-mail and databases.

Flexibility

Wireless computers can go where wired ones can't go. You can move laptops around easily, of course, but a wireless network also enables you to place desktop computers in places where you can't or don't want to run wires, and to move computers at will, without regard for where network connections are available. Old homes or business offices are often a challenge to wire because they lack accessible ceiling or wall spaces. Businesses that occupy several buildings or include outdoor spaces can be networked most easily with wireless, eliminating the need for long cable runs. Finally, wireless networks make giving network access easy to houseguests or customers who bring their laptops with them and need temporary network or Internet access.

Cost Savings

Pulling cable is often a significant expense for businesses because it's labor-intensive. Designing and installing wired networks also can be costly. Families and businesspeople who use individual dial-up accounts to reach the Internet can save money on Internet access by installing a wireless network that enables everyone to share a single account. You can also save the cost of printers and other shared peripherals by networking a single device and giving everyone on the network access.

Beginning a wireless network could cost more than starting a wired one (if you don't count the time required to wire your building) because you need to buy wireless equipment for each computer you intend to add to the network, as well as a wireless *access point* (a device that makes it possible for wireless devices to communicate with one another). Wireless costs are higher because most modern computers include Ethernet connectors you can use to connect the devices on a wired network. But that shared Internet access will help the network pay for itself quickly, and you might find it's easier to telecommute from home with wireless access available throughout your home.

Scalability

Scalability is the capability to expand a network after initial installation. In business, this capability is essential to manage growth efficiently in your organization. You don't need to add infrastructure (cables and network management devices) to give a new employee access to a wireless network. With a wireless-equipped laptop, the new worker can join the network even before the work area is ready. Wireless access points can support 15–150 users, depending on the device's horsepower. In a wired environment, you'd need Ethernet hub ports for each network device. To support 30 users, you'd need to buy and connect four 8-port Ethernet hubs, adding a new one each time your user base increases.

At home, scalability is less of an issue because, typically, fewer users exist and little significant growth is anticipated.

Wireless Technology Overview

Several types of wireless technologies have been applied to wireless networking. These differ by frequency and by a variety of other characteristics related to range, signal strength, spectrum used, and speed. Most wireless networks use radio frequencies (RF) to transmit signals between stations. Infrared (IR) networks also exist, but they don't provide the same range or flexibility as RF-based networks. Infrared technology, for example, is a great way to remotely control a television, a hand scanner in a grocery store, or even to facilitate short-range communication between a PDA and a laptop. However, IR signals can't pass through opaque objects, and their range is limited to a few feet. Most, but not all, radio-based transmissions can travel tens or hundreds of feet and aren't confined to a single room or line of sight.

Frequency

Wireless network devices operate within specified frequency ranges. The use of radio frequency bands is subject to regulation by national governments. In the United States, the Federal Communications Commission (FCC) requires licenses for the use of some segments of the broadcast spectrum, including those used by radio broadcasters and cell phone operators. Wi-fi networks must operate in one of two unlicensed areas of the spectrum: the 2.4-to-2.4853 GHz bands or the 5 GHz band between 5.15 and 5.825 GHz. These frequencies are among those set aside for industrial, scientific, and medical (ISM) uses. Despite the exclusive sounding name, ISM band access isn't restricted to particular users. Because these areas of the spectrum are accessible for a variety of uses in addition to data networks, some areas, like the 2.4 GHz bands on which wi-fi networks operate, are rather crowded. Other occupants of the 2.4 GHz space include microwave ovens. The 5 GHz bands available for network use are among the U-NII (Unlicensed National Information Infrastructure) bands defined by the FCC. These frequencies are much less crowded than the 2.4 GHz ISM bands.

Spectrum

Although no license is required in the 2.4 GHz and 5 GHz frequency bands, the FCC does impose some regulations on equipment. These rules ensure that wireless transmissions don't use excess bandwidth and that devices don't interfere with other users of the band by too-powerful broadcasting signals. In addition to rules about power use, designed to prevent interference on the band, the FCC requires wireless networking equipment to use one of three spread-spectrum technologies to communicate with other devices. *Spread spectrum*, as the name implies, spreads wireless signals across a swath of the band in which the network operates, rather than transmitting at a single frequency, as does narrowband communication. Spread spectrum uses more bandwidth than narrowband, but it offers the advantage of better reliability, security, and data integrity.

The three types of spread-spectrum communication found in wireless networks are direct sequence spread spectrum (DSSS), frequency hopping spread spectrum (FHSS), and orthogonal frequency division multiplexing (OFDM). In an FHSS environment, signals hop among a series of subchannels in a random pattern understood by both transmitter and receiver. Each hop consists of a short burst of data, and the amount of time between hops is referred to as *dwell time*. Although DSSS also spreads transmissions over multiple channels within a given frequency range, no hopping occurs between frequencies. Instead, a binary string called a *spreading code* creates redundant transmissions, increasing the chances that signals and data will reach the intended receiver intact. The sending wireless device must use the same spreading code as the sender for signals to pass between them. Restricting the devices to a particular code, rather than using several, reduces the interference potential on the channel used by the two devices. OFDM makes efficient use of available spectrum by dividing it into subchannels and sending a portion of a given data transmission over each one.

The question of which spread-spectrum technology is best is largely a moot one for wireless network builders because the developers of each networking technology, along with standards organizations that approve them, have all picked the methods that match their technologies. The methods can't be used together. As wireless networking technologies are described in the next section, I'll note the spectrum method used by each.

Current and Future Wireless Networking Technologies

Radio-based wireless networks come in several varieties. Most of the technologies available today have several characteristics in common, including the use of either the 2.4 or 5 GHz radio bands and spread-spectrum technology. Even their network structures are similar. In most wireless schemes, you build a network by connecting radio transmitters to computers and PDAs and then use a central access point to manage the network. Under most networking schemes, you can also build a network without the central access point. Here's a quick look at the major wireless networking standards.

IEEE 802.11

The Institute of Electrical and Electronics Engineers (IEEE—pronounced *I Triple E*) develops and approves standards for a wide variety of computer technologies. The organization creates working groups of technology experts representing vendors and the scientific/engineering community to study, review, and approve proposed standards on which new products can then be based. IEEE designates networking standards with the number 802. Wireless networking standards—a subset of 802—are designated by the number 11. Hence, IEEE wireless standards fall under the 802.11 umbrella. Ethernet, by the way, is called 802.3.

The first IEEE wireless standard, adopted in 1997, was simply called IEEE 802.11. This was an RF-based standard operating in the 2.4 GHz frequency band, with a maximum throughput of 2 Mbps. (By way of comparison, wired Ethernet operates at 10 Mbps). A revision of the standard was originally dubbed 802.11 High Rate for its improved speed (up to 11 Mbps). By 1999, 802.11 High Rate had been renamed 802.11b, and 802.11a, a higher-speed standard using a different spread-spectrum method, had been added. In 2002, 802.11g joined the ranks of approved wireless standards. These standards are described in detail in the next few paragraphs.

In addition to the three current networking standards, IEEE 802.11 includes task groups that are working on standards that will, when approved and implemented, compliment 802.11a, b, and g. IEEE 802.11i, for example, is aimed at beefing up wireless network security, while 802.11e addresses quality of service (QoS) issues that are important in large wireless networks. Once these standards have been adopted, they can either be folded into one of the networking protocols or simply made available to vendors who want to add features to their 802.11a, b, or g products.

802.11b

As mentioned earlier, 802.11b is an updated and improved version of the original IEEE 802.11 standard. A detailed description of 802.11b is provided in Chapter 2. Today, no commercial products based on plain old 802.11 are available. In fact, few 802.11-only products were ever marketed. Apple Computer introduced the first widely available 802.11b products, which it dubbed Air-Port, in 1999. The product line consists of a wireless access point (Apple calls it a base station) and a PC card for Macintosh laptops. Apple didn't invent 802.11b, but the company was first to popularize the technology with computer buyers. Most wireless networking products today are based on 802.11b.

802.11b networks operate at a maximum speed of 11 Mbps, slightly faster than 10-BASE-T Ethernet, providing a more than fivefold increase over the original 802.11 spec. The 802.11 standard provided for the use of DSSS and FHSS spread-spectrum methods. In 802.11b, DSSS is used.

802.11a

Approved soon after 802.11b, IEEE 802.11a operates in the 5 GHz frequency band and provides speeds up to 54 Mbps. 802.11a uses the OFDM spread-spectrum method. While 802.11b products appeared shortly after the standard won approval from the IEEE, 802.11a devices only began appearing in 2002. When compared to the crowded 2.4 GHz band where other 802.11 standards operate, the 5 GHz band used by 802.11a is wide open, with few other uses competing for access. The FCC has allocated a greater swath of the 5 GHz spectrum to wireless networking than is provided in the 2.4 GHz ISM bands. The wider band provides more channels and bandwidth for wireless communication.

Although how successful 802.11a wireless will become is currently unclear, large companies and organizations will probably adopt the technology in higher numbers than will consumers and small businesspeople. For one thing, 802.11b has a tremendous head start, with a large number of products available at reasonable prices. For another, 802.11a isn't compatible with 802.11b, so you can't use an existing 802.11b-equipped laptop to log on to an 802.11a network. Even if support for older equipment isn't important—if you're starting a network from scratch—802.11a equipment is and will probably remain more expensive than the alternatives.

802.11g

In 2002, the 802.11g Task Group approved the third IEEE networking standard, after a heated battle between supporters of two competing proposals. As approved, 802.11g has a maximum speed of 54 Mbps. It uses the same OFDM spread-spectrum technology found in 802.11a, with an option allowing vendors to provide an enhanced version of OFDM in addition. Like 802.11b, 802.11g operates in the 2.4 GHz band, and it's backward-compatible with the older standard. Because 802.11b and g can work together, the next generation of wireless networking products for consumers and small business will probably feature 802.11g, or a combination of 802.11b and g.

Bluetooth

Before 802.11 roared onto the scene, Bluetooth was there. With early backing from industry heavyweights like IBM, Intel, and Erickson among many others, Bluetooth was touted as the technology that would bring wireless into homes and businesses. Bluetooth isn't a brainchild of the IEEE. With support from its backers, the standard was developed by the Bluetooth Special Interest Group.

Like 802.11b and g, Bluetooth is a radio-based technology that operates in the 2.4 GHz band and uses FHSS. Bluetooth's top speed is 1 Mbps, with a range of approximately 50 feet. Despite its limitations and the primacy of IEE 802.11, Bluetooth isn't dead. Instead of being promoted as a local area networking (LAN) standard for communication between computers in different rooms, Bluetooth is now promoted as a PAN (personal area network) technology, suited for communication between computers and peripherals located close to one another or for synchronization of PDAs and host devices. One day, Bluetooth might give us wireless keyboards and monitors or automate communications between household devices. New evidence that Bluetooth has staying power came early in 2002 when Microsoft and Apple (Microsoft was an original Bluetooth backer) both announced initiatives to bring Bluetooth support into their products. The Bluetooth Web site is at http://bluetooth.org.

HomeRF

HomeRF, like other technologies I've described, is a radio-based standard operating in the 2.4 GHz band. The initial version of HomeRF offered a maximum speed of 1 Mbps, but the newer HomeRF, called HomeRF SWAP (Shared Wireless Access Protocol) can reach speeds of 10 Mbps. Like Bluetooth, HomeRF uses FHSS. A few HomeRF products are available, but the standard remains significantly behind 802.11 in the marketplace. The promoters of the technology see HomeRF as an all-inclusive standard that can move both voice and data around a home network, but they don't promote it as a solution for business. Learn more about HomeRF at http://homerf.org.

HiperLAN

HiperLAN/1 and HiperLAN/2 were developed in Europe by the Broadband Radio Access Network (BRAN) group within the European Telecommunications Standards Institute (ETSI). To date, HiperLAN has made little noise in the United States. Both versions operate in the 5 GHz band and, unlike the 802.11 protocols, HiperLAN is primarily intended to facilitate communication among wireless stations, rather than routing it through a central access point. HiperLAN/1 reaches top speeds of 24 Mbps, while HiperLAN/2 can provide a maximum of 54 Mbps of bandwidth. The HiperLAN/2 Global Forum Web site, at http://www.hiperlan2.com, has more information.

How Wi-Fi Fits In

If you glanced at the cover of this book, you might be asking yourself what 802.11a, b, and g have to do with wi-fi. In fact, they're one in the same—sort of. By 2001, the term "wi-fi" had become a popular substitute for the more

Figure 1.1
A HomeRF network looks a lot like a small wi-fi network: a device called a connection point (CP) performs the functions of a wi-fi access point and adds a gateway to the telephone system, allowing voice transmission.

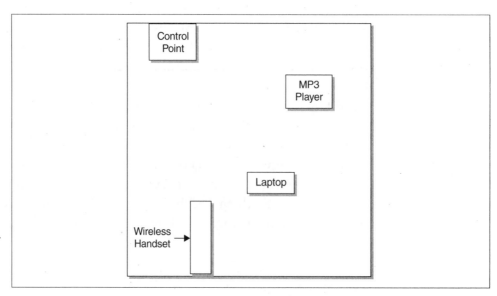

Figure 1.2
HiperLAN/2 supports networks that include multiple access points, overlapping to form continuous wireless coverage.

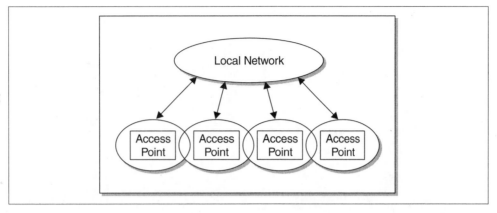

unwieldy IEEE 802.11 in the computer press. Enter the Wireless Ethernet Compatibility Alliance (WECA), which adopted wi-fi as an easily understood brand for all qualifying 802.11b products. WECA was formed by product vendors to promote IEEE 802 and to develop a certification program designed to ensure that wireless products are fully compliant with the 802.11 standard. WECA tests and certifies products and grants vendors whose products meet the requirements permission to use the wi-fi logo on their equipment and marketing materials.

At press time, wi-fi certification applies only to 802.11b products. WECA has announced its intention to expand wi-fi certification for 802.11a and, by the time you read this, you might be able to buy certified 802.11a devices. 802.11g products are expected to become eligible for wi-fi certification shortly after IEEE finally ratifies that standard. WECA's Web site describes the wi-fi certification process and lists products that have passed it: http://www.wirelessethernet.org.

Because wi-fi certification currently applies only to 802.11b and because 802.11b dominates the wireless LAN world—especially for consumers and small businesses—this book focuses primarily on building networks around that standard. Much of what you read here, though, is applicable to other 802.11 technologies. I point out those overlapping areas as the book progresses.

Figure 1.3
The wi-fi logo on a product package indicates the device is fully compliant with the IEEE 802.11b standard and has passed WECA's certification tests.

Chapter 2

IEEE 802.11 In Depth

This chapter is for everyone who likes to know how things work. You could build a wi-fi network without reading it, but you'd be missing an explanation of the technology underlying wi-fi. Understanding the details of the 802.11 standard can help you assess the strengths and limitations of wi-fi networking, as well. You'll also gain the background you need to understand the features of wi-fi equipment, its limits, and how future innovations will build on current technologies. Concepts introduced in this chapter are referred to throughout this book.

As you learned in Chapter 1, wi-fi refers to the IEEE 802.11 wireless networking standard. At press time, wi-fi specifically refers to the 802.11b standard within the IEEE 802.11 family. This chapter covers the family and the individual standard prevalent today. First, let's look quickly at the components of a wi-fi network. Next, you'll get a bit of networking background that shows you how wi-fi networks compare to wired ones operationally. You'll get a glimpse into the layers that make up the wi-fi protocol stack and see what each one does. Next, you'll learn about the various wi-fi network designs and the implication that using each one has for building your network. The last stop on your tour of wi-fi is the supporting standards developed by the IEEE to add new capabilities and features.

Parts of a Wi-Fi Network

All wi-fi networks include stations, usually network adapters installed in or connected to computers. A network adapter, required for each device on the network, includes a radio transmitter/receiver and (usually) an antenna to boost the radio's signal. Most wi-fi networks also include at least one access point (AP), a device that manages the network and extends its range. Like a wi-fi station, the AP contains a radio and usually has an external antenna. Management software allows the access point to authenticate network users, provide security, and share resources over the network.

Wi-fi stations and access points can communicate and exchange data if they all adhere to the same wireless standard. That process begins at the radio. All radios on the network must operate at the same frequency to transmit and receive each other's signals. To turn radio signals into packets, devices must also adhere to the same wireless standard, which specifies the frequencies at which the radios communicate, as well as a number of other requirements for communication among them.

The OSI Reference Model

Like all networks, wi-fi networks are built on the Open Systems Interconnection (OSI) reference model, a seven-layer framework that describes the structure of a network and how communication takes place from the lowest level (the physical network) to the highest (specific software applications). The OSI model (Figure 2.1) is a convenient way to think about a network's structure because understanding how a given function relates to other network activities is easier. The OSI model is a hierarchy. Low-level network functions, such as identifying the physical medium used by a network and decoding radio signals, for example, occur at lower layers. Higher layers govern how transactions are conducted and, at the top, the rules for specific network applications, like file sharing, printing, and so forth. Not all networking standards or protocols must make use of all OSI layers. Think of a contract between the buyer and the seller of a home. The contract specifies the financial terms of the transaction, the timing of the transaction, and conditions under which the sale will take place. But it doesn't address how the buyer and seller will get to the closing. Transportation for each party is a high-level detail that is irrelevant to the signing and executing of the contract for the house.

Different kinds of network applications and processes use different layers of the OSI model, based on where the network device or application needs to interact with its counterparts. All IEEE 802 standards operate at the physical and data-link layers. These include IEEE 802.3, commonly referred to as the *Ethernet spec*, 802.5 (Token Ring), and 802.11, the wireless protocol that's the subject of this book. Protocols at higher levels of the reference model, such as TCP/IP, NetBIOS, and AppleTalk, to name a few, are completely independent of these lower layers. Higher-level protocols simply use the lower layers as a platform on which to operate.

Figure 2.1
The seven-layer
OSI reference
model defines
everything about
a network;
IEEE network
specifications
operate at the
physical and
data-link layers.

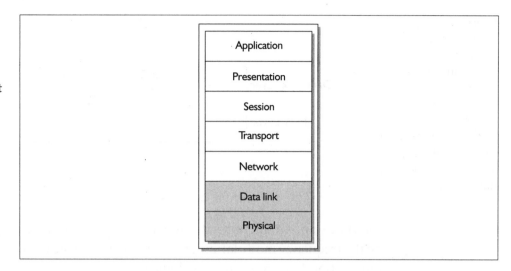

Layers and Sublayers

Many IEEE standards, including 802.11, allow different versions of a particular layer to be "plugged in" to the OSI framework. This enables multiple variations of a single standard to exist, but they can maintain continuity with their siblings. The 802.11b standard, for example, adds a new high-speed physical layer to those specified in the original 802.11 spec. (More about this in the next section.) Multiple-layer types within the same layer are usually expressed horizontally when a protocol's OSI structure is described visually, as shown in Figure 2.2.

Layers often have multiple jobs within the hierarchy. These tasks are typically divided into sublayers that take responsibility for a specific slice of the layer's work. Sublayers pass information from the layer below to the next sublayer and on to higher layers. Communication goes in both directions, from higher to lower layers and to any sublayers present. Dividing a layer, like the data-link layer, into sublayers also allows networks that are otherwise different to use a common sublayer.

All IEEE 802 networks, for example, use a common upper-level data link sublayer called the 802.2 Logical Link Control (LLC). This sublayer encapsulates packets it receives from lower levels of the network for transfer to upper layers. Below the 802 LLC is a Media Access Control (MAC) sublayer (Figure 2.3). The MAC's job is to manage access to the network medium and

Figure 2.2
This IEEE 802.11
PHY shows the
different layers
supported by
the standard.

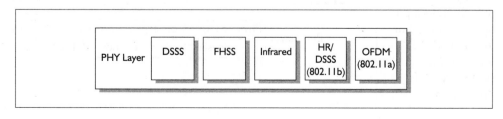

Figure 2.3
All IEEE 802
protocols
communicate at
the physical- and
data-link layers;
specifically, IEEE
802 specs employ
LLC and MAC
sublayers at the
data-link level.

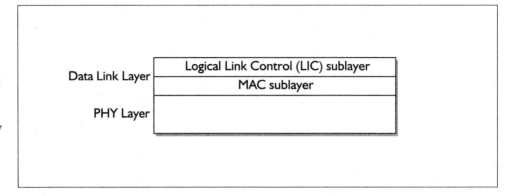

each 802 standard includes its own MAC layer. The 802.11 MAC layer builds on the frequency modulation provided by the physical layer, managing communication between wireless devices—access points and stations. MACs associated with wired network protocols have no radio-related responsibilities but, like the 802.11 MAC, they regulate access to the network.

The Physical (PHY) Layer

The physical (PHY) layer is the lowest in the OSI reference model. PHY layers define the method of communication over the network. The 802.11 PHY layer structure is divided into two sublayers: the Physical Layer Convergence Procedure (PLCP) and the Physical Medium Dependent (PMD). The PLCP sublayer serves as a go-between for the PHY and data link (MAC) layers, passing data from the radio to the network. The PMD sublayer transfers data from the PLCP into the air. Figure 2.4 shows the PHY and MAC layers and their sublayers.

The original 802.11 specification provided for three separate physical layers: one each for DSSS and FHSS, and a third layer for diffused infrared. The original 802.11 specified a top data rate of 2 Mbps under DSSS, 1 Mbps for FHSS. By adding a physical layer specific to a particular type of spread spectrum, the 802.11 Task Group was able to provide a substantial speed boost when 802.11a and 802.11b were approved. In 802.11b, the new layer supports High Rate (HR) DSSS, while 802.11a uses an OFDM layer.

Figure 2.4
The PHY layer is
divided into two
sublayers, each of
which plays a part
in delivering data
from the 802.11
radio to the
MAC layer of
the network.

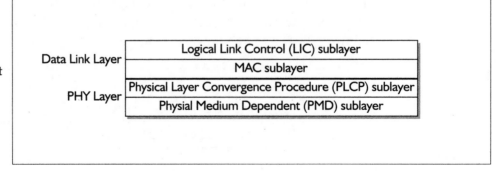

The Media Access Control (MAC) Layer

The 802.11 MAC layer performs carrier sensing and transmission/receiving of frames. While different 802.11-based standards use different physical sublayers, the MAC layer has the same characteristics for all versions of the standard. Although they aren't identical, the MAC used by wi-fi bears a great resemblance to the one used by Ethernet, with unique features to support wireless-only requirements. Like Ethernet, the wi-fi MAC uses carrier sense multiple access (CSMA) as a gatekeeper for the transmission medium (the air for wi-fi and the cable for Ethernet). Where Ethernet uses CSMA/CD (collision detection) technology, wi-fi employs CSMA/CA (collision avoidance) technology to prevent signals from colliding in the air. Ethernet uses collision detection because, though inconvenient, collisions on a wired network can be managed. But sending and receiving transmissions from the same radio at the same time isn't possible, however, so 802.11 uses CA to prevent collisions before they occur.

The MAC layer performs a number of station and distribution services. Station services relate directly to the way wireless devices communicate with one another. Distribution services relate to communication managed by access points.

Station services in 802.11 are

❑ **Authentication** A wireless device seeking to associate with another nearby station or access point must authenticate itself with the other device before being allowed on the network. Many access points are set to use the open systems form of the authentication service, however, meaning any device seeking to join the network will be authenticated. The alternative is *shared-key authentication,* which first requires a station to provide a shared key (password) to the access point. The key passes from one station to the receiving station via its own secure communications channel. This method requires Wired Equivalent Privacy (WEP) be used by both stations. The privacy service described in this section is built on the authentication service.

❑ **Deauthentication** When a device seeks to disassociate itself with the network, the deauthentication service severs the connection.

❑ **Privacy** Wired Equivalent Privacy (WEP) is intended to emulate the level of security available in a wired network, where intruders must have a physical connection to the network to gain access to data. In a wireless network, data travels over the air and could easily be intercepted by someone with a wi-fi radio who is within range of the network. With WEP enabled, data traveling between wireless devices is encrypted and uses either a 64-bit or a 128-bit key. To decrypt the data, a user must be authenticated as a member of the network and provided with the required access key. As you learn in Chapter 10, WEP is far from secure, primarily because the encryption algorithm used to generate shared WEP keys can easily be used to retrieve and use those keys to gain access to networks where WEP is enabled.

❏ **MSDU delivery**   The MAC Service Data Unit (MSDU) service is responsible for making sure data reaches its intended recipient.

Distribution services of the 802.11 MAC are

❏ **Association**   To communicate with an access point and with other stations on the network, a wireless device must be associated with an access point. In a network consisting of multiple access points, devices can communicate with devices associated with several access points, but a device can only be associated with one access point. The access point passes association information along to other parts of the network.

❏ **Disassociation**   When devices leave the network, either because they move out of range of the access point or the access point terminates the connection, the device is disassociated from the network.

❏ **Reassociation**   When a device changes its association, the reassociation service provides information about the change. *Resuscitation's* primary function is to transition mobile devices from one access point to another.

❏ **Distribution**   When information is sent from one station to another on a wi-fi network, the distribution service ensures the data reaches its intended destination.

❏ **Integration**   Wi-fi devices can communicate with wired networks or other non-802.11 networks using portals. The integration service, in concert with the distribution service, ushers data through the portal and on to its destination outside the wi-fi network.

Frequency Spectrum and Wi-Fi

Earlier in this chapter, you were introduced to the frequency modulation methods used by IEEE 802.11 networks. Let's look at the workings of each of the methods: DSSS, FHSS, and OFDM.

802.11b and DSSS

In Chapter 1, you learned that under DSSS, data is transmitted within a designated frequency band (2.4–2.485 GHz, in the case of 802.11b in the United States). A pseudorandom binary string, called a *chipping code* is used to transmit data. In this arrangement, multiple bits represent a single bit of information. These bits are transmitted within the same amount of time it would take to deliver a single bit. The receiving side of a DSSS transaction uses a filter correlator to "unspread" the data, removing the chipping code and delivering the data as it was originally transmitted.

DSSS allows three different modulation methods, each of which provides for a different data transmission rate. Differential binary phase shift keying (DBPSK) and differential quadrature phase shift keying (DQPSK) are used respectively by the 1 Mbps and 2 Mbps versions of the original 802.11 spec. These techniques map data transmissions into two (DBPSK) or four (DQPSK) phases, encoding data when the phase changes. The use of four bits, rather than two bits, allows a DQPSK-based system to operate at twice the speed of DBPSK.

HR/DSSS, the PHY layer used by 802.11b, uses the third DSSS method, Complementary Code Keying (CCK). Using DQPSK to modulate the signal, CCK achieves a 5.5 Mbps or 11 Mbps data rate by dividing the chipping code used to transmit data into a series of 8-bit symbols. The result it this: CCK encodes and transmits more information during each phase shift than DQPSK does alone.

802.11a and OFDM

Like HR/DSSS, the OFDM physical layer is an extension to the 802.11 standard. OFDM is used by 802.11a and will probably become a part of the 802.11g spec when it's approved. OFDM's advantages include high data rates, up to 54 Mbps under both 802.11a and g.

You might call the OFDM way of doing things "divide and conquer." Instead of creating a large data pipe to deliver data, OFDM transmits bits using a number of subchannels, operating in parallel (orthogonally) on different frequencies. Like parallel processing in the supercomputer world, OFDM allows the individual processor (subchannel) to concentrate on a small amount of information, unburdened by other tasks. When all the subchannels are glued together (multiplexed) at the end of a data transmission, the result is high throughput. OFDM channels overlap, but the presence of unique identifiers within each channel substantially diminishes potential interference. In 802.11a, which operates in the 5 GHz frequency band, each

OFDM channel is 20 MHz wide, with 48 data subcarriers per channel (plus six subcarriers to handle overhead).

Like the DSSS physical layer, OFDM supports several data rates, using different frequency modulation techniques to achieve each one. OFDM data rate tiers are 6 and 9 Mbps, 12 and 18 Mbps, 24 and 36 Mbps, and 48 and 54 Mbps. The lower two tiers use DBPSK and DQPSK, respectively. The third tier adds quadralator amplitude modulation (QAM) to DBPSK. The 48 and 54 Mbps tier combines QAM with DQPSK.

QAM, like phase shift keying, expresses encoding in terms of data bits per symbol. 16-QAM, used in the 24 and 36 Mbps OFDM tier, encodes 4 data bits using 16 symbols per subchannel. 64-QAM, used in the 48 and 54 Mbps tier, uses 64 symbols to encode 16 bits per subchannel.

FHSS

Although the original 802.11 standard provides a frequency-hopping physical layer, FHSS isn't used by any current 802.11-based implementations. As laid out in the spec, FHSS provides data rates of 1 and 2 Mbps. Like OFDM, FHSS splits data to be transmitted over the available frequency band using subcarriers. The pattern is generated with a pseudorandom algorithm. Unlike OFDM, which transmits data over multiple subchannels in parallel, FHSS transmits data in small bursts at specified intervals, hopping among frequencies within the available band. The hopping pattern must be known to both sender and receiver, as is the *dwell time*, the interval during which signals use a particular frequency.

Network Topology

A network's *topology* is the layout and structure of the network. Wi-fi uses two topologies, the Basic Service Set (BSS) for networks consisting of devices that are all within range of one another or of a single access point. Extended Service Set (ESS) networks allow multiple wireless cells to overlap, expanding the range of a single network greatly. An ESS consists of multiple BSS networks.

Two types of BSS networks exist—ad-hoc (also called independent or peer-to-peer) and infrastructure. An *ad-hoc* network consists of computers or other wi-fi devices that communicate directly with one another. *Infrastructure* networks, on the other hand, consist of an access point that manages communication and security for devices associated with it. All communication between devices in an infrastructure network flows through an access

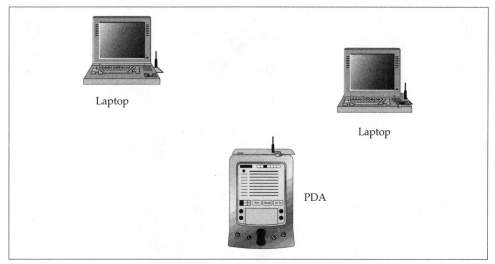

Figure 2.5
An ad-hoc network includes wireless devices communicating directly with each other via the air.

point. Even if two laptops are physically nearer to one another than to the access point that forms their network, signals travel from the sending laptop to the access point, and then to the receiving device. Wi-fi devices can't be on both an ad-hoc and an infrastructure network simultaneously.

Ad-hoc networks, like the one shown in Figure 2.5, are easy to set up and they work well when you need to build a temporary link between computers. Infrastructure networks (shown in Figure 2.6), on the other hand, are better suited for permanent wireless networks for a couple of reasons. First, an access point makes sharing Internet access among connected devices easy. Computers that want to join the network must authenticate themselves with the access point or they will have no access to other devices on the network. If you plan to share files or printers on a long-term basis, an infrastructure network also makes this possible.

Second, an infrastructure BSS provides greater range than an ad-hoc network because mobile devices needn't all be within range of one another. Instead, each device must be able to reach the access point. This allows devices that aren't within range to take share files, for example, as long as both can see the access point.

Extended Service Sets

Just as many large wired networks are a collection of smaller networks, a wireless ESS (Figure 2.7) consists of overlapping coverage areas in which devices can roam between several access points without having to disassociate from the original access point. This capability greatly expands the normally short range of a wi-fi network. ESS networks are also critical in public spaces or buildings where wireless coverage must be widespread and redundant.

Figure 2.6
A BSS infrastructure network relies on an access point to provide network access, security, and management to connected stations.

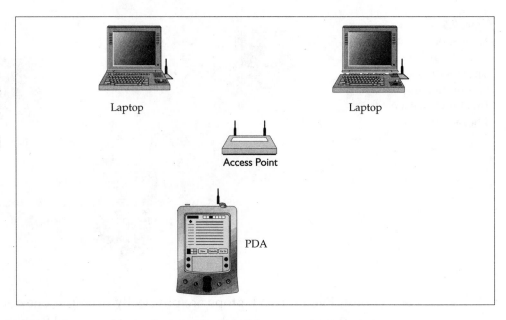

An ESS is formed by first connecting each access point to a backbone network of some kind. The network could be (and usually is) a wired Ethernet network or some other kind of network with a link layer (layer 2) communications medium. The wired network might exist only to connect the access points or it might provide Internet access and local network services for the wireless ESS.

A Distribution system (DS) is the means by which APs communicate between themselves. Access points within the ESS act as bridges between the

Figure 2.7
An ESS network consists of several access points that can be spread over a large area to create a larger, continuous coverage area for wireless devices. A backbone network connects access points (and, thus, the BSS networks they control) to one another.

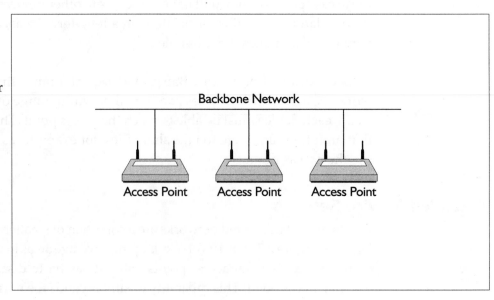

BSS networks that form the ESS, allowing any station on the network to communicate with any other station, and making it possible for devices to move between segments of the network. This only works, however, if the access points are all configured as members of the same network. The capability of access points to communicate in this way is specified in the 802.11 standard and is referred to as the DS. Access points are all given the same network name and security access settings but each communicates on a different radio channel. (This is done to limit interference between access point radios.) If a device moves out of range of the AP to which it was originally associated, it's automatically reassociated with another access point if one is in range and if that access point is set up to accept new stations seamlessly. Figure 2.8 shows an ESS with three overlapping networks. From a network design point of view, it's a good idea to position access points so that their coverage areas overlap, preventing gaps in accessibility for roaming stations.

From the user's point of view, joining an ESS is identical to connecting to a network with a single access point. A user associates with an access point within range of his or her wi-fi-equipped device. If the user moves out of range of that access point, access to the network is provided by another access point within the ESS. Associating with the new access point to send and receive data isn't necessary. This is made possible by the 802.11 DS.

For access points to work together in an ESS, they must support an interaccess point protocol (IAPP). IAPPs make it possible for all access points in the ESS to know about stations associated with all other APs. Without this information, one access point can't deliver data to a recipient associated with a different AP. IAPP isn't a single standard, but a type of protocol that has been implemented differently by different access point vendors. As a practical matter, this usually means all access points in an ESS should be purchased from a single vendor. A standard IAPP is among the IEEE 802.11 working group's current projects.

Figure 2.8
Overlapping coverage areas ensure that devices moving between BSS cells within an ESS won't lose access to the network.

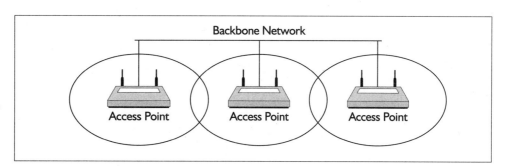

Supporting 802.11 Standards

This chapter concentrated on aspects of the IEEE 802.11 standard that are identical in versions a, b, and g. As you learned in Chapter 1, the three differ in the way they use spread-spectrum radio technology and in the frequency at which they operate. Because many features required to make 802.11 a robust standard were either not planned for or were delayed in the interest of quick ratification of the a, b, and g standards, IEEE has created task groups to develop supporting standards that can be plugged into the main protocols to add new features. At press time, none had been approved or integrated into 802.11 networks. These supporting protocols follow the 802.11 naming conventions and come with their own letter designation. Current supporting protocols are

❏ **802.11e (Quality of Service)**   *QoS*, as it's known in the parlance of network management professionals, gives some data packets priority over other packets. QoS is considered critical to make 802.11 a robust standard, suitable for use as a medium for voice and data communication, as well as multimedia.

❏ **802.11h (Spectrum Manager 802.11a)**   Unlike Ethernet, wireless networks aren't good listeners. While devices using Ethernet delay data transmission until they're sure the line is clear, 802.11 transmits at will and doesn't wait for a response from a station or access point. The result is both an overburdened network and potential radio interference. Although this problem affects all 802.11 standards, Task Group H is specifically working on a supplement to 802.11a. Making the 5 GHz standard less noisy will give it access to European Union countries, where HiperLAN/2 (also operating in the 5 GHz band) currently has a market advantage.

❏ **802.11i (Enhanced Security)**   Motivated by the documented weaknesses in WEP, the encryption scheme built into 802.11, IEEE is developing a new security method to replace it. Currently called Temporal Key Integrity Protocol (TKIP), the proposal being reviewed by Task Group I will probably boast longer encryption keys that change over time for enhanced security, rather than the permanent, relatively short keys that WEP uses.

Chapter 3

Choosing a Wireless Access Point

An access point (AP) is the device at the center of most wireless networks. The job of an access point is to provide Internet and local network access to wireless devices, to maintain network security, and to provide a bridge between wired and wireless computers on the network.

This chapter introduces you to wi-fi access points, their features, and how you can choose a wi-fi access point that meets your needs. (You learn how to set up wireless access points in Chapter 7.) I use several popular access points as examples, describe key features, and help you to decide how best to choose one for your home or business. You also learn about the different kinds of access points and how the names their manufacturers give them can sometimes be confusing.

All types of radio-based wireless networks can use access points as management and communication hubs. Although the focus of this book and the examples in this chapter refer specifically to wi-fi APs, access points have the same job, and many of the same features, in all radio-based wireless networks. In short, much of what you read in this chapter applies whether you're starting an 802.11a, an 802.11g network, or sticking with wi-fi.

Do You Need an Access Point?

As you learned in Chapter 2, it's possible for computers with wi-fi network adapters to communicate wirelessly without an access point in *ad-hoc mode*. In *ad-hoc mode*, you can share files or play network games with another wireless computer. Ad-hoc mode is best used for short-term wireless resource sharing, however. Besides offering a better way to share Internet access and manage the local network, infrastructure mode networks—the kind that use access points—support more users and include network management features. You also need an access point if you want to create a local network that has both wired and wireless devices, including shared Internet access, printing, and file sharing for all. In short, get an access point if you want to build a permanent wireless network. A variation on ad-hoc mode is the *software access point*, basically routing software running on a computer that contains a wi-fi network adapter. Many Linux hobbyists build their own homemade access points for fun, reclaiming an old, underpowered computer as the host. A few vendors sell "access points" consisting of a Linux-based computer, one or more wireless radios, and router software. PC and Mac users can also set up software access points. You learn how in Chapter 9.

Access points can be put into two broad categories: enterprise-capable units designed to meet the needs of medium and large offices, and inexpensive offerings for the Small Office/Home Office (SOHO) user. Enterprise access points boast professional network management features, support for high-end security protocols, and tight integration with other equipment used in large networks. Current leaders in this category include Cisco, Agere/Orinoco (formerly Lucent), and Nokia. Consumer access points do the same job as their pricier cousins, even offering some firewalls for security, access logging, and other management features useful in small networks. These are likely to support fewer users, though, and to provide user-oriented documentation and configuration tools. SOHO units can also generally be used to share a broadband Internet connection. Because the range of an access point is determined by the wireless standard it supports (as well as conditions in your home or office), not the contents of the box, an expensive unit won't increase the coverage area of your network. You'll need an external antenna for that, or multiple access points. Enterprise-level APs usually support an interaccess-point protocol (IAPP), which provides a means to create a large wireless network by joining several access points in a distribution system (DS).

Most consumer/small business access points that use the wi-fi standard cost less than $250, while enterprise-capable units can run from several hundred to more than $1,000. Leading consumer vendors include Intel, D-Link, Linksys, Agere/Orinoco, NetGear Proxim, and 3Com. The focus is on consumer and small-office grade access points for the remainder of this chapter, but what you learn here can get you started if you're considering more advanced products.

Is One Access Point Enough?

A single access point can usually provide full wireless coverage for a mid-sized, single-family home or a small office or store, assuming no major interference or obstructions exist. Wi-fi devices can receive signals within 300 feet or so of the access point. In an ideal setup, the access point is centrally located, giving you coverage in all directions. You might experience interference from metal-filled walls or from other 2.4 GHz devices in your building, though. You will learn more about wireless interference in Chapter 12.

You can extend the range of your network by adding access points or by attaching a high-gain antenna to your access point or wireless network adapters. High-gain antennas enable radio signals to travel further, enabling you to place wireless devices further away from the access point than would otherwise be possible. An external antenna added to a wi-fi device, such as a laptop, gives the user the flexibility to roam farther from the access point or it can put the device within range of an access point that isn't centrally located. Chapter 5 introduces you to antenna options for both access points and wireless computers.

The best way to determine whether you might need a second access point or an additional antenna is this: Take some quick measurements of the distance between the spot where your primary access point will live and the farthest point you want to cover with a wireless signal. If you want to add an access point to the home office upstairs, measure the distance between your office and the garage or backyard deck where you plan to use a laptop. If your business office is a shed in the parking lot behind the store, measure the distance between the shed and the front door of your store, or the distance to a location in the store where you might want to put the access point. If you need to cover an area greater than 100–300 feet, you'll probably need an antenna or a second access point. Don't buy these things right away, though. Read Chapter 5 to learn about antenna options, and then read Chapter 12 to learn how you can plan your network and choose equipment to cover the area at the lowest cost. At this point, having a general idea of the amount of space you need to cover should be enough. In Chapter 12, you learn about access point features that make it easier to create a single network with multiple APs.

Access Point Parts

Most access points are small boxes, with an antenna or two protruding from the top. A few vendors, including Apple and Agere/Orinoco, build stylish units that look like flying saucers or shark fins. Whatever their design, access points are much the same inside. All wi-fi access points contain at least one radio (2.4 GHz in the case of 802.11b, 5 GHz for 802.11a), software to manage the access point and the wireless network, and ports to link the access point to the Internet connection (modem or broadband) and to a wired network. Although most access points have external antennas, some antennas are hidden inside the AP's case.

The Radio

All wi-fi access points and network adapters communicate via radios. The radio inside determines which wireless standard (802.11b, a, or g) the device supports.

Access point radios are tucked inside the case and most aren't upgradeable or removable—at least in consumer models. A few access points, however, including Asante's FriendlyNet models (Figure 3.1), contain a PC slot that accepts the same network adapters sold for use in laptops. You might need to buy a card when you buy the AP or it might be included. Access points with multiple PC slots give you the option of adding a second radio to expand your network. Empty radio slots also make it theoretically possible to install radios using two different wireless standards in the same access point box. In this way, you could add 802.11g support to an existing 802.11b access point by simply sliding in a new radio. And, chances are good that, by press time, vendors will be selling dual-radio APs as a way to

Figure 3.1
Asante's
FriendlyNet
Wireless
Cable/DSL router
has two slots for
wireless radios.

provide maximum compatibility between existing networks and new wireless standards.

Wi-fi radios differ in one major way: they're based on one of several chipsets. Lucent and Intersil (whose 802.11b chipset is called PRISM-2) are the leading providers, selling their chips to most of the major vendors of wi-fi equipment. You'll find Lucent chips in products from Agere/Orinoco (formerly Lucent), Apple, Compaq, and IBM. PRISM-2 vendors include NetGear, Linksys, and D-Link. Other vendors sell chips that are the basis for 802.11a and 802.11g radios.

Basic chipset features are identical from the user's point of view, but a good idea is to buy access points and network adapters that use the same ones. Although all wi-fi chipsets adhere to the 802.11b standard by definition, incompatibilities do crop up, causing configuration problems for some users. The easiest way to make sure all your wi-fi devices use the same chip is to buy them from a single vendor. The single-vendor approach can also be helpful if you're dealing with technical support who will be more knowledgeable about issues related to interoperability of their own products. They'll also be less likely to blame your problem on a chipset or product with which they're unfamiliar.

Battling Chipsets

Wireless technologies become IEEE standards once they're approved by the 802.11 task group associated with each. The groups evaluate proposed standards, including competing implementations, and they vote to ratify the final product after a set of specifications is agreed on. In the case of 802.11g, two companies—Intersil and Texas Instruments (TI)—proposed incompatible versions of the spec to the Task Group. Intersil's would have provided greater speed, but no backward-compatibility with 802.11b, while TI's offering was wi-fi friendly and slower (22 Mbps). Both companies hoped to dominate the chipset market for eventual 802.11g radios. Following protracted debate, the Task Group agreed on an 802.11g spec based on elements of both companies' chip designs—backward-compatible with a potential 54 Mbps throughput. At press time, the final spec hasn't been ratified, but approval of the basic spec is expected in late 2002. Also likely is that Intersil and TI will each sell 802.11g chipsets with enhancements over the dominant spec.

Connectivity

SOHO access points typically sit between your broadband Internet connection (cable or DSL modem) and a local wired network. An Ethernet WAN port provides a connection between the AP and your broadband modem. One or more 10/100BASE-T LAN ports provide a place to connect wired devices to the network. Better APs include several LAN ports, sometimes including an uplink port, specifically intended for an Ethernet hub. In a wired network, all computers and networked printers are connected to an Ethernet hub, allowing everyone to communicate with every other device on the network. You can make a faster wired network by connecting all wired devices to a switch, rather than a hub. Like a hub, a switch facilitates communications among all networked devices but, instead of forcing all devices to share the same network data pipe, switches dedicate an individual data channel to each switched port. This results in faster communication among all devices because they don't have to compete for network capacity. Access points' Ethernet ports are typically switched ports.

With two to four Ethernet ports, most home users can connect all existing Ethernet devices directly to the access point, eliminating the need for a separate Ethernet hub. If you have more computers than access point ports, you can connect an inexpensive Ethernet hub to the uplink port on the access point, to enlarge the network.

Some consumer access points include a serial port that can be used to connect a dial-up modem. If you plan to use dial-up as your primary Internet access, make sure the AP supports that arrangement. Some models, including the D-Link DI-714, shown in Figure 3.2, provide the modem port for backup access—when a broadband connection is down. Apple's AirPort Base Station contains a modem. Most APs have only the port, so you'll need both a modem and a modem cable.

If you don't have a networked printer, consider an access point that includes a printer port or a print server. At press time, most access points that support shared printing have parallel ports. You might have trouble finding one that supports USB printing. The advantage of an AP-based print server is that you can make non-Ethernet printers available to wired and wireless network users, and offload print server tasks from a workstation or server to the access point. This is a particular advantage at home, where the family could need to share a single printer.

Figure 3.2
D-Link's DI-714 access point has a WAN Ethernet port, an RS-232 modem port, and four 10/100 Ethernet ports.

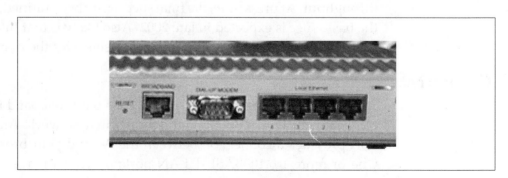

Antennas

Like an AM/FM radio, access points receive (and transmit) further with a good antenna. Most APs include one or two external antennas, though a few antennas are fully contained inside the case. Many also include a port for a range-extending antenna that can increase your AP's reach by hundreds of feet or, in extreme cases, miles. Access point vendors and radio equipment vendors sell antennas that match your wireless network's frequency. If you need to provide wireless connectivity over an area larger than the 100–300 foot radius provided by 802.11b networks, choose an AP that includes an external antenna jack. Also, make certain you can find a compatible antenna—lots of antennas operate on the 802.11b frequency, but you might need an adapter to use one.

Box Design

If you're starting a wireless network at home or if you're taking an architecture firm or design house wireless, style could either be important to you or an added bonus. If you're adding an access point to an existing business network, though, things like stackability and mounting options could be important. Many home-oriented APs aren't stackable and might not have screw holes for mounting them to a wall or rack. Interestingly, the flying-saucer-shaped Air-Port does include a wall mount. Linksys' BEFW11S4 broadband router has a nice modular-locking mechanism that lets you connect and stack several devices. Zoom and D-Link sell rectangular, stackable units. Figure 3.3 shows three access point box designs.

Figure 3.3
D-Link's DI-714 Wireless Broadband Router and the Zoom ZoomAir IG-4165 Wireless Router look like other access points, while Agere's Orinoco BG-2000 sports a shark fin design.

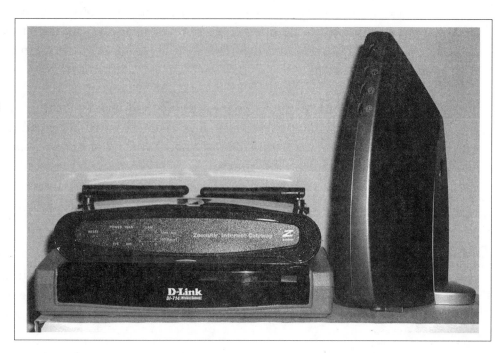

Internet Access, Networking, and Administration

Access point setup software gives you access to Internet and network configuration, security options, and device administration tools. Many access points use a Web-based management interface, though some, like Buffalo, also include or require Windows-based tools. Apple's AirPort Base Station requires a Mac to administer the access point (though a few freeware alternatives are available on the Web). A few APs allow administration from a vendor-neutral Linux tool or via a command-line interface. Although Web-based administration definitely dominates, a good idea is to be sure the access point you want can be managed from the operating system you have.

Shared Internet Access

A major feature of all wireless access points is the capability to share an Internet connection. The access point assumes the role ordinarily played by a computer connected directly to a broadband link—the access point requests a connection, provides network configuration information, and then delivers Internet access to computers on the network. Two features allow access points to work with nearly any broadband Internet connection: PPPoE support, and DHCP client capability.

Point-to-Point Protocol over Ethernet (PPPoE) is a method used by some ISPs to connect DSL or cable users to their network. If your ISP requires a PPPoE connection, you need an access point that supports it. Fortunately, most do, but the lack of PPPoE support is a deal killer unless you're willing to find another ISP. Dynamic Host Configuration Protocol (DHCP) client capability means the access point can obtain its IP address for itself from your ISP, rather than using a static one. This feature is almost universal in SOHO-oriented access points.

As mentioned in the section titled "Connectivity," some access points support dial-up Internet access. If you have a dial-up connection, you'll need an access point with a modem port and a dial-up modem. Finally, if you use AOL to access the Internet, you'll only be able to go online wirelessly with Apple's AirPort Base Station access point. AirPort uses custom scripts to dial AOL and pass Internet information from AOL to your wireless network.

DHCP Server

Every computer on the Internet has an *IP address*, a numeric address that identifies it online. IP addresses are either *static*, meaning they never change, or *dynamic*, meaning they're assigned when you join a network (usually when you reboot your computer) or when you connect to the Internet via dial-up. Many ISPs assign IPs dynamically and let customers use one IP address at a time to connect to the Internet. To share an Internet connection with computers on your local network, you need an IP address for each one. Just as the ISP assigns addresses when users connect, access points can assign addresses with a built-in DHCP server. This tool gives wireless and wired machines access to your network and to one another, via TCP/IP. When combined with Network Address Translation (NAT), which allows multiple devices to share a single public IP address, all computers on your network can use the address assigned to you by an ISP.

The difference between DHCP servers is small and all access points have them. Most, but not all access points, also offer NAT. Some AP models offer nifty DHCP server extras that enhance convenience and even some added security.

For example, several access points enable you to set a time limit on DHCP leases. When the lease expires, the connected device loses access to the network. You can also tell the access point how many clients to allow on the network at any given time. This can control bandwidth use and lock out unwanted network eavesdroppers.

If you use a file or print server, or even if you share files or play games with someone else in your home or office, it's handy for devices on the network to count on having the same IP address each time they join the network. Without such a feature, users receive the next address available from the AP's DHCP server. A DHCP server that ties IP address assignment to the unique MAC address of a client ensures desktop shortcuts and bookmarks stay correct. D-Link's DI-714 access point/router allows you to reserve IP addresses as shown in Figure 3.4. This feature isn't available in all access points, so shop carefully if maintaining IP addresses over time is important to you. The feature goes by slightly different names: D-Link calls it IP address reservation.

Public Versus Private IP Addresses

The IP address you use to connect to the Internet, whether static or dynamic, is a public one that identifies your PC uniquely. Public addresses are recognized on the Internet and let you connect to servers using other public addresses. Local networks often use private IP addresses. Although their format is the same as a public IP, they aren't within the range of addresses recognized on the Internet. If, for example, your IP address is 192.168.0.1 or 192.168.1.106, you have a private address. The number 192 at the beginning of an IP is a good indication the address is private, though other private ranges exist.

Figure 3.4
D-Link's DI-714 Wireless Broadband Router lets you reserve IP addresses for specific clients by name.

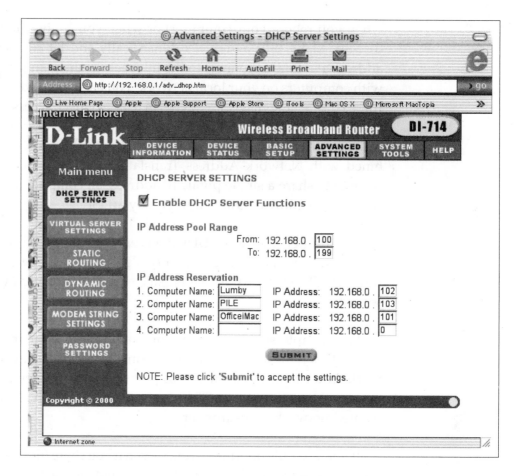

Using private IP addresses is a way to create a TCP/IP network without regard to outside connectivity or whether you have enough public IP addresses to serve your local network. Private addressing is also secure because outsiders can't connect to a network that uses them.

But, you're thinking to yourself, I want all the computers on my network to connect to the Internet from my private network without having to buy a public IP address for each one. This is possible if your network includes a means of sharing a public Internet address. Access point routing features and NAT provide this capability for wi-fi networks. The AP's DHCP server assigns a private IP address to each device on the network and connects to the Internet itself using a public address. Internet packets are passed from the access point to local machines. NAT displays a single IP address to the outside world—the one assigned to your access point.

Firewall

Firewalls protect computers that are behind them from outside attackers or other unwanted connections from the Internet. They do this by blocking access to the means by which specific Internet applications send and receive information.

Internet applications like e-mail, the Web, and FTP each use communications channels called *ports* to communicate. Each application has a port number assigned to it (more than one, in some cases), which it uses to perform a specific kind of transaction. These ports are numbered. Web page requests (using the HTTP protocol) use port 80. File transfer protocol (FTP) transactions use port 21, and so on. Your favorite game, instant messenger program, and Windows file share all have numbered ports associated with them, too.

If a port on a computer that's connected to the Internet is open, anyone who knows the computer's IP address can communicate with it, either with an application that's designed to communicate by that port (a web browser, in the case of port 80) or by special software that checks to see what ports are available on your computer. With these port-scanning tools, an attacker can probe an unprotected computer, flood it with packets, or create other mayhem. Certain ports, including port 80, are popular targets for hackers, because access to these ports provides opportunities to exploit an unprotected computer. By blocking all ports you don't need, a firewall ensures that unwanted visitors can't get in. Firewalls can be set up to allow for access to and from certain ports. That's how many servers operate. An e-mail server computer run by your employer that isn't also a Web server might be protected by a firewall that blocks access to port 80, but leaves e-mail-related ports available.

Access point firewalls shield clients on the local network by blocking access requests that originate from the WAN port—where your network connects to your Internet access device. Computers on the local network can communicate freely with one another and can also connect to Internet sites.

Once again, a firewall is a standard access point feature and is usually enabled by default. Access point firewalls don't have as many access control features as do firewall software packages. Most firewall software is designed not simply to wall off a network, but also to watch for attacks and allow limited access to specific servers on the LAN. Content filters enable firewall users to control inbound traffic based on keywords or URLs. Software packages designed to filter objectionable content before it reaches your home computer are a kind of content filter. Firewalls are also sometimes used to prevent outbound access from specific computers or applications.

Access point firewalls do the basic job of isolating the network from intruders. You can also allow outside access and most give you the capability to expose one local computer or port to the Internet. These features are known as DMZ and port forwarding. You'll also find content filtering in a few access points.

DMZ

A DMZ, as in Demilitarized Zone, is a computer that's outside a firewall. Computers on the Internet can connect to all available ports on a DMZ machine, enabling you to use it as a public Web or file server, for example. Most access points support a single DMZ machine.

Port Forwarding

You might not need to leave all local computers' ports unprotected by your access point's firewall. Instead, you can choose to expose individual ports to the outside world. Some vendors call this feature port forwarding, while others call it virtual server.

Port forwarding enables you to choose one or more computer and one or more specific ports that will be exposed to the outside world, while the rest of the network remains protected. For example, to make a Web server available, you would expose port 80 on the computer running the server. Even though surfers can find your Web site, they won't be able to access other applications—say, a local file server—whose ports are behind the firewall.

Port forwarding is widely available in consumer access points and can be used to open individual ports on several computers on your network, if you choose. Although the feature is straightforward, some management interfaces are better than others. While some products require you to know and enter individual ports, others provide a handy pull-down menu, listing the most common ones. A few enable you to expose a range of ports, in case your server needs to provide access to several applications.

Under the heading Special Applications, some access points provide preconfigured port-forwarding options for networking gaming. The ZoomAir 4165 Cable/DSL Router, for example, provides preconfigured port forwarding for MSN Gaming Zone and Battle.net, as shown in Figure 3.5. Ports are made available for gaming when the access point receives a trigger packet.

Content Filters

Although access points do a good job of enabling you to open or lock down access to computers on your network, most don't offer the content filtering features available in personal firewall applications. Many parents use content filters to keep their kids from finding or receiving objectionable content. Businesses might use filters to block sites or fend off spam e-mail. Access

Figure 3.5
The ZoomAir
IG-4165 Wireless
Gateway/Router
includes
preconfigured
trigger- and
port-forwarding
options for MSN
Gaming Zone
and Battle.net.

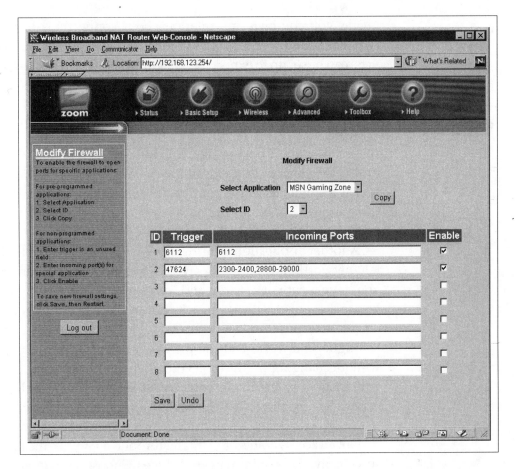

points that offer content filters, including NetGear's MR314 Cable/DSL
Router, enable you to exclude incoming content based on keywords or
source domain.

If you need serious content filtering, especially if your goal is to protect
kids, don't rely exclusively on access point-based filters. They lack the sophisticated filtering of software that's designed to block objectionable sites, e-mail,
and files. Content filtering can be used to block specific sites, though, so if
you're determined to keep your employees from checking out postyour-
resume.com, by all means find an access point that will filter that domain.

Logging and Alerts

You can use a firewall simply to deflect intruders or you can use it to warn of
attacks when they occur. Most firewall software can log a full range of information about intruders, evaluate the risk to your network, and alert you to
repeated attacks.

Although many access points log incoming and/or outgoing activity, few
do a good job of using their logging features to alert you to intruders or even

giving you complete information about connections to your access point. NetGear's MR314 and Agere's Orionco BG-2000 (and some of their other products) can be set up to export the system log. The NetGear product lets you send the log by e-mail at regular intervals or when suspicious events occur.

Routing and Bridging

Access points all bridge the wireless network to the wired one to which they're connected. *Bridging* simply means the two network segments function as a single network: You can mount file servers or use network printers from either segment of the network.

Another application of bridging allows access points to link multiple distant networks. For example, say you operate a business in an office building. You have a network (wired and/or wireless) and a fast Internet connection. You make a deal with another tenant in the office building to share Internet access. By connecting a wireless bridge to your network and another to your colleague's network, you can provide Internet access to the remote network without changing anything on your or your colleague's network. For example, with long-range antennas, you can extend this idea over hundreds of feet, or even miles, enabling you to bridge your home network to your office network.

Not all access points offer this feature and a few, like the Linksys' WAP11, are specifically marketed as wireless bridges. Choose a bridging access point, for example, if you need to provide wireless coverage for two buildings.

Some APs are marketed as routers or residential gateways. By definition, you need a router or gateway to share Internet access—data to and from the Internet is routed to your local network. In fact, most wi-fi products aimed at consumers—whether they're called access points, routers, or residential gateways—provide Internet access sharing. On the high end, though, access points could simply facilitate wireless networks and bridge them to the wired world. Some devices identified by their manufacturers as routers provide dynamic and/or static routing. Both are features that are only useful when the access point is part of a group of networks that already contains other routers. Static routing lets you specify the path data uses to move between routed networks, while dynamic routing allows the path to be determined in real-time by the current layout of the larger network.

Finally, you can purchase access points that route AppleTalk, the network protocol used by older Macintosh computers. Because all modern Mac operating systems can communicate fine via TCP/IP, you won't need AppleTalk, even if you have Macs, unless you have an AppleTalk-only printer. Vendors who sell AppleTalk-capable access points include Apple, NetGear, Zoom, Agere/Orinoco, and Buffalo.

Security

Firewall security protects your local network from Internet-based intruders who seek to do harm by connecting to computers on your network via TCP/IP. A firewall won't protect you, however, from uninvited guests who seek to join your network by connecting to it with a wireless network interface card. Anyone carrying a laptop within range of your network can either connect to it easily or simply monitor the data being transmitted. If that happens, your firewall is useless.

Wi-fi has a basic layer of security called Wired Equivalent Privacy (WEP), which uses encryption to mask network data. In addition, access points have access control features that restrict access to all but "known" wireless devices. Also, security features exist to protect the access point's administrative interface. And, finally, many APs enable you to establish a connection to a virtual private network or to use proprietary access methods established by security-conscious companies that allow their employees to work from home.

WEP

WEP is part of the IEEE 802.11 standard and is supposed to make it impossible for anyone to decipher data being transmitted over a wireless network. WEP uses the RC4 encryption cipher to scramble data packets as they move between devices on the network. To view data in its unencrypted form, you must have joined the network and entered the correct WEP key—a series of alphanumeric characters or a hexadecimal number. The access point manages WEP-based access.

Two levels of WEP encryption exist—64-bit (sometimes called 40-bit) and 128-bit. These levels refer to the number of bits that form the encryption key. The greater the number of bits, the stronger the key. To use 128-bit encryption, access points and network adapters must support the higher level. Almost all currently available access points provide 128-bit encryption and they all also support 64-bit keys. In the early days of wi-fi, 128-bit encryption commanded a premium. Today, it's hard to find a 64-bit only access point or network adapter.

Unfortunately, WEP encryption isn't bulletproof. Security experts have proven the encryption keys can be easily obtained by laptop-toting crackers who drive or walk within range of your WEP-protected network. Freely available software allows these mischief-makers to automate the process, giving them quick access to your network. Most home users needn't worry about crackers and should use WEP to provide a basic layer of security. Businesses shouldn't depend on WEP alone, especially when you need to protect sensitive data.

Access Control

With a bit of work, you can improve the security of your network by limiting access to specific wireless devices. Access control features allow 802.11 access points to identify each wireless device by the MAC address of its wireless network adapter. NetGear's MR314 can display a list of currently connected wireless devices and their MAC addresses. This feature makes it easy to find and use device MACs to create a list of trusted network users. If your AP doesn't display MAC addresses, you need to find and copy them into the fields provided in the AP's management software.

Most, but not all, APs provide MAC-based access control and most home users probably don't need it. Like WEP, access control isn't a complete security solution. Crackers can spoof or copy MAC addresses they know to be valid on a network they want to join. A disadvantage of access control is you must manually add the MAC address of each new device you want to add to the network. This can be inconvenient if, for example, you often need to provide temporary wireless access to your network.

VPNs and External Security Standards

Many corporations and other large organizations use virtual private networks (VPNs) to provide secure remote access for their employees. A *VPN* provides a secure connection from a computer to a remote network, encrypting all the data that passes between them. If your employer uses a VPN, get a home access point that supports VPN passthrough and the particular protocol your employer uses. The same goes for a multioffice organization, in which you might want to reach the headquarters VPN from your field office's wireless network.

VPN passthrough allows a computer that gets its Internet access through a NAT-enabled access point to connect to a VPN to which you have access. Because NAT masks the true IP address of devices on your network, the VPN won't recognize and admit your computer unless the AP also provides passthrough.

A number of VPN protocols exist. Three of the most common are IPSec, PPTP, and L2TP. Check with the administrator of the VPN you need to access to determine which kind of passthrough access you need at home or in your remote office.

Proprietary Security

In an attempt to provide greater security than what's offered by WEP and access control, vendors, including Cisco, have developed proprietary schemes to secure wireless networks. Access points don't provide these high-level security features themselves but, instead, support access to secure networks for networks using compatible access points. In this way, these security measures are like a VPN: You need them only if you intend to connect to a server that requires them.

Remote Administration Dial-In User Services (RADIUS) is a security server. Users log into the server and are authenticated, enabling them to connect to and use network services protected by the server. Data on the network is encrypted, but with a much stronger algorithm than WEP's. Lightweight Extensible Authentication Protocol (LESP) is a Cisco security protocol found in that company's access points and supported by Apple's AirPort Base Station. The Base Station also supports RADIUS, as do many high-end access points. Most SOHO-class APs don't provide support for these tools.

Access Point Protection

Just as wireless networks are vulnerable to intruders, access points themselves, through their management software, are also subject to tampering. An attacker taking control of an access point could change its settings, locking out legitimate users, disabling security measures, learning WEP keys, and so forth. Access points with Web-based management tools are especially vulnerable because anyone who is on the network, either a stranger or an authorized user, can connect to the access point by typing its IP address into a browser. APs that use operating system-based tools are vulnerable to people with a copy of the administrative application.

The most basic way to protect the access point is to password-protect its management tools. This isn't WEP encryption, which protects the network, but a traditional password required to manage the device. All access points provide password protection, but some go several steps beyond. Agere's Orinoco BG-2000 and the D-Link DI-714, for example, restrict access from an IP address other than the one used to configure them initially. You can override this feature or you can specify IP addresses with administrative privileges. A nifty twist on this feature provided by Agere/Orinoco is the capability to specify that only wired (or wireless) clients can connect to the admin tools.

Special Features

So far in this chapter, you've learned about features you'll find in most wi-fi access points. Some special features aren't generally available, but are must-haves for some people.

AOL Support

If America Online is your Internet service provider (ISP), Apple's AirPort Base Station is the only game in town when it comes to wireless. Although other APs support dial-up access, they can't deliver AOL-based access to your network. Apple made a deal with AOL in 2001 and, through a set of custom scripts, the AirPort Base Station cannot only dial AOL from its built-in modem, it can also deliver shared Internet access to clients on an AirPort network.

Print Servers

The easiest way to share a printer with everyone on a wireless network is to connect it directly to the access point. APs with print server capability can accept and line up print jobs from both wired and wireless clients. Access points from D-Link, Zoom, and Linksys, among others, include printer ports. Some companies include the words "Print Server" in the names of products that offer this feature, while others simply include a parallel port on one or more of their products.

If you use network printing, you won't need a print server. You can connect an Ethernet printer that communicates using TCP/IP to the wired network, just as you would any other wired device.

Access Point Checklist

You learned a lot about access point features in this chapter. If you think shopping for the right AP will be a challenge, fear not. The good news is the majority of SOHO APs include most important features. A few rise above the rest when it comes to ease of use and value, and a few dogs exist. The best way to choose the right one, though, is to identify features you can't live without and move on from there. For example, if you know you'll need an external antenna to maximize your AP's range, ignore products that don't include a jack for an external antenna. Likewise, if you want to print to a wired, AppleTalk printer, your AP needs to provide AppleTalk support and include an Ethernet port for the printer.

Here's a list of the most important access point features:

❏ DHCP/NAT

❏ Multiple switched Ethernet ports

❏ External antenna jack

❏ Configurable firewall

❏ 128-bit WEP encryption

❏ Access control

This list is general and applicable to all wi-fi buyers. You might find you need features I haven't included on this short list, like dial-up modem support, PPPoE, VPN passthrough, or AppleTalk routing. If you need these or other features described in this chapter, add them to your personal checklist and start shopping for the right AP.

At this point, you might ask yourself how to find information about the access points you're considering. I'm pleased to say most AP vendors provide helpful information on their Web sites and some online merchants offer comparison shopping tools. Go beyond the press releases and product marketing flyers on the vendor sites. Download the PDF user guide and data sheets that most companies offer. You can learn a lot from the user guide, not only about features, but also about the aesthetics of each AP's management software. Is it confusing, pretty, filled with help screens for your edification? Chances are the user guide will provide screenshots, so take a good look.

You'll also find reviews of wi-fi APs in major computer magazines and on Web sites like Practically Networked (www.practicallynetworked.com).

Chapter 4

Network Adapters and Interfaces

Although many high-end laptops now include wi-fi radios as standard equipment, most portables and desktop don't include them. Onboard wireless, like Ethernet before it, will eventually be ubiquitous but, for now, chances are you'll need to buy wi-fi network adapters—also called network interface cards (NICs)—for most computers and handheld devices you want to add to your network.

In this chapter, you learn about your wi-fi NIC choices, including options available for laptops, desktop machines, and handheld devices. As the wi-fi (802.11b) access points, discussed in Chapter 3, have much in common with other 802.11 devices, more similarities than differences exist across the 802.11 network adapter spectrums. I point out those instances where newer technologies mean different interface characteristics as you move through this chapter.

Anatomy of a Wi-Fi Network Adapter

A *wi-fi network adapter*, like the one shown in Figure 4.1, consists of a 2.4 GHz radio and a connector that matches one of your computer's I/O ports. In most cases, there's also an antenna to extend the range of the radio. If not, the NIC will include a connector for the antenna.

Most wi-fi radios are contained within a Type II PCMCIA card (usually referred to as a *PC card*). This form factor makes good sense because most computers on wireless networks (at least at press time) are laptops with PC slots. For desktop PCs, you need a PCI-, USB-, or ISA-based NIC. To maximize

Figure 4.1
This Orinoco
Silver card is
a typical wi-fi
device: a PC card
containing a radio
with an antenna
attached to the

efficiency and volume, most manufacturers have built desktop NICs and access points around PC card radios, providing slots or adapters that accept the radios. Aside from making some of these products a bit cheaper than they otherwise would be, another advantage of this approach is that you can theoretically upgrade wireless clients and APs with new radios as technology evolves— simply switch radio cards to move from one standard to the next.

A 2.4 GHz antenna is integrated into one end of almost all radio cards. Apple's AirPort card, which is based on an Agere/Orinoco (formerly Lucent) radio, and works only with AirPort-compatible Macintosh computers, doesn't include an antenna, but connects to an antenna built into all AirPort-compatible Macs. Figure 4.2 shows three typical PC card network adapters.

Just as you can extend the range of many access points by plugging in external antenna, wi-fi cards often include an antenna port. You might need to buy an adapter that supports the antenna you want to use, but adapters and

Figure 4.2
The D-Link Air
and Lucent
Orinoco Silver
cards include
antennas. Apple's
AirPort card has
no antenna, but
it connects to an
antenna inside
the Macintosh.

the antennas themselves are widely available. See Chapter 5 for a detailed discussion of antenna options.

Kinds of Network Adapters

You might notice that I sometimes refer to wi-fi devices as network adapters and sometimes simply as network interface cards. This is because, while all these devices include a PC card radio, some require an adapter or plug into your computer via a USB cable. The point? You have several choices of wi-fi network adapters and not all vendors take the same approach. Each is described here, and then you get some help in choosing the best one for each computer on your wi-fi network. Table 4-1 compares the types of wi-fi network adapters available.

PC Cards

Almost all laptop computers contain one or two PCMCIA slots that accept Type II PC cards. Most wi-fi radios are Type II, CardBus-compatible cards. *CardBus* is the 32-bit version of the PCMCIA standard and is supported by all modern laptops. If you have an older laptop, check to see whether its PCMCIA slots support CardBus.

Card Type	Pros	Cons	Notes
PC Card	Easy to install, inexpensive, compact, and compatible with more non-Windows laptops than PCI or USB alternatives	Not directly compatible with desktop PCs	Default choice for laptops
PCI	Provides wi-fi access for almost all desktop PCs running Windows, affordable	Requires installation; driver conflicts possible	Choose adapters and radios from a single vendor
ISA	The only option when all PCI slots are full	Compatibility problems, requires extra IRQs, few products available	
USB	Portable, compatible with desktops and laptops, flexible placement options enhance wireless range	Somewhat expensive	

Table 4-1
Choose the Right Kind of Wi-Fi NIC Based on Your Computers, Your Need for Portability, and Your Budget.

PCI and ISA Network Adapters

Most wi-fi vendors sell a PCI card for desktop PCs. A few, including Agere/Orinoco, D-Link, and Buffalo Technology offer ISA options. In most cases, the required equipment for a desktop PC consists of an adapter (sometimes called a *sleeve* or *card holder*) that you install into an open ISA or PCI slot, and a PC card radio that slides into a slot in the adapter (Figure 4.3). In some cases, you must buy the two devices separately, while other vendors sell the adapter and card together.

PCI or ISA will be the only option for some desktop PCs and you might find these network adapters, with their direct access to the PC's system bus, are the fastest way to go. Internal devices like these could also be a bit cheaper than USB adapters (see the following section). Some disadvantages exist to PCI or ISA, though. First, you must open the computer to install the card holder. Second, you might also find that, even in a Windows plug-and-play world, the PCI or ISA card requires a bit of troubleshooting. You need to install driver software for both the card holder and the wi-fi radio. The best way to minimize configuration and compatibility problems is to purchase the PCI/ISA card and wi-fi PC card from the same vendor.

If you have both PCI and ISA slots available for a new wi-fi adapter, choose the PCI option. ISA configuration is sometimes more troublesome and might require you to use two valuable interrupt request lines (IRQs) instead of one. If you must use an ISA adapter, choose one from a reputable vendor who offers good and free technical support. More about hardware and driver setup in Chapter 8.

Figure 4.3
When installed in a PCI or ISA card holder, the D-Link Air PC card can provide wireless access for a desktop PC.

Apple Power Macintosh computers, like PCs, contain PCI slots, but no current wi-fi adapters support them directly. A few vendors do offer open source drivers that might work with some PCI cards and older Mac operating systems. If you choose this path for taking an old Mac wireless, be sure to test both the adapter and the driver before you buy.

USB Adapters

Perhaps the most flexible kind of wireless network adapter is a USB device. Unlike a PCI/ISA adapter, a USB unit requires no installation. Just plug it in to a free USB port on your computer or USB hub. Almost all modern PCs—both desktops and laptops—include USB ports, so wi-fi adapters can be moved between computers easily and quickly if there aren't enough to go around. Speaking of moving around, you can often enhance reception by repositioning a USB device in relation to your wi-fi access point. Figure 4.4 shows the Agere/Orinoco USB device. It's vertical orientation gives it good radio reception characteristics. Other USB devices are more boxy in shape.

On the downside, wi-fi USB devices could compete for resources with other USB peripherals attached to the same hub, slowing down network access. You might also need to add a USB hub if you've already maxed out a

Figure 4.4
Agere's Orinoco USB NIC is a stylish little thing. Although you can't see it, the unit contains a PC card radio and an antenna.

PC's USB ports. Finally, USB devices come at a bit of a price premium because of their consumer-friendly packaging.

Special Network Adapters

A few vendors offer special kinds of network adapters for devices that don't have connectors for standard PC, PCI, ISA, or USB cards. Ethernet converters and PDA modules are two of these.

Ethernet Converters

Ethernet devices, primarily printers, that can't be outfitted with a standard wi-fi NIC can be added to a wireless network with a print server. Agere/ Orinoco and Linksys (Figure 4.5) sell devices that provide a port for the printer, an Ethernet port to connect the printer to the wired network, a wi-fi radio, and an antenna. With the print server device connected to the printer, wireless devices on the network will be able to print to it. See Chapter 11 for more details on print server operation.

PDA Modules

Some, but not all, PDAs can join a wi-fi network. Intel's Xircom-branded SpringPort Wireless Ethernet module works with Palm OS-based PDAs.

PocketPC devices, including the Compaq IPaq, HP Jornada, and Casio Casiopia can join wireless networks, but you'll need a compact flash (CF) card to beam wi-fi signals to these devices. CF cards slip into a sleeve in these

Figure 4.5
Linksys' PrintServer connects directly to a printer or a wired network via an Ethernet port.

and several other PocketPC and Handheld PC (HPC)-based handheld devices. Like PC card radios, CF cards include an antenna that protrudes from the top of the handheld device.

When looking for a CF card, be sure the card supports the handheld device you use. D-Link's compact flash radio, for example, works with handhelds based on StrongARM and MIPS processors, but not SH3 devices. Some HP Jornadas use StrongARM, while others are based on SH3 chips.

NIC Drivers and OS-Compatibility

Wi-fi radios themselves are a lot alike. Once you choose the type of card you want, you might spend most of your shopping time evaluating different products based on price. If you're a Linux or Mac user, your choices might be limited by the availability of drivers for the card because most vendors ship only Windows drivers. Linux users can download open source drivers that support the most popular PC cards and, with a bit of troubleshooting, can use most current products. Mac users whose computers aren't AirPort-compatible have severely limited choices. Agere/Orinoco products are compatible with older Mac laptops, and Proxim sells a Mac-compatible USB NIC. Third-party drivers also provide Mac OS X and OS 9 compatibility for a number of PC cards. For details on OS compatibility and driver options for all major operating systems see Chapter 8.

Chapter 5

Antennas and Accessories

Adding antennas, repeaters, management software, or other tools to your wi-fi network can enhance its performance and give you access to new wireless applications. This chapter describes a wide variety of tools you can add to your network. Some of them are well suited to a home or small office environment, while others are intended for large organizations or community network installations. A range of products is included here to give you a better idea of what's possible in a wi-fi environment.

The bulk of this chapter is dedicated to antennas. Adding an antenna to your access point can significantly extend the range of your wi-fi network and connecting one to a laptop puts you within reach of more access points. First, you're introduced to antenna technology that's applicable to wi-fi. Next, you learn about the different types of antennas available, which ones work best indoors and out, and how to decide which antenna is best. From there, it's on torepeaters and bridges that you can use to extend the reach of your network.

Antenna Basics

Antennas increase the range and coverage of wi-fi networks. They radiate the modulated radio signals into the air, so that can be received by other radios. Antennas don't boost the level of available signal—they merely focus the signals generated by radios.

Nearly all wi-fi network adapters and access points come equipped with some kind of antenna and those that don't, like Apple's AirPort cards, are connected to an antenna within the host computer. Built-in network adapter antennas are particularly weak, both because of their location (at one end of a

PC card) and their high directivity. As you see in this chapter, highly directional antennas are desirable when pointed toward other wireless devices. But that directivity harms the network adapter's range if you don't have it aimed at an access point. Interestingly, those wi-fi-equipped laptops often provide better antenna performance than do add-on network adapters. That's because vendors, including Apple and Toshiba, build antennas into their laptop cases, usually inside the LCD display, rather than stuffing an antenna into the network adapter This arrangement gives the antennas "room to breathe" and more exposure to incoming signals from all directions.

Access point antennas are usually vertical, low-gain omnidirectional or dipole antennas that provide significantly more gain than most network adapter antennas, but a lot less than the external antennas you learn about in this chapter.

Most access points and some network adapters support external antennas. External AP antennas often replace the ones that come as standard. Long-range antennas typically connected to an access point. In large networks, multiple access points might be used, each with its own external antenna. Wi-fi signals can travel up to 12 miles when an antenna is well placed (on a rooftop, for example) and not blocked by buildings, trees, or other obstructions. You must maintain a line-of-site connection between two remote points for antennas to carry radio signals over long distances.

A number of antenna types work well in wi-fi environments. A wide range of gain levels and physical antenna configurations is available. But before you learn about these, I'll define some important antenna terminology. Understanding the meaning and interrelationship of these terms is critical to choosing the antenna that's right for your situation.

Antennas all have several characteristics that contribute to the quality and strength of the signal they provide

❑ **Bandwidth**   In a radio transmission, the range of frequencies (the 2.4 GHz band, for 802.11b) available for data is referred to as *bandwidth. radiationBandwidth* also refers to the speed at which data travels over a given path.

❑ **Gain**   While *pattern* describes the shape of the signal transmitted by an antenna, *gain* describes the degree of directionality of the antenna. Highly directional antennas, those whose signals propagates in a straight line, without losing signal along the way, provide higher gain than those who distribute their signal in a wider pattern. Gain is measured in dBi, or sometimes, dBd.

❑ **S/N ratio**   The strength of a radio signal, relative to the noise in the environment, generates the signal-to-noise (S/N) ratio for a transmission. This is measured in decibels.

❑ **Radiation pattern**   Different types of antennas produce different patterns of coverage in the air. *Directional antennas,* for example, modulate the signal in a linear pattern, in the direction the antenna is pointed. Omnidirectional antennas, however, cover a radial pattern around the antenna.

❑ **Beamwidth**   Related to radiation pattern, an antenna's *beamwidth,* usually expressed in degrees, refers to the area in which the antenna's power is at its peak. You can use the rated beamwidth to calculate the width of the coverage area of the antenna. Beamwidth usually, but not always, refers to the horizontal plane.

❑ **Polarization**   The electromagnetic waves emitted by an antenna travel either horizontally or vertically. The polarization of antennas on each end of a transmission must match to minimize gain loss. A poor polarization match generates signal noise.

❑ **Isotropic antenna**   Antenna gain is expressed in *dBi,* a measure that compares the antenna's gain to an *isotropic antenna*—a theoretical antenna with zero gain/loss.

Types of Antennas

Antennas come in a variety of shapes and sizes. As described earlier, when defining antenna radiation pattern, the shape of an antenna has a great affect on its range and coverage area. You can buy small antennas suitable for attaching to a network adapter in a laptop or large units for mounting on a rooftop. In between are choices for indoor access points and even units that can be mounted in vehicles or on poles in public spaces. Choosing an antenna is a tradeoff between coverage area and signal strength. Antennas designed to provide coverage to a large area won't provide the same signal strength as a directional antenna with the same rated power.

Omnidirectional Antennas

The signals from an omnidirectional antenna are radiated outward from the antenna in all directions, creating a dome-shaped pattern, as shown in Figure 5.1. Omnidirectional antennas are pole-shaped and work best when pointed upward.

Figure 5.1
The Agere /Orinoco antenna is an omnidirectional antenna that's well suited for use with a laptop or a desktop PC. The shape of the radiation pattern is drawn on this image.

Because omni antennas can provide a signal over a large area, but lack the directionality needed to deliver maximum signal to all clients, they're best used in areas where client radios are spread out over a large area and are at approximately the same height as the omni antenna. The coverage dome is also subject to interference, which dilutes the antenna's signal. An open coffee shop or office space makes a good environment for an omni, especially if the antenna is placed high above obstructions that could cause interference.

The greater the gain of an omni antenna, the flatter the signal dome becomes, resembling a pancake in the case of a 12 dBi antenna. In all omni antennas, but especially in large ones, the poorest signal occurs immediately above and below the antenna, making these the worst locations to place a wireless device. Thus, high-gain omnis can create dead spots in close proximity to them. Even in an environment where you want to spread the signal over a large area, a lower-gain antenna might provide better coverage.

Sector Antennas

Think of a sector antenna (sometimes called a *corner reflector*) as an omni with more direction in life. *Sectors* are flattened antennas with a reflector behind the antenna surface to direct the signal forward or—if the antenna is placed on the ceiling or tilted—downward. Sectors can be vertical, flattened poles or horizontal ones. They provide signal in a radius up to 180 degrees, but no more because the reflector prevents them from radiating a signal behind the antenna. Because sectors are more directional than omnis, they can be used to focus wi-fi signals in a small area and they're less subject to signal noise, also because of the reflector. Sector antenna gain ranges from 4 to 10 dBi.

Sectors are often used where all wi-fi devices are in the same area and in the same direction in relation to the antenna. You could also use several sector antennas, each covering an area where wi-fi clients are concentrated. Again, the blocking characteristics of the barrier behind the antenna reduce interference in environments where multiple networks operate within close proximity to one another.

Yagi Antennas

Yagi antennas are intended for long distance, point-to-point situations. They could look like rooftop TV antennas or they might be housed in cans or tubes. Yagi antennas are directional, with a beamwidth of perhaps 15–60 degrees. As such, they provide higher gain than sector antennas (6–21 dBi), as shown in Figure 5.2. You can achieve high gain by using an extremely long yagi antenna mounted on a roof and pointed toward another antenna located at your destination.

Panel Antennas

Panel antennas are flat and solid in construction. They provide between 12 and 22 dBi gain but, because of their flat design, they suffer from wind-related path loss in outdoor environments. *Panels,* also called *patch antennas,* are highly directional and, thus, suitable for point-to-point environments. Panels are sometimes preferred for aesthetic reasons, see Figure 5.3.

Figure 5.2
The HyperGain
Radome Enclosed
yagi antenna has
a beamwidth
of 30 degrees
and 14 dBi gain.

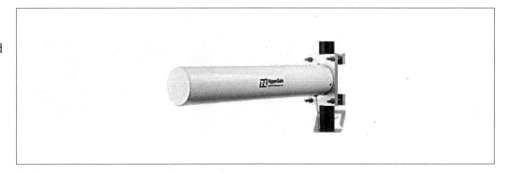

Figure 5.3
This 18 dBi panel antenna from NetNimble measures 16.5 inches' square.

Parabolic Reflectors

Parabolic reflectors can be square or round. They're suited to rooftop or other outdoor installation. Some parabolic antennas consist of a wire mesh, while other are solid in construction. They also vary widely in size, as shown in Figure 5.4. Parabolic antennas generate high gain (up to 27 dBi) and are directional. Several configurations of parabolic antennas exist—some are round, some have an irregular parabolic shape. Like yagis, parabolic antennas make a great choice for point-to-point links, providing even higher gain. On the downside, parabolic antennas sometimes lack the aesthetic appeal of other antennas.

Other Types of Antennas

All sorts of antennas can be used with wi-fi. Varieties you might encounter include *dipoles* (the type usually supplied with access points), mobile whips,

Figure 5.4
Here are three parabolic grid antennas: an 18 dBi grid and a 21 dBi dish from Andrew Systems, plus a small (2-inch diameter) Radio Waves dish.

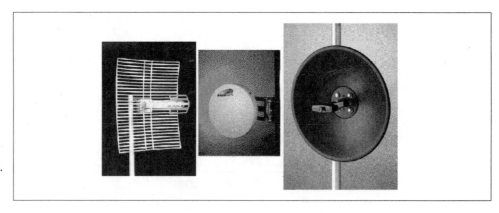

and corner reflectors. Although many antennas of these types weren't built specifically for wi-fi applications, you can use any antenna that operates in the 2.4 GHz band.

Connectors and Cabling

To use an antenna with your access point or network adapter, you typically need a length of coaxial cable and a connector that matches the antenna you're using. You might also need an adapter for your network adapter or access point.

Coaxial cable connects an antenna to a wireless device. You should use good quality cable that's rated for the 2.4 GHz band and make the cable as short as possible. That's because cable is a source of attenuation (signal loss) that could significantly impair the range of a high-gain antenna. Consider thin coaxial cable, with an attenuation of 3 dB for every four feet of cable. Cables from Times Microwave's LMR series are good choices. LMR cables offer different degrees of attenuation. You should check with your antenna vendor to be sure you select the best specific cable for the run length you need. In fact, ordering cable in the length you need it, with the proper connector attached, is the best (though not the cheapest) way to limit the amount of cable-related attenuation.

Like cables, connectors introduce signal loss. Although a variety of connector types are electrically compatible with 802.11, the three that best combine support for the 2.4 GHz band and minimum signal loss are SMA, TNC, and N connectors. All are available in male and female versions, so be sure to order the connector type that matches and has the opposite polarity of your antenna's connector.

SMA connectors are small and threaded. Some coax cables might be too thick to use with SMA connectors, but you can use TNC connectors with thicker coax varieties. Of the three connector types, N is the most popular in the 802.11 world. You can find many antennas marketed specifically for wi-fi that have an N connector. Again, be sure your connector of whatever type is the opposite gender of the one on the antenna. Although you can buy adapters that reverse connector polarity, these adapters, and others that intervene between antenna and radio will attenuate signals significantly.

Home-brew Antennas

Many hobbyists and others knowledgeable about radio and antenna technology choose to build their own antennas. Some folks assemble antennas from scratch, while others adapt antennas not designed for wi-fi, by adding custom elements and connectors. Either way, building your own antenna requires specific knowledge of the calculations needed to obtain the correct frequency and gain, as well as an understanding of the FCC's Part 15 regulations, which pertain to the level of signal amplification allowed in the 2.4GHz ISM band. Fortunately, the Internet provides a wide array of antenna information, as well as many sources of components for your building project. Some examples of homebrew antenna projects appear in Table 5-1. A variety of home-brew antenna plans are also available. A few of these are spotlighted, but please use these plans at your own risk.

Choosing Antennas

Picking the right antenna or antennas requires you take several factors into account. First, consider the antenna's job. Linking remote sites via a point-to-point link calls for a high-gain, highly directional antenna on each end, such as a yagi or parabolic grid. The right antenna for a point-to-multipoint environment, where the antennas delivers signals from a central access point to many remote networks, depends on the shape of the space to be covered, interference in the environment, and, of course, the distance to be covered. As indicated earlier, omnidirectional antennas create a 360-degree coverage area, but they don't provide the gain of a highly directional antenna.

Name	URL	Notes
Primestar Dish	http://www.wwc.edu/~frohro/ Airport/Primestar/Primestar.html	Use a Primestar satellite TV dish as a wi-fi antenna
Pringles Can	http://www.oreillynet.com/cs/ weblog/view/wlg/448/	With a potato chip can and a few items from the hardware store, you can build an omni antenna
Vertical Collinear Antenna	http://205.159.169.11/reference/ antennas/2ghz_collinear_omni/	

Table 5-I
A Number of Plans for Homebrew Antenna Are Available on the Internet.

The Right Antenna for Your Environment

Let's look at some common environments and the antenna types that work best in each. Every situation is different, of course, but you can make some generalizations about the layout of areas requiring wi-fi coverage.

❏ **One-story Home**   A typical one-story home can usually be served effectively by the dipole antenna connected to the access point if the AP is centrally located and not hindered by obstructions. If your home is large or if placing an access point in a central location isn't practical, consider adding an external omni antenna to your laptop's network adapter card.

❏ **Two-story Home**   Although wi-fi signals can travel between floors of a building, you might find your AP's antenna doesn't provide the coverage you need to reach all areas of your home. Again, locating the antenna centrally can improve your reception significantly. Placing the access point on the second floor can also help distribute the available signal throughout your home. To cover a large area, add an omni antenna to an access point located in the center of the upper floor.

❏ **Small Office/Retail**   Depending on your office's physical configuration, you might be able to use a single omnidirectional antenna to provide full coverage. If a portion of your space is separated from the rest or if you need to locate your access point at one extreme of the environment, choose a more directional antenna, such as a parabolic grid.

❏ **Warehouse**   The most efficient way to cover a large contiguous space is with multiple omnidirectional antennas with overlapping coverage areas.

❏ **Large Office**   Although omni antennas provide the broadest coverage area and could be the best choice for open office environments, you might find adding directional antennas necessary to concentrate coverage in a conference room, lab, or other area with lots of users. This could also provide security advantages if you choose to limit coverage in those areas to prevent unauthorized access to the network.

❏ **Point-to-Point**   To bring wi-fi signals from one building to another within the same area—on a corporate campus, for example—you might be able to use two high-gain omnis or a pair of panel antennas. Because panel antennas are more directional than omnis, consider their placement carefully to be sure they have good line-of-sight coverage. To link sites that are more than a half mile apart, you need long-range, highly directional antennas at each end. Yagis are typically the best choice because of their high degree of directionality, but high-gain parabolic dishes can also be used.

❏ **Outdoor Open Space**   Providing wi-fi coverage to an outdoor area, such as the quad on a college campus or a city park is a challenge because signal loss is so high outdoors. High-gain sectors can effectively beam signals in point to multipoint environments and omnis can provide coverage to large areas.

Calculating Antenna Range

A number of factors affect the range an antenna will cover in a wi-fi environment. The raw gain number for the antennas you choose, as well as its directionality, provide the basis for your range calculation, but they don't tell the full story. Some level of interference occurs in all environments, reducing the range of your antenna, especially if it isn't positioned in a way that minimizes obstructions. As you learned previously in this chapter, the cable and connectors placed between the antenna and the access point can also significantly reduce the antenna's actual gain.

The process of determining the range you need is called calculating your *link budget*. You might perform these calculations on your own or you can use one of several link budget calculators you'll find on the Internet. These include Wireless Network Analysis from Green Bay Professional Packet Radio (http://members.gbonline.com/~multiplx/wireless/wireless.main.cgi), Electro-Comm's Interactive Wireless Network Design Utilities (http://www.ecommwireless.com/calculations.html), and RFPROP (http://www.users.dircon.co.uk/~netking/freesw.htm), a Windows-based calculator. Preparing a link budget is a crucial step if you're building a long-range, point-to-point link but it's less necessary when you're providing coverage to an indoor area, such as your home or a single-floor office.

To determine a link budget yourself, you need to perform two calculations: first, determine the *path loss*—the amount of signal lost between the two ends of the transmission. Second, calculate the effective gain of your antenna by subtracting losses associated with cables and connectors. Third, and finally, subtract the path loss from the effective gain.

You can calculate path loss over an unobstructed path using the following formula:

$$L = 20 \log(d) + 20 \log(i) + 36.6$$

where *L* equals path loss in decibels, *d* equals distance in miles, and *f* equals the specific frequency in megahertz. To obtain the frequency number, you need to choose the channel on which your network will operate. This tells you the frequency on which that channel operates. Table 5-2 shows each channel's frequency in megahertz, as allocated in the United States and Canada. The allocation ranges are slightly different in Europe and Japan.

Note: a path loss calculation only tells you how much signal will be lost over an unobstructed distance. Obstructions or improper antenna placement will generate additional losses.

To calculate the amount of gain each antenna will provide, you need to subtract all your losses from the antenna's rated gain. The formula looks like this:

Antenna gain – pigtail loss – cable loss – connector loss – other losses = effective antenna gain

To obtain loss numbers for cables and connectors, check out the specs for each piece of equipment you use wih your antenna and plug the loss numbers into the formula.

The formula for your point-to-point link's total gain looks like this:

Total gain = (Site *A* effective antenna gain + Site *B* antenna gain) – path loss

Channel	Frequency
1	2401-2423
2	2406-2428
3	2411-2433
4	2416-2438
5	2421-2443
6	2426-2448
7	2431-2453
8	2436-2458
9	2441-2463
10	2446-2468
11	2451-2473

Table 5-2
Each Wi-fi Channel Occupies a Portion of the 2.4 GHz Frequency Band

Antenna Specs Checklist

You've learned all you can about antennas. You memorized the terminology associated with them. Perhaps you even chose a lovely spot on your roof or wall where your new antenna will be located. When you begin shopping for antennas, though, you still might find yourself wading through a wide array of products, unsure which ones meet your needs. So, let's look at antenna specs, given what you've learned in this chapter.

❏ **Frequency**   When shopping for antennas, first be sure the unit operates in the 2.4 GHz frequency band. An antenna's specs might indicate the device works between 2.3 and 2.5 GHz. That's OK, of course, but anything outside a range that contains 2.4 GHz won't be compatible with 802.11b or 802.11g. If, on the other hand, you need to boost the range of an 802.11a network, you must use a 5 GHz antenna.

❏ **Antenna type**   Next, look for the antenna type you need: omni, yagi, sector, grid, and so forth. Antennas names might differ among manufacturers. You might want to examine the antenna visually and look at a data sheet to determine whether an antenna has the directional characteristics you want. For example, a 360 degree antenna is omnidirectional, even if it isn't labeled as such.

❏ **Beamwidth**   More specifically than the general antenna type, most directional antenna specs include the beamwidth in degrees, enabling you to plot the coverage area based not only on the distance from one antenna to the other, but also on the portion of the radius that's covered.

❏ **Polarization**   If you're using multiple antennas to link remote sites, be sure the units you select have the same polarization (horizontal or vertical). Vertically polarized antennas have a higher profile, and they make the best choice when you face land and water obstructions to your signal. Horizontal polarization is best when buildings are the primary obstacles. Some antennas provide a choice of polarization, even dual or circular polarization.

❏ **Gain**   This is often the first spec antenna buyers look for. The raw gain of an antenna means little without considering the other factors on this check list. As you learned in the previous section, many factors reduce the real gain your antenna will achieve, as does its directionality and placement in the environment. Use the gain calculations in this chapter to help you determine how much gain you need.

❏ **Connectors** As discussed in the connector section, your antenna will either be connected directly to a wireless device or you'll need to acquire connectors, cables, and adapters to make the link. If you can find an antenna whose connector matches your wi-fi device (N-female to N-male, for example), you'll experience reduced attenuation in the signal.

Wi-fi antenna equipment is available from a number of sources online. See Appendix B for an exhaustive list.

Bridges and Repeaters

A *network bridge* connects two segments of a network. With a bridge in place, devices on each segment of the network can see and communicate with devices on the other segment, as if all devices were on the same segment. Most wi-fi access points act as bridges between the wireless and wired portions of the network, allowing a wireless laptop to print to a wired printer or a wired workstation to download files to the laptop.

A wireless bridge isn't the same as an access point that bridges wired and wireless segments. Instead, *wireless bridges* connect two remote wired networks, either within the same building or over long distances, as shown in Figure 5.5. You could do the same job with a wired bridge with cabling with a leased line between remote offices, but a wireless bridge can be an inexpensive way to accomplish the same goal.

Figure 5.5
The Linksys
WAP11 is a
wireless bridge
and access point.

With wireless bridges connected to each wired segment, the two segments can function as a single network. The bridges exchange packets bound from one network to another, wirelessly. Wireless bridges can also function as access points, meaning each network can include wireless clients when such a unit is used.

You can buy or build a wireless repeater to extend wi-fi coverage from one site to another. This arrangement is useful if you don't have a good line-of-sight relationship between antennas on either side of the wireless link. A repeater receives a wireless signal from one site, amplifies it, and transmits it to a site out of range of the site where the signal originated. A repeater consists of two wi-fi radios and an amplifier that delivers signals from one location to another, via the radios (Figure 5.6). A repeater is a useful way to extend wireless coverage over a distance that's greater than that over which wi-fi equipment can transmit or in environments where line-of-sight problems impede the performance of antennas.

Software

You needn't buy extra software to build and run a wireless network. The drivers required for network adapters ship with these products, though you might need to download open-source software to use a particular card with Linux or Mac OS X. This is because most driver software provided with network cards is for Windows.

Software packages exist that help you manage and analyze your wireless network. Most of these are intended for administrators who need to find and close security holes within a large wireless network or who want to locate other networks in their community.

Figure 5.6
A repeater receives signals from one site, amplifies them, and transmits them to a remote site. The repeater consists of two wi-fi radios.

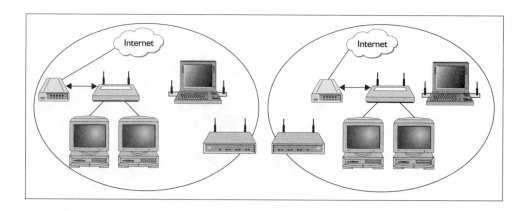

Software for managing and analyzing wireless networks is in its infancy. Sophisticated tools network administrators use to keep tabs on wired environments have yet to become available to the same degree in the wireless world. Some good tools do exist, though, including a variety of freeware and shareware programs for scanning the air for wireless networks or assessing signal strength. You can also buy applications that analyze wireless network traffic, even though these are usually overkill for home or small business networks. Scanning and security auditing software tools are discussed in Chapter 10 and network analysis software appears in Chapter 13. Appendix B lists a variety of drivers, network analysis tools, and other applications you can use to get more from your wireless network.

Chapter 6

Choosing Internet Access

Shared Internet access is a primary reason many people site for starting a wi-fi network. The capability to share is built into nearly all access points and setting it up is a simple matter in most cases. But to share access, you must choose a provider and configure the access point to work with the service you buy. This chapter provides helpful advice for choosing a new Internet service provider (ISP), working with an existing provider to meet the needs of wireless users, and determining whether any special services are required. You also learn about the types of ISP services and connections available.

How Wi-Fi Internet Access Works

Most owners of home and small office wi-fi networks use the wireless connection to provide shared Internet access to computers on the local network. An access point can act as a router between the Internet and your network, routing Internet data around the network, and bridging the wired and wireless segments of the network. Using the AP to distribute Internet access is usually the easiest way to share and the best way to provide security for users. This is because access point firewalls shield the network from intruders.

For the most part, the same Internet accounts and methods of getting connected don't differ, whether or not you're sharing the account with a wireless network. You can purchase Internet access from a local or national ISP, a phone company, or a cable company. And you can use the equipment the provider recommends to make an Internet connection—a cable or a DSL modem, or a dial-up modem. In a wireless environment, the access point usuallyconnects to the cable, DSL, or dial-up modem just as a single computer does in an environment where Internet access isn't shared (Figure 6.1).

Figure 6.1
In a typical wi-fi environment, the access point links your Internet access device and the local network. Wired and wireless computers depend on the access point for Internet access.

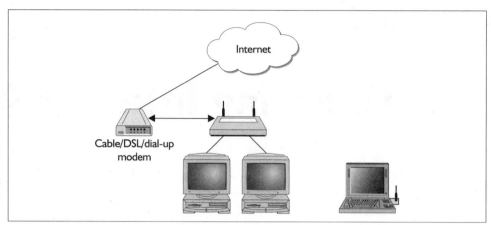

The Data Link

To share Internet access with networked users, you need to do some hardware setup and software configuration. The process works like this: connect the access point to the modem, and then configure it with your user name and password. Use the IP addressing method and other settings supplied by your ISP. When IP setup is complete, your access point will be able to connect to the Internet, log on to your account and use or acquire a valid IP address. To share the Internet with local network users, the access point must route packets from the Internet to the local computers. This is usually accomplished by using the access point as a DHCP server that provides local IP addresses to each connected device. You can also assign private IP addressees in the same subnet as the access point's local address to each device. Identifying the access point as the router enables everyone on the network to reach both the access point and the Internet beyond. You will learn about this process, with practical examples, in Chapter 7.

Once configured to obtain an IP address and/or use the access point as a router, all computers on the network will be able to reach to the Internet by launching a web browser or other Internet application. If you use dial-up to connect, launching an application will activate the modem as it does in a single-user situation, unless another network user is already online.

Sharing a connection this way provides more than an affordable access method: you'll also have the benefits of the firewall built into your access point. Although some firewalls aren't customizable, almost all give you the capability to shield the IP addresses of individual computers on your network with Network Address Translation (NAT), as described in Chapter 3. No configuration is required; simply turn NAT on and surf without fear that an individual computer's IP address will be broadcast over the Internet. Instead, the IP address assigned to the access point—which usually changes each time you connect to the Internet—identifies your network, no matter who's using it. If your access point's firewall can be configured to prevent specific kinds of incoming and outgoing access, then it will protect all devices on your network.

Hardware and Connections

Access points include a 10-BASE-T Ethernet port for broadband devices. In an enterprise setting, this port might connect the access point to a network backbone. When the access point provides direct Internet connectivity, the broadband port connects the AP to the cable, DSL, or satellite modem—any method that uses Ethernet.

A few APs include a dial-up modem, to which you connect with an RJ-11 cable from the access point to the phone outlet. Far more provide a serial port to which you can attach a dial-up modem. Whether it's built-in or external, using dial-up to connect adds some steps to the configuration of your AP. Instead of setting up a dial-up connection in your operating system (OS) or using software supplied with the modem, you need to enter the ISP phone number and other information specific to the modem in your access point's config software. With the modem configured to dial the Internet from the access point, you can add wired and wireless clients, just as you would with a broadband connection. Configure each to obtain its IP address from the access point (if you're using the AP's DHCP server) and set the access point as the network router.

Nontraditional Setups

It's not crucial for an access point to be the conduit for Internet access. The AP can act as just another node on a wired network, with a connection to a backbone network via a hub or router that provides Internet access to all wired clients. The AP's job is to manage communication between wireless clients, as well as to bridge communication between them and the wired devices. But even if the AP isn't providing Internet access to wired clients, it needs to deliver access to wireless ones, unless you don't intend to provide Internet access to wireless devices at all. If you don't plan to use the AP to provide IP addresses locally, you only need to connect the AP to the network, configure its wireless properties, and disable its DHCP server software.

Internet Access Choices in Detail

The most basic decision you must make about acquiring Internet access for a wireless network is how that access will be provided: broadband or dial-up, cable or DSL, and so forth. Your decision will be based on your budget, the degree to which fast access is important, and the options offered by ISPs in your area.

Dial-Up Access

The cheapest, most widely available way to get on to the Internet is with a 56K modem and a dial-up Internet account. At $10 to $20 a month, dial-up access is much more cost-effective than other methods, though it's a much slower way to surf the Web. To use a dial-up connection in a wi-fi environment, you must have a dial-up account, a modem, and an access point with either an integrated modem or a modem port. You also need a phone line that can be dedicated to Internet access. In short, the only new item you'll likely need to provide for wireless dial-up is an access point.

Despite its simplicity and low cost, you should think carefully before opting for dial-up. It's one thing to surf the Web with a 56K modem when you're the only user on the line, but sharing a connection with a second simultaneous user, much less three or four, will severely reduce the speed of your connection, even if you're all performing low-bandwidth tasks. If one of you begins a large download or a multiplayer game, speeds could become intolerable for everyone. Think carefully about how many simultaneous users your network will have and what each will be doing on the Internet.

Aside from the obvious speed benefits, a broadband connection offers instant Internet access from the wireless network. Modem connections usually remain disconnected until a network device opens a browser, tries to check e-mail, or engages some other Internet application. Although dial-up's slow speed is a given, you might not be prepared for the slowdowns you experience when sharing a dial-up Internet connection with several simultaneous users. Even though this is somewhat rare today, some dial-up accounts are metered, meaning every connection costs money. The monthly cost of an Internet connection that's shared with several clients could be difficult to manage.

If your Internet use is generally limited to checking e-mail and viewing text-based web sites (a more typical office usage pattern), you might be able to get by with dial-up access. Dial-up could also serve you well if you use your network primarily for local applications, with little need for Internet access. Some parents might prefer this scenario as a way to keep their kids from harm's way on the Internet. In some cases, a dial-up connection used by one person might only need to be shared when wireless devices connect. An inexpensive dial-up connection could be just the thing.

AOL

Most dial-up ISPs provide a phone number that gets you connected to the ISP's network, and then takes you directly to the Internet. America Online's dial-up accounts bring you into the AOL service which, though it does provide access to Internet sites, doesn't pass you directly through as other ISPs do. For this reason, you can't normally use an AOL account to provide shared Internet access on your network unless you have an Apple AirPort Base Station (Figure 6.2). Because of an agreement between Apple and AOL, AirPort owners can dial into AOL with the built-in modem and share access with wireless clients, using scripts supplied with the base station. Each user needs his or her own account to reach the AOL service, but all can connect to the Internet once the base station has connected via AOL. This is a neat setup for those who already have an AOL dial-up account and would rather not switch but, instead, simply want to go wireless.

Broadband Options

Consumers and businesspeople in most areas of the country can purchase some form of broadband Internet access. In most metropolitan areas, you can choose among several options. Broadband options include cable, DSL, satellite, and ISDN. While dial-up connections provide a maximum speed of 56 Kbps, even the slowest broadband connection method—ISDN—operates at a minimum speed of 64 Kbps. Cable and DSL speeds range from 128 Kbps to 384 Kbps for home users and up to 1 Mbps plus in high-use business environments. Broadband also offers the distinct advantage of continuous, immediate access to the Net for everyone on the network. The primary downside is that broadband access, though rapidly decreasing in price, is still slightly more expensive than dial-up. If, however, you dedicate a phone line exclusively to Internet access, the combined cost of an AOL account and the phone line isn't much less than some broadband options, especially if you already have cable television (a requirement for cable-based Internet access) in your home or business. The cost is most important to home users and others who don't use the Internet frequently.

Figure 6.2
The Apple AirPort Base Station supports dial-up access via AOL.

Let's look at the various types of broadband access and see how each affects the wireless network.

Cable

Cable television companies that have upgraded their physical plants with fiberoptic cable can and usually do offer broadband access via their networks. Internet access is typically delivered by an external cable modem. In single-user setups, the cable modem connects to a computer via an Ethernet cable. Cable service is often available to business users as well, including access to the network for multiple computers. In all cases, cable TV service is a prerequisite.

Cable offers the advantage of being widely available and fairly simple to install for the provider. This reduces cost to the customer. Most homes, even in small communities, can be or have been wired, and a high likelihood exists that Internet users and home network builders already have cable TV. On the other hand, cable companies that haven't upgraded their systems to fiber probably won't offer data service because their infrastructure isn't capable of supporting it.

The maximum download speed for cable-based Internet access can be as high as 2 or 3 Mbps, with an upload limit usually below 160 Kbps. The theoretical maximum download speed is as high as 27 Mbps, but you won't achieve that kind of speed. For one thing, the speed of the provider's connection to the Internet imposes a limit. More significantly, cable bandwidth is shared with other customers. The number of households using the bandwidth depends on the infrastructure provided by the cable company.

Despite the fact that bandwidth is shared, cable does provide considerable potential speed. Cable provides more speed than low-end ADSL if many others aren't constraining the network. For customers who already have cable TV installed, adding Internet access could be the most affordable way to go.

If you use a cable modem, be sure to invoke your access point's firewall. Without a firewall, some network resources, could be vulnerable. Security measures taken by cable companies—including the blocking of ports commonly used for file sharing—generally keep most users safe from attackers, however. Another problem affecting a small number of cable modem customers is the use of one-way or telco-return cable modems, which prevent hardware-based Internet sharing. If your cable company doesn't offer a two-way modem option, then choose DSL or dial-up.

DSL

Digital subscriber line (DSL) delivers data via telephone lines. No new cabling is required and DSL doesn't require a phone line be dedicated to the service. You can make and receive voice calls while using a DSL-equipped phone line to connect to the Internet. Because DSL service uses phone wiring, it's most often sold by a local telephone provider and is only available in areas where the phone provider has upgraded its infrastructure to deliver DSL from a nearby central office facility. Because DSL degrades over long distances, subscribers must be located within range of a phone company's central office facility. Although DSL emanates from the phone company, federal law requires it make its lines available to broadband providers. Because of this law, many ISPs resell DSL access, adding their own ISP services on top.

DSL comes in a number of flavors. Asynchronous DSL (ADSL) is the most common in residential and small office settings. ADSL is the slowest and most affordable type of DSL and subscribers must be within a few miles of a phone company central office. DSL speeds are expressed with two numbers: upstream (upload) and downstream (download). With ADSL, download speed is greater than upload speed. This works out fine for most Internet surfers and even for those who need to operate low-traffic Internet servers. Many providers offer several ADSL speeds, ranging from 128 Kbps upstream/384 Kbps downstream, to 800 Kbps upstream/8 Mbps downstream.

ISPs often select a specific type of DSL to offer their customers. Some varieties you might encounter are the following:

❏ **HDSL**   High-bit-rate DSL requires two phone lines and has a top speed of 1.5 Mbps, upstream and downstream.

❏ **RADSL**   Rate-adaptive DSL service, unlike ADSL, can operate at different speeds, depending on the condition of the telephone line. The modem adjusts throughput accordingly.

❏ **SDSL**   Synchronous DSL has a top speed of 2 Mbps and requires a dedicated phone line. SDSL is most often used in businesses where high speed is critical and where the capability to share a phone line isn't particularly important.

❏ **VDSL**   Very-high-bit-rate DSL boasts top speeds of 52 Mbps downstream. VDSL requires the use of fiberoptic cable. Distance between the central office and the subscriber must be under a mile. VDSL isn't widely available as yet.

The lowest-speed versions of ADSL are usually affordable. The required phone line is usually already installed and can be shared. Because ADSL providers generally find themselves in competition with one another and with the local cable company, consumer prices are typically on the decline. Availability and customer service failures are the most frequent complaints from would-be DSL users. Because fiberoptic upgrades haven't penetrated all areas, it might be impossible to get DSL in a rural area, in a sparsely populated part of a metropolitan area, or where the phone company sees limited growth opportunities. Customers can wait for weeks or months to get DSL installed. They can also find customer service lacking from phone companies still reeling from mergers and other changes that can make it tough to get a problem addressed quickly.

Satellite

Satellite-based Internet access is most common where cable and DSL service is unavailable—in rural areas. The service is available everywhere, but usually costs more than cable or DSL when those services are available.

Like other broadband services, satellite download speeds are significantly faster than uploads. In fact, real-world upload speeds resemble dial-up more than cable or DSL. On the download side, satellite offers speeds comparable to DSL.

Pulling the Internet down from outer space comes at a hefty price. The satellite receiver and modem can cost up to $600, with monthly residential rates around $70 at press time. You could also be required to sign a service contract.

You can share a satellite-based Internet account, but you might be unable to do it with a wireless AP. In fact, StarBand, a satellite provider owned by Gilat Satellite Networks, Microsoft, and EchoStar Communications, only supports sharing with a Windows-based gateway application supplied with your account. To provide Internet access to wireless users, you must add a second network interface to the PC, which acts as the Internet gateway. The first network interface connects the satellite modem to the gateway, while the second joins the gateway computer to your wi-fi access point. This setup creates a network in which wired and wireless computers can surf the Web, but won't be able to share files or a printer. Finally, Linux and Mac-only networks won't be able to use satellite because the gateway software must be installed on a Windows computer. You can add non-Windows clients to the network, though.

Internet Account Features

A typical Internet account provides a single IP address and access to the ISP's network via dial-up or broadband. With these services, you can share the account with network clients as described in this chapter. If, however, you want to run your own web server or provide network users with access to e-mail, you'll need to purchase one or more additional services.

❏ **Multiple e-mail accounts**   Many ISPs offer a number of e-mail accounts to each customer. You can easily configure each computer on your network with a separate e-mail account, provided your ISP offers enough to go around. Providing e-mail accounts is inexpensive, so look for an ISP that enables you to create five to ten accounts. Visitors to your network or people who get their e-mail access elsewhere can check their mail while connected to your network. All the required configuration is done in the user's e-mail program.

❏ **Static IP addresses**   Most ISPs include one dynamic IP address with a home or small business account. To run a web server or other Internet server, though, you need static IP address for each server. You can run multiple instances of a server (supporting multiple web sites, for example) on a single computer. Larger business accounts often include a block of static IP addresses, which the organization can assign to individuals or to Internet servers that need a constant location on the Net. Most broadband ISPs will sell you a single static IP address or blocks in multiples of eight. Although prices vary and some providers might not offer this service, you can generally buy a single IP address for $10 to $25 per month. (By the way, additional dynamic addresses will also cost you.) To use a static IP address on a network where a wireless access point acts as a DHCP server, you can assign the static IP address to the access point and use its DMZ or port-forwarding feature to direct web server traffic to a computer on the local network. See Chapter 7 for more details.

❏ **DNS and domain registration**   For Internet users to find a server on your network, users must be able to communicate with it by IP address or by domain name. The name (www.myownwebserver.com) must be registered as a valid domain name and its IP address must be known to the Internet's domain name system (DNS). You can register your domain yourself or have your ISP do it. Domain registration fees are typically $35 a year (paid every two years), plus whatever fees your ISP charges to access its DNS system and to complete your registration for you. You could choose to register a domain yourself, whether or not you've acquired a static IP address for it. If you change ISPs later, you can update your IP information with the registrar.

❑ **Web hosting**   If you don't want to run your own server, you can purchase space on your ISP's web server. You could also choose to register and use your own domain or you might elect to go with a URL supplied by the ISP (www.isp.com/mywebsite). The latter option is cheaper and usually perfectly adequate for individuals, but most businesses opt for their own domain, hosted by an ISP or web hosting company. When you allow someone else to host your site, you decrease the chances that it'll go down because of a power failure or machine crash. If you're not an expert web developer, but you want to add a search engine, forms, and other features that require scripting behind the scenes, stick with an ISP or hosting service, whose server supports these advanced options. Your hosting company might also be able to help you develop a site that takes advantage of the host's server capabilities.

Account Sharing Issues

You might wonder whether Internet sharing is kosher as far as ISPs are concerned. After all, the accounts they sell come with a single IP address, right? Fortunately for you, most ISPs are realistic about Internet sharing. They realize many people have found ways to share a single account and, even in situations where multiple users have access, the impact of a few extra users on their network will be minimal. Other ISPs haven't yet taken a position on sharing because they're currently looking for a pricing model that enables them to take advantage of the ease of sharing connections. A few are selling packages that include both a broadband modem and wireless-sharing capabilities.

Many ISPs draw the line at sharing that goes beyond the boundaries of your property, however. In a wired network, it's impossible to share a connection with computers that aren't within physical reach of your Internet access device. In the wireless world, though, signals can easily travel outside the walls of your building and beyond, especially if you installed an antenna on the roof.

Some Internet sharing is purposeful, such as when network owners sell neighbors their network's SSID and/or WEP key. Many residential users make agreements with neighbors to share a broadband connection and split Internet access costs. That's what ISPs fear and hope to prevent. In other cases, a passerby with a wi-fi network card and network discovery software, such as NetStumbler, finds a network without a WEP key and joins. The owner of a wi-fi network nearby might not object to people joining the network and surfing the Web. In fact, this could be the plan all along (wink wink, nudge nudge).

Whether you've agreed to share your Internet connection with a neighbor or simply left your network open to passersby or patrons at the coffee shop next door, you could be violating your ISP's service agreement. AOL/ Time-Warner and AT&T have investigated unauthorized sharing and sent legalese-filled e-mails to customers they think are sharing in violation of their contracts.

So far, these attempts to prevent cross-property-line sharing aren't widespread and many ISPs ignore or allow it. As yet, no law suits have been brought and some community wireless activists believe that sharing can't be prevented by ISPs. A number of communities and user groups have built large public-access wireless networks with the blessings of ISPs (though some have done so without such approval). If you're not sure how your ISP feels about sharing, read your contract or ask. If you don't find out for sure, share at your own risk.

Because sharing restrictions relate only to Internet access provided by an ISP, you face no potential hassles when you simply provide access to your network. In this case, you're simply allowing your neighbors or business associates in a nearby building to join your local network. You can restrict Internet access with your access point firewall if you choose, providing yourself a line of defense if someone from your ISP happens to drive by with a network sniffer.

Chapter 7

Setting Up and Configuring Access Points

Now, it's finally time to begin building your network. I hope you've chosen an access point (AP) and network adapters that meet your needs. If you plan to share Internet access with wireless users, you should also have some sort of Internet account and access method available in your home or office.

In this chapter, you learn how to plan a wireless network, as well as how to set up and configure APs. The chapter begins with a short discussion of your network design options: How does your new wireless capability integrate with an existing network, how do you start a network from scratch, and so forth. For a more detailed discussion of network planning and design, see Chapter 12. Next, you learn about AP placement, including ways you can maximize the wireless coverage area. The next task is to set up AP hardware. Finally you learn about basic and advanced AP configuration. This process is illustrated by example and introduces you to APs that include nearly all the features you might encounter when you set up your own AP.

Planning Your Network

Network planning can be an involved process in the corporate world. Professional planners who build large networks for corporations, universities, and even medium-sized businesses go through extensive design and planning phases before they ever lay a cable or place an AP. They determine the needs the network must meet, the area and users it will cover, any obstacles to building it that exist, and the time and budget available to do the job. With this background information in hand, professional network builders evaluate different types of technology and specific products before coming up with a workable plan for the network. This exhaustive process enables the network designer to ask and answer questions about what the network must accomplish for its users: access to shared computer resources, ease of communication among people who need to share information, and the most efficient use of available funds and time.

Although your home or small office network won't require the same level of planning as a corporate installation, the principles are the same. Before you set up an AP and create a network, ask yourself what the network is intended to do, who it will serve, and where wireless coverage is needed. If you expect that obstacles exist to the network you want to build, know what they are and consider options for overcoming them. Your goal should be to develop, in a simple statement, what your network is for, such as the following:

"I want to provide wireless coverage throughout my home and back yard, so our family can connect to the Internet from anywhere on our property."

"I want the kids to be able to print from their computer to the inkjet printer in my home office."

"I want to use my laptop to connect to our business network from the shed behind the store."

"I want to provide Internet access for a computer lab in my school."

"I want our salespeople to have easy access to e-mail, the Web, and our company server when they come in from the road."

Last, but not least, plan for growth. If you're running a business network, you might need to add capacity later so more users can connect or to cover an expanded office area. Even if you're beginning a home network, consider your future needs. Will your toddler son need a computer someday? Are you thinking of building a home office over the garage in a few years?

Once you have a concrete idea of what your new or improved network will do, you can begin the practical steps of setting up the AP and configuring it for local and Internet access.

Setting Up an Access Point

The location of your AP matters because the radio coverage it provides in your home or office radiates outward in a dome-shaped pattern from the device. The more centrally located your AP is, the broader the coverage area within your own property will be. Locating an AP at one end of your house provides great signal from the immediate vicinity (and probably to your neighbor's house), but you might find the radio signal doesn't reach all areas within your building. Likewise, positioning an AP on a high shelf or even mounting it on the wall will deliver more of the radio's signal. A high vantage point minimizes obstructions that can impede the radio signal.

Interference

Building materials can have a significant affect on radio-signal strength. While wood and uncoated glass don't contribute significantly to signal interference, metal does. Keep your access point away from walls or ceilings with lots of metal, as well as air ducts. In some cases, it is better to lower the AP to avoid close proximity to an air duct. Tinted glass windows can also generate interference. Interference can also come from other devices in the 2.4 GHz frequency band, including newer cordless phones and poorly shielded microwave ovens. If possible, locate the AP at least 25 feet away from strong sources of interference. Remember, the same materials that interfere with your access point affect all wi-fi devices. Even if you place your AP well, you might find coverage is better in some areas of your property than others. My kitchen, for example, has metal cabinets that decrease reception.

Although you can assess interference in your environment with spectrum-analysis tools, a simpler way is to set up the AP in a convenient location, and then test your network's signal strength by walking around your property with a wi-fi-equipped laptop. Open the configuration utility provided with your wi-fi network adapter and observe the signal strength indicator as you walk. This can help you identify "dead spots" that could indicate interference with your wi-fi adapter or the AP. If you find the signal is weak within 100 feet or less of your AP, you probably have an AP-based interference problem.

Connectivity Issues

To provide Internet access to wireless users, you need to connect the access point to your broadband or dial-up modem. The best option is to place the modem near the centrally located AP. If that's not practical, you either need to move the modem, if possible, or choose a less-than-perfect location for the AP near the modem. You can buy a long Ethernet cable (no more than 100 feet or so), and find a convenient and aesthetically pleasing way to run it from AP to modem. If you're using a dial-up modem as an Internet access device, it must be located within a few feet of the AP and within reach of a telephone outlet.

Your location options could also be limited if you need to connect wired Ethernet devices to the AP's LAN ports. Your options include extra Ethernet cabling or the use of an Ethernet hub between the AP and the local wired devices. This approach could be best if you're adding wireless to an existing Ethernet network. In my house, for example, a small Ethernet hub preceded my wi-fi access point as the center of my network. All wired computers and my printer were connected to the hub via Ethernet cable (see Figure 7.1). To avoid rearranging things to accommodate the access point, I plugged an Ethernet cable into one of my AP's LAN ports, connecting the other end to my hub's uplink port. All wired devices retained access to one another and to the wireless ones communicating with the AP. If your hub doesn't have an uplink port, you need a cross-over Ethernet cable, which you can find at a local electronics shop.

The primary drawback of including an Ethernet hub for wired devices in this way is this: While the AP's LAN ports are switched—providing each device connected to the AP with a dedicated network channel, the hub's ports are shared, meaning all devices connected to the hub share the same channel. In a busy office network, this arrangement could decrease network performance. The best way to solve this problem is either to eliminate the hub from the equation by connecting all wired devices to the AP or to replace the hub with an Ethernet switch.

Figure 7.1
In my home network, some devices still connect to the network via a wired Ethernet hub. This hub is, in turn, cabled to an AP.

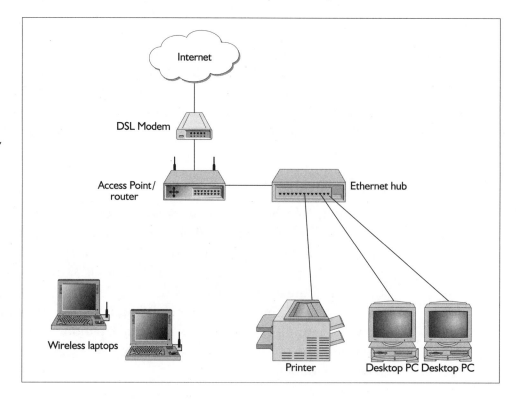

Chapter 12 covers a variety of wireless network setup options in detail, focusing mostly on what these options enable you to do with your network, but also addressing the physical layout of APs and other devices.

Basic Access Point Setup

In this section, you learn how to set up an access point to perform two basic tasks: managing communication between wireless computers on your network, and sharing a connection to the Internet among wired and wireless computers. You learn how to perform these setup functions using the Linksys BEFW11S4 Wireless Access Point/Router, an inexpensive product, which is, in many ways, typical of the APs described in Chapter 3. To illustrate alternative ways of setting up an AP and special features not found in the Linksys product, other products are used as examples in the section "Outbound Filtering."

Linksys BEFW11S4 Access Point/Router

Like most consumer-grade wi-fi APs, the Linksys product provided is both an 802.11b access point and a router that enable you to share a broadband Internet connection with wired and wireless users on your network. The BEFW11S4 (Figure 7.2) includes a four-port 10/100BASE-T Ethernet switch, to which you can directly connect wired computers and printers, as well as a wide area network (WAN) port for your broadband modem. The BEFW11S4 doesn't support dial-up access. The router supports 128-bit WEP encryption, and includes a DHCP server, NAT, and a firewall.

Figure 7.2
The Linksys BEFW11S4 access point/router is typical of wi-fi APs available for home and small-business users.

Connect the Hardware and Configure the Setup Computer

Get started by shutting down your computers and broadband modem. Next, connect your AP to AC power and to your broadband modem, using the WAN or broadband port on the AP. The easiest way to set up an AP for the first time is to connect a computer directly to the access point and run the AP's administration software from the setup computer. Connect an Ethernet cable from a LAN port on the AP to the Ethernet port on the computer you want to use to administer the AP, as shown in Figure 7.3. You can change this physical setup later if it isn't convenient. Most AP packages, including the Linksys model, include an Ethernet cable you can use to link the computer to the AP. By the way, you can set up an AP from a wireless computer in most cases. To do so, you either need to know the default SSID for the AP (sometimes noted in the documentation) or how to use a network adapter driver that can scan for APs automatically. If you enable WEP encryption during the setup process, however, you'll immediately lose your wireless connection to the AP. These little inconveniences are the reasons that I recommend you set up your AP from a wired computer.

With the hardware ready to go, you'll need to verify that your setup computer is ready to connect to the AP. Most APs, including the Linksys, require that your computer be set up to obtain an IP address automatically. Yours could already be set up this way, especially if you've been using the setup

Figure 7.3
This typical setup configures the AP for the first time: the laptop on the left is connected to a LAN port on the Linksys AP/router, which is connected to a DSL modem, and the modem connects to the Internet via a telephone line.

computer to connect to the Internet from a broadband modem. Start the setup computer and check its TCP/IP settings.

❏ **Windows**   The specifics vary, but you open the Network control panel, and then open the TCP/IP properties. Choose to obtain an IP address automatically and close the Properties window.

❏ **Mac OS X**   Open System Preferences, and then open the Network panel. If the Network panel is inaccessible, click the lock and enter an administrator password. Be sure Built-In Ethernet is selected. Choose Using DCHP from the Configure menu. Click Apply, and then close System Preferences.

❏ **Mac OS 9**   Choose DHCP Server from the Configure menu in the TCP/IP control panel.

The procedure for doing this under Linux varies, depending on both the distribution and the wi-fi network adapter driver you're using.

Now restart the setup computer, along with the AP and the broadband modem. When you restart, the setup computer will obtain its IP address from the AP, enabling you to communicate with it.

Like most APs, the Linksys example access point uses web-based administration software. The AP contains the web server software and HTML pages that make up the interface. You can set up the AP from any modern web browser and operating system (OS).

Initial Setup

With the Linksys AP connected to a desktop PC and to a DSL modem, you're ready to begin setup. Be sure you have information about your the configuration requirements of your Internet service provider (ISP) on hand before you begin. You'll enter information about how you connect to the Internet and how it should obtain an IP address from the ISP's server.

1. Open a web browser and type **192.168.1.1** into the Location field. An authentication dialog box appears (Figure 7.4).

2. Leave User Name blank and type **admin** in the Password field. Click OK.

3. The first setup screen appears, as shown in Figure 7.5. If your ISP requires a hostname and/or a domain name, enter them in the fields provided. Otherwise, leave them blank. These fields aren't widely used. You might need one or both of them if you maintain your own Internet servers at your business site.

Figure 7.4
A user name and password authentication protect the AP from unwanted access.

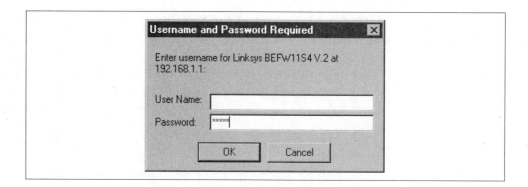

4. Leave the IP address unchanged, unless you have a specific reason to change it. This is the private address your AP will use on the local network. The AP's public IP—the one it will share with all users of your network—will be obtained in a later step. Entering the private IP in a web browser, as you did in Step 1, brings up the AP setup tool. You can change the address to another private IP if you want, but don't forget to write down the new address. All computers using your AP as a DHCP server will use this address as their *gateway* or router address. Leave the subnet mask unchanged. A *subnet mask* tells the domain name system to what subnet an IP address belongs.

5. Leave Wireless enabled if you want to allow wireless clients to join your network.

6. Change your AP's Service Set ID (SSID). Choose a name that's meaningful to you in some way, but that doesn't provide more information than you want to laptop-toting strangers within range of your network. If your business is in an office building, where users could see multiple APs from their laptops, leaving the AP's name set to "Linksys" or "default" guarantees confusion. I once came across an SSID that revealed the AP owner's home address. Not a good idea.

7. Disabling Allow Broadcast SSID to Associate hides the SSID from scanning software, making your network invisible to anyone who doesn't know the SSID. Doing this provides security against unwanted visitors to your network.

8. Leave the Channel set to 6 unless this AP will be part of an Extended Service Set (ESSS). In that case, you would distribute the channel assignments for members of the ESSS to different channels. You learn more about this configuration in Chapter 12.

Figure 7.5
The most important configuration options for the Linksys AP appear on the opening screen of the administration tool.

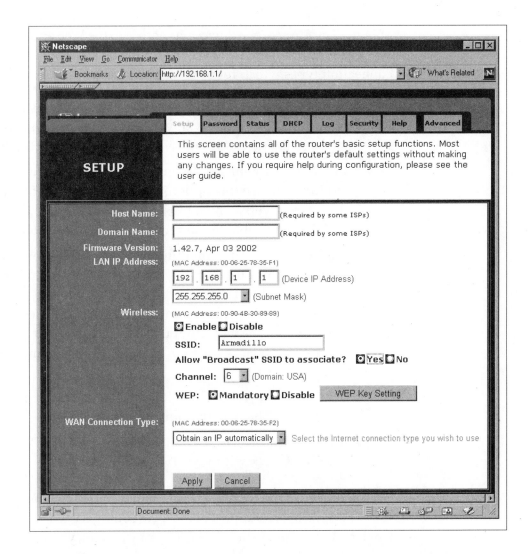

9. To require anyone joining your network to provide a WEP key, leave the Mandatory box checked. To leave your network completely open to anyone within range, click Disable. Be aware that disabling WEP removes all security from your wireless network. (You can choose a WEP key now by clicking the WEP Key Settings button. See the section entitled "WEP" for details.) For now, let's complete the Internet setup process. Figure 7.5 above shows the administration screen with settings chosen for my office network.

Setting Up Internet Access

To connect to the Internet, the AP (or any computer) must obtain a valid, public IP address. If you use an ISP to reach the Internet, that IP address is provided by the ISP in one of several ways. Once the AP or local computer has obtained an address, the device has access to the Web and any other Internet services. The Linksys AP we're using in this example provides five WAN connection types which follow:

❏ **Obtain an IP automatically**   Most ISPs use this method. When you connect to the server, your access point requests an IP address and keeps it until you disconnect from the Internet.

❏ **Static IP**   If your ISP assigned you a permanent public IP address, choose this option. Static IPs are most often used by Internet servers, which must maintain the same address to be reliably accessible to other computers on the Internet.

❏ **PPPoE**   A variation on dynamic addressing, Point-to-Point Protocol over Ethernet (PPPoE) is used by some DSL and cable ISPs to provide a means of authenticating users when they attempt to connect to the Internet. Older OSes required you to use a custom application from the ISP to log on and request access to the ISP's server. If your ISP requires PPPoE connection, your AP must support it.

❏ **RAS (for SingTel users)**   Remote Access Service (RAS) is used in Singapore. Check with your ISP for details.

❏ **PPTP**   Point-to-Point Tunneling Protocol (PPTP) is used in Europe. Check with your ISP for details.

You must use the connection method specified by your ISP. If you don't know it, contact tech support before proceeding. When you choose a method from the WAN Connection Type pull-down menu, you first see a screen indicating the settings you've chosen so far have been applied successfully. PPPoE settings appear in Figure 7.6. If further WAN configuration is required, the initial screen returns with new fields.

When you've entered information required by your ISP, click Apply to save your settings and to acquire and/or activate your IP address. Test your connection by opening a new browser window and connecting to a web site.

WEP

Wired Equivalent Privacy (WEP) is the most basic way to prevent unwanted access to your wireless network. Although WEP security isn't bulletproof, as you learn in more detail in Chapter 10, you should enable it unless you want to provide unlimited access to both your network and your shared Internet connection.

 I.   Be sure WEP is enabled and click the WEP Key Setting button.

Figure 7.6
Settings for PPPoE include fields for your user name and password.

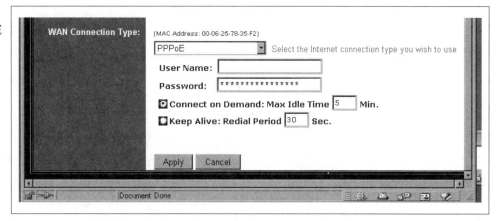

2. Choose 64-bit or 128-bit encryption in the WEP Key Settings window, shown in Figure 7.7. You need to stick with 64-bit encryption if any of your wi-fi network adapters are limited to 64-bit. Applying 128-bit encryption could also reduce your network's speed somewhat, but it's the more secure option.

3. An encryption key can be entered as an *alphanumeric passphrase* (made up of numbers and letters) or a *hexadecimal passphrase* (a base 16 code used by computer programmers, consisting of numbers

Figure 7.7
Set encryption options in the WEP Key Settings window.

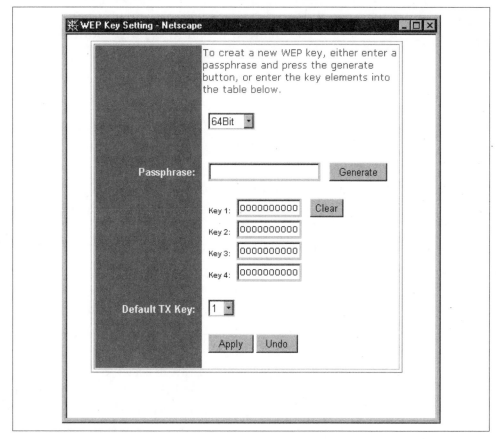

from 0–9 and letters A–F). To use the passphrase method, enter a phrase less than 31 characters and click the Generate button to create an encryption key.

4. Click Apply.

DHCP Server Setup

Most APs enable the built-in DHCP server by default. This means once the AP is configured to connect to the Internet and all the hardware connections are properly made, a computer joining the network will obtain an IP address from the AP, and then be able to connect to the Internet. You probably won't need to make changes to DHCP settings unless you want to disable the server or change the rules by which clients can use your DHCP server. If you're already using a local DHCP server, you'll want to disable the DHCP server.

Click the DHCP tab at the top of the screen. Figure 7.8 shows the DHCP configuration screen. Click Disable to deactivate the DHCP server if you choose. Here's a rundown of the remaining settings on this screen:

❏ **Starting IP address**   All IP addresses provided by your DHCP server fall within the range, 192.168.1.0–192.168.1.255 (unless you changed the address range on the previous screen). The starting address is the first one available for members of your network. If you changed the address range, addresses are allocated from the range you chose.

❏ **Number of DHCP users**   You can restrict the number of simultaneous users on your network by limiting the number of DHCP addresses available.

❏ **Client Lease Time**   Limit the amount of time a dynamic address is active.

❏ **DNS**   Your ISP provides one or more DNS addresses. The Internet uses the Domain Name System (DNS) to match up URLs with IP addresses.

❏ **WINS**   If your network uses the Windows Internet Naming Server (WINS), enter a WINS address.

Click Apply to save any changes you make on this screen.

Basic Access Point Security

Because all your AP's settings are accessible from the web-based administration application, using a password to prevent unwanted access is important. The default password can easily be guessed, and any wireless device that can

Figure 7.8
By default, the DHCP server is enabled and set up to provide an IP address for up to 50 users.

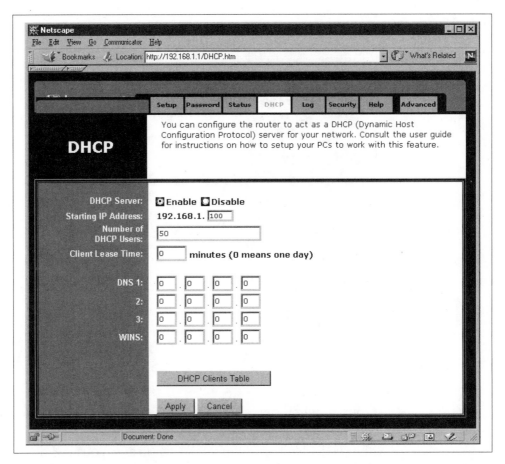

join your network and get an IP address from your AP will have access to the admin tools. To change the password, click the Password tab, and then type a new password when the Password screen appears (Figure 7.9). Click Apply.

The Password screen also includes options for allowing UPnP services (described in the section "Port Forwarding") to return the router to factory-default settings.

Create the Network

At this point, you've configured all the settings you need to set up a wireless network. The remaining settings enable you to monitor the network, add security options, and configure the firewall. You can reach these tools at any time by connecting to the AP as you did at the beginning of this section. Now, let's light up the wi-fi network.

If you want to use the setup computer wirelessly, shut it down and unplug the Ethernet cable that connects it to the AP. If you need to connect other wired devices to the AP, do so now, using the access point's local area network (LAN) ports. If you're using an Ethernet hub or switch to connect a

Figure 7.9
Protect your AP's
configuration
options by giving
it a password.

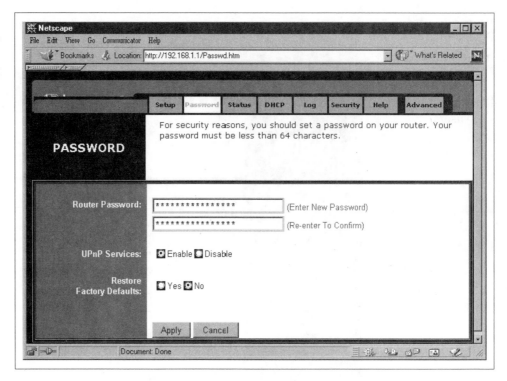

group of wired devices to the AP, connect the hub to the AP using the AP's uplink port (Figure 7.10). Note, the uplink port found on the Linksys BEFW1154 isn't a universal AP feature. If your AP doesn't have an uplink port, connect to the hub's uplink port from one of the AP's LAN ports.

Figure 7.10
Connect wired
devices to your
AP's LAN ports.
The WAN port
connects to your
broadband
modem.

To add wireless computers to your network, you need to install network adapters and set up drivers for each, as described in Chapter 8. Because your AP is already broadcasting wi-fi signals, the wireless computers can connect to the network once you provide the AP's SSID and WEP key. Once each computer is connected (wirelessly or via Ethernet), test the connecting by launching a web browser.

Advanced Access Point Configuration

Beyond the basic configuration and setup options described in this chapter, many APs offer advanced features you can use to provide additional services on your network or customize access to particular parts of the network. In this section, you learn about the advanced features of the Linksys AP/router, as well as a few features available in other products.

Running Your Own Internet Server

When you type a URL into a browser, the Domain Name System (DNS) matches the alphanumeric name with the corresponding IP address to retrieve the page. DNS servers around the Internet communicate with one another, passing domain names and corresponding IP addresses from one server to the next to keep the system current. When you connect to an Internet site using a domain name, a DNS server looks up the corresponding address. When you purchase or activate an Internet domain, the name and the IP address corresponding to it are entered in the DNS, enabling other Internet users to reach your server by typing in the domain name. To host an Internet server in your home or office, the server needs a static IP address the DNS can match with its URL (http://www.mylittleserver.com). You can run a server from your network if you've purchased a static IP address from your ISP and the server URL points to that IP address. Many ISPs will register a domain name for you and provide DNS service to it by linking the domain and the static IP address you acquired from the ISP. To add a server to a wi-fi network, you have two options: configure your network so the server connects to the Internet separately from the rest of the network, using its own address, or share the server's static IP address with your local wi-fi network. The advantage of sharing a static IP address is that the server can be fully accessible from the rest of your network (for uploading new web pages, for example), and you needn't purchase an additional static IP address. The main drawback is that busy networks and busy Internet servers could drag down one another's performance. You can use your AP's firewall to protect the network, while allowing server traffic to flow freely, using the AP's DMZ and port-forwarding features.

Set Up the DMZ

DMZ stands for Demilitarized Zone. In networking, a *DMZ* computer is outside the network firewall, making it fully accessible from the Internet. Other computers on your local network remain behind the firewall. The computer you use as a DMZ host must use the same IP address at all times. Some APs enable you to reserve a particular address for the server computer, while others don't have this feature and require you to switch from dynamic to static IP addressing on the server computer. In this case, you assign the DMZ host an address within the range managed by your DHCP server. (Be sure to enter the AP address as the gateway or router address for the DMZ computer.) In either case, you use the AP's administration software to designate the DMZ host.

The Linksys router takes the latter approach. You must assign static IP, such as 192.168.1.110, to your DMZ. To verify the address you chose isn't already in use on your network, click the DHCP tab in the administration tool, and then click the DHCP Client Table button. You'll see all DHCP client computers on your network (Figure 7.11), listing each by name, IP address, and MAC address.

To set the DMZ, follow these steps:

1. In the Linksys administration tool, click the Advanced tab (see Figure 7.12), and then click the DMZ Host tab.

2. Enter the last one-three digits of the DMZ IP address.

3. Click Apply.

Figure 7-11
The DHCP client table lists computers, including their IP addresses, that are or have been connected to your network.

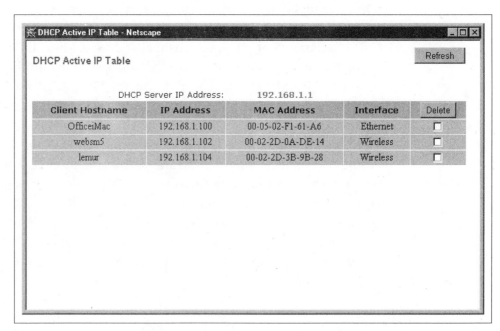

Figure 7.12
Enter the address
of your DMZ host.

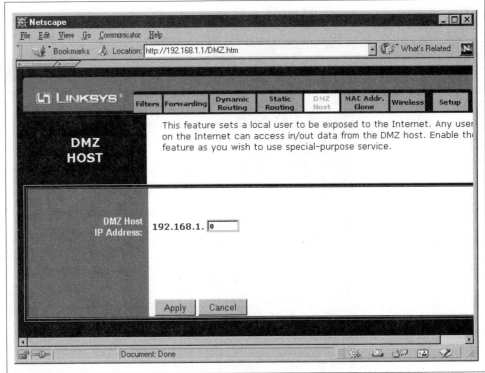

To verify operation of your DMZ, enable the Internet server and connect to it from a computer outside your network.

Port Forwarding

Port forwarding, like a DMZ, enables you to expose network servers to the Internet. Unlike DMZ, port forwarding limits that exposure to one or more specific ports. (Port forwarding is sometimes referred to as *virtual server*.) You can use this technique to provide limited access to multiple computers. You could, for example, expose only ports 20 and 21 on a particular computer to run an FTP server, while running a gaming server on another machine. Leaving all other ports closed protects the computer from unwanted access.

Setting up your server for port forwarding is identical to DMZ setup. You should either give the port-forwarded computer a static private IP address or, if your AP supports it, reserve an address for that computer. Next, assign ports and servers. For the Linksys AP, follow these steps:

1. In the Linksys administration tool, click the Advanced tab, and then click the Forwarding tab. You can choose ports to be forwarded on this screen (Figure 7.13). Or, if you're using Microsoft's Universal Plug and Play (UPnP) system, click the UPnP Forwarding button.

2. Enter a name for the application whose port you want to forward in the Specialized Application field of the first column.

Figure 7.13
You can open ports for any Internet application on one or more computers on your network.

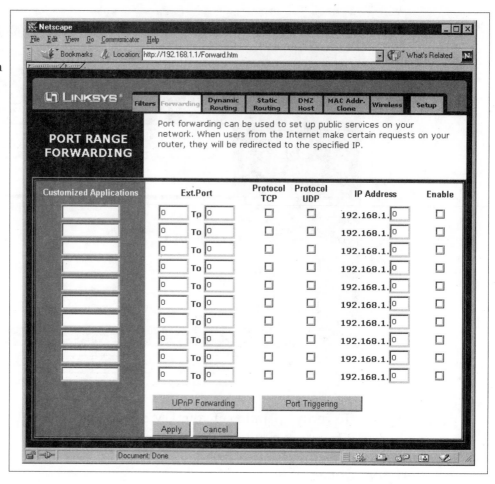

3. In the Ext. Port columns, enter the port number or the range of ports to open. To determine which ports are required for the server software you're using, consult your server's documentation.

4. Enable TCP and/or UDP, depending on the type of port you're enabling.

5. Enter the final digits of the computer's IP address in the IP Address column.

6. Click Enable to activate this port.

7. Repeat the process for all ports you want to forward, and then click Apply to save your changes.

To use the UPnP screen (Figure 7.14), click the UPnP Forwarding button on the Forwarding screen. UPnP is a Microsoft-networking architecture, which enables PCs that support it to automatically connect to and use remote services and devices as if they were connected directly to the PC. If you host a UPnP device, remote users can connect to it. To enable remote connections to a UPnP device that's behind your firewall, you must open a port for it.

Figure 7.14
The UPnP
Forwarding
screen lists
the appropriate
ports for
popular Internet
applications.

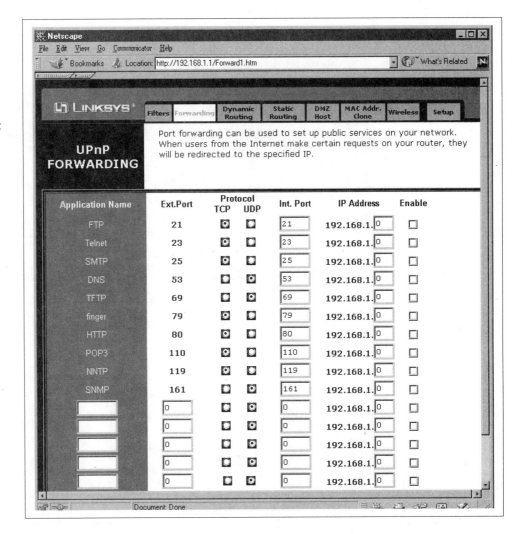

Internet gamers often need to set up custom port-forwarding setups. Some APs provide direct support for gaming environments like Battle.net and the MSN Gaming Zone. The ZoomAir IG-4165 AP/router has specific options for these and other gaming setups (Figure 7.15). If your AP doesn't provide automated support for gaming, you might be able to accomplish the same thing with port forwarding.

Outbound Filtering

Firewalls prevent unwanted traffic from reaching your network via outside networks, including the Internet. They can also be used to prevent access to the Internet by particular computers and/or from specific ports. This feature is found in most firewall software, but it isn't provided by all access point firewalls. A few APs can filter incoming or outgoing content by keyword, such as a web site name or an objectionable phrase in e-mail, and some can restrict access to or from outside IP addresses that you specify.

Figure 7.15
The ZoomAir
IG-4165 supports
access to Batle.net,
MSN Gaming
Zone, and ICU II.

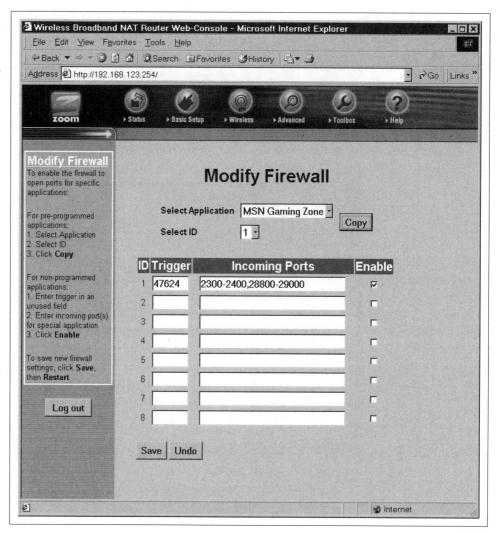

The Linksys BEFW11S4 filter is based on internal IP address, Internet port, or MAC address. To filter based on an internal IP address, you need to set the IP address for that computer. To filter several computers on your network, set the IP address for each within a range, say, 192.168.1.5–192.168.1.10, giving each machine whose IP address isn't filtered a number outside the filtered range. Computers whose addresses you filter will lose all access to the Internet. You can also choose to filter based on a computer's MAC address (eliminating the need to set static IP addresses, but requiring you to copy each machine's MAC).

Or, you can filter by Internet port. This prevents access to the filtered port by any computer on the network. The example access point doesn't enable you to filter some ports on some computers, while others retain full access. You must choose one approach or the other to use filtering. To set up content filtering, follow these steps:

1. Click the Advanced tab. The Filters tab is selected.

2. To prevent outgoing traffic from a range or IP addresses, enter the range in the first row of the Private IP Range section of the screen (Figure 7.16). To filter a single IP address, enter it in both fields. Choose additional ranges if necessary.

3. Click Apply.

To filter by Internet port, preventing all network users from using the selected port, enter the port range or individual port number (in both fields) in the Filtered Private Port Range area of the Filters screen, and then click Apply.

❑ *MAC address filtering* has two functions: like IP or port filtering, it can be used to restrict local access to the Internet. MAC address filtering can also be used as a security measure if you suspect an unauthorized person is repeatedly connecting to your network. First, you must find the MAC address (a 12-digit number unique to each network adapter) of the device you want to filter. You can find your network adapter's MAC address in several ways: In Windows 95, 98, and Me, choose Start | Run. Next, type **winipcfg** in the Run field, and then click OK. Choose your Ethernet or wireless adapter from the menu and copy the MAC address (aka the Adapter address).

Figure 7.16
Filter a range of IP addresses to prevent computers using them from connecting to the Internet.

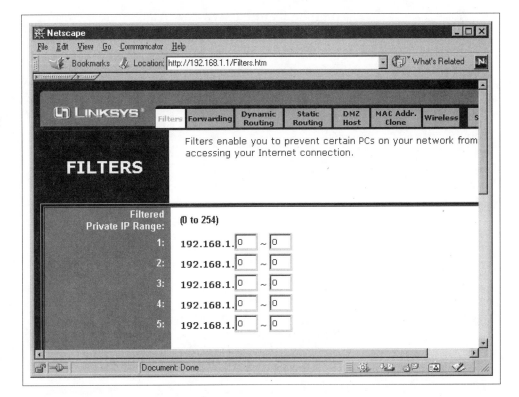

❏ In Windows NT, 2000, and XP, choose Start | Run and type **cmd.,** and then click OK. Type **ipconfig/all** in the command prompt window. IP address information appears, as shown in Figure 7.17. Write down the physical address for your network adapter.

❏ In Mac OS X, open System Preferences, and then open the Network pane. Select your network adapter and write down the physical address shown.

❏ If a client whose MAC address you want to filter is currently connected to your AP and the AP provides a listing of current connections or displays them in the system log, get the MAC address information from there.

❏ Look at the back of your wi-fi network adapter or Ethernet card. Its MAC address can often be found on the bar code tag.

To filter a MAC address, click the Edit MAC Filter Setting button on the Filters screen and enter addresses in the fields provided.

Keyword Filtering

Parents who have used filtering software to protect their kids from objectionable material are familiar with content filters. *Content filters* watch for the occurrence of certain words on a web page, e-mail, or chat room conversation and stop the material before it reaches a protected computer. Although this isn't a common feature of wireless APs, some, including the NetGear MR314 provide keyword filters. In NetGear's case, you block web sites or newsgroup messages that include keywords you specify (Figure 7.18). You can set a

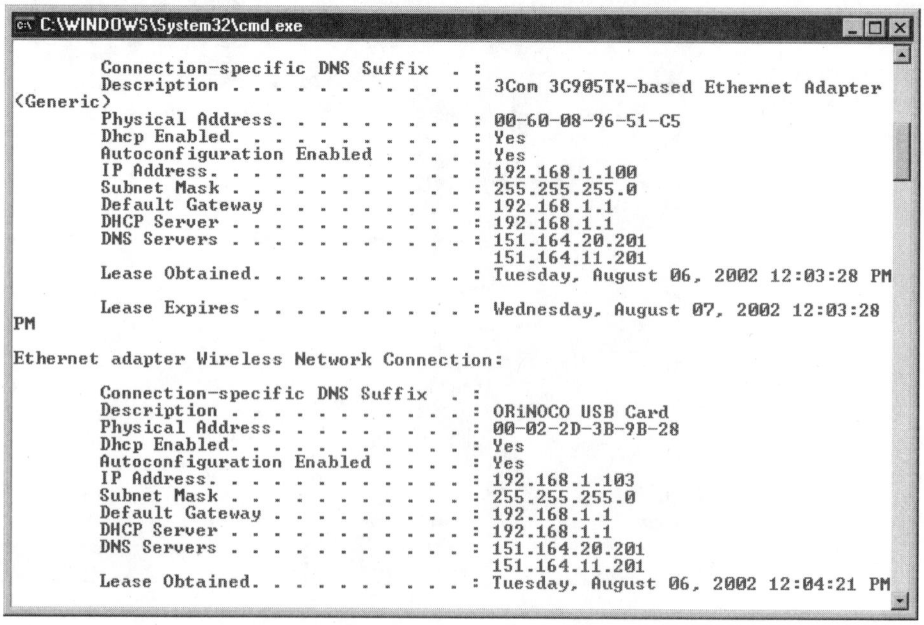

Figure 7.17
This PC contains both a built-in Ethernet card and a wireless USB network adapter. Each has a MAC address.

```
C:\WINDOWS\System32\cmd.exe

        Connection-specific DNS Suffix  . :
        Description . . . . . . . . . . . : 3Com 3C905TX-based Ethernet Adapter
(Generic)
        Physical Address. . . . . . . . . : 00-60-08-96-51-C5
        Dhcp Enabled. . . . . . . . . . . : Yes
        Autoconfiguration Enabled . . . . : Yes
        IP Address. . . . . . . . . . . . : 192.168.1.100
        Subnet Mask . . . . . . . . . . . : 255.255.255.0
        Default Gateway . . . . . . . . . : 192.168.1.1
        DHCP Server . . . . . . . . . . . : 192.168.1.1
        DNS Servers . . . . . . . . . . . : 151.164.20.201
                                            151.164.11.201
        Lease Obtained. . . . . . . . . . : Tuesday, August 06, 2002 12:03:28 PM

        Lease Expires . . . . . . . . . . : Wednesday, August 07, 2002 12:03:28
PM

Ethernet adapter Wireless Network Connection:

        Connection-specific DNS Suffix  . :
        Description . . . . . . . . . . . : ORiNOCO USB Card
        Physical Address. . . . . . . . . : 00-02-2D-3B-9B-28
        Dhcp Enabled. . . . . . . . . . . : Yes
        Autoconfiguration Enabled . . . . : Yes
        IP Address. . . . . . . . . . . . : 192.168.1.103
        Subnet Mask . . . . . . . . . . . : 255.255.255.0
        Default Gateway . . . . . . . . . : 192.168.1.1
        DHCP Server . . . . . . . . . . . : 192.168.1.1
        DNS Servers . . . . . . . . . . . : 151.164.20.201
                                            151.164.11.201
        Lease Obtained. . . . . . . . . . : Tuesday, August 06, 2002 12:04:21 PM
```

Figure 7.18
You can block web sites and newsgroups containing the keywords you specify, using NetGear's keywords filter.

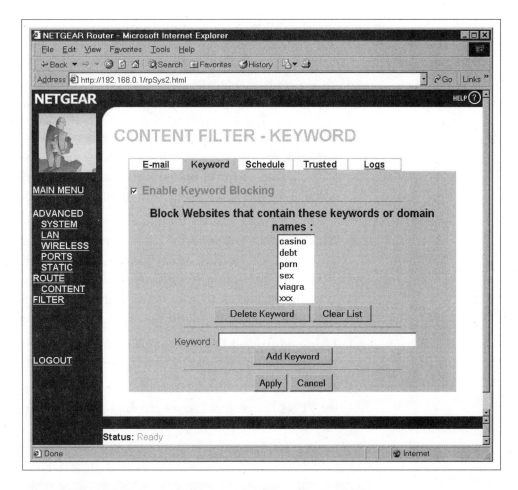

schedule so, for example, blocking only occurs when the kids are home from school. You can also designate one computer (by IP address) whose access isn't subject to blocking.

Enhanced Security

In addition to WEP and firewall protection for the local network, and password security for the AP, many APs include additional security measures that protect both the network (wired and wireless) and restrict access to the AP. Many businesses will want to implement these security measures, especially where a risk exists that intruders or unauthorized employees could otherwise tinker with the configuration of the AP and defeat basic security. Most home users won't need to go beyond the basics.

Network Security and VPN Support

Advanced network security features usually address allowing or blocking specific kinds of transmissions between your network and the Internet. They're more specific than port filtering or address blocking. Virtual private network (VPN) support is also covered here because the pass-through method used to allow a connection from your wi-fi network to a corporate VPN bears a similarity to the network security features.

Advanced security features in the Linksys AP appear on the Filters screen (Figure 7.19), below the port-filtering options. These are the following:

❏ **Stateful Packet Inspection (SPI)**   When a packet enters your network, bound for a specific IP address, the destination address is compared to the source of the request to verify they're the same. This provides protection against attacks done by using fake IP addresses on the network.

❏ **Blocking WAN Requests**   This option prevents anyone outside your network from pinging your AP or performing port scans. Attackers often ping IP addresses to determine if they're valid, and then move on to scan valid addresses for open Internet ports through which they might be able to penetrate your network.

❏ **Using Multicast Pass-Through**   Enabling this option allows multiple transmissions to specific recipients at the same time.

❏ **IPSec and PPTP Pass-Through**   These protocols are each used by VPNs to create a secure channel for communication between

Figure 7.19
Block unwanted or invalid access attempts and enable access to a corporate VPN using these security options.

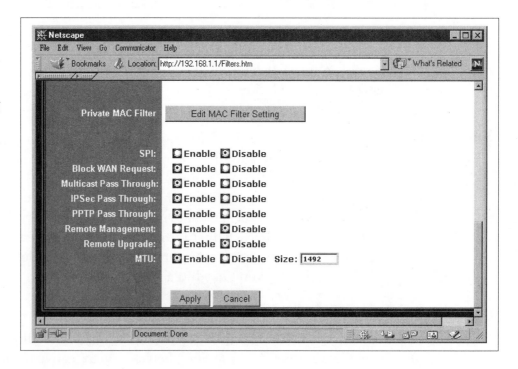

a corporate network and remote users. If you need to connect to a corporate VPN, enable the option that applies.

❏ **Use Maximum Transmission Units (MTU)**   This option controls the maximum size of packets that can be transferred into your network. Enabling MTU activates a field where you can enter a value. Linksys documentation recommends you use a value between 1200 and 1500, and that DSL users choose a value of 1492, if this feature is enabled.

Access Point Security

The private IP address you enter to reach your AP's administration software makes the AP inaccessible to the outside world. Or, does it? With an AP configured to connect to the Internet, the public IP address your network shares is also the AP's IP. In other words, a web surfer who knew your public IP address could enter it and connect to your AP administration software. In most cases, this isn't a problem because IPs are assigned dynamically by an ISP and change each time you make an Internet connection and AP passwords keep intruders out. If you have either static IP address or a poorly thought-out password, your AP is at risk, however. In addition, it's possible for wireless intruders to join your network and guess your AP's private IP address.

Many APs defeat unauthorized access to the administration software by requiring the AP can only be reached from a specific IP address or a MAC address. In some cases, you can only manage the AP from the computer you first used to configure it. Access from a different computer requires you to change settings in the administration software.

If you need to connect to your AP from outside your network—while traveling, for example—you can allow remote access from a specific IP address or domain. Other requests from outside the network are rejected.

Linksys imposes no restriction on local access to the AP administration software. Any computer on the network can connect to it via browser, but you'll need a password to make changes. If you're concerned about local security, be sure to specify a password, as described earlier.

Orinoco's BG-2000 and D-Link's DI-714 APs both restrict local connections. Try to connect to the access point from a computer other than the one you used to set it up and you'll be denied access. You can, of course, override this limitation, either giving all local users access or switching the administrative access from one computer to another.

Remote management is disabled by default on most APs. You can enable it on the Linksys BEFW11S4, on the Filters screen. Other APs, including the ZoomAir IG-4165, let you choose a specific remote address that can connect to the AP. To manage the Zoom AP remotely, I enabled remote management and provided my office IP address (Figure 7.20).

Routing

AP/router combinations often provide specific routing functions that go beyond simply negotiating communication between a local network and the

Figure 7.20
Enter an IP address in the Remote Administrator field to manage the AP from outside your local network.

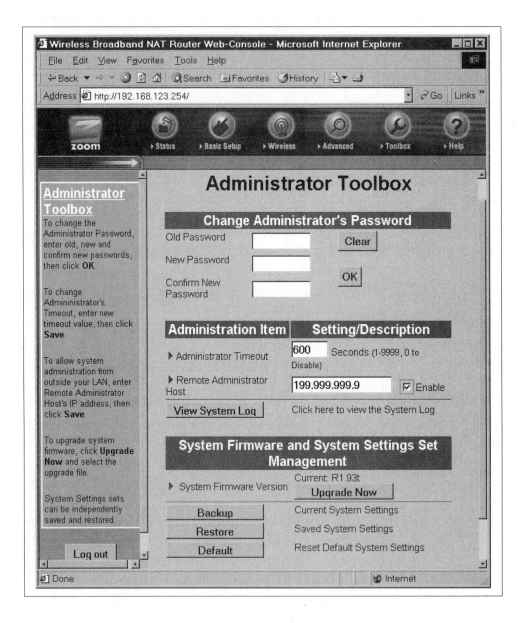

Internet. They're usually divided into dynamic and static routing functions. Although some support both, finding routers that support one—usually dynamic—of the two is common. The Linksys' example product provides both. Like most consumer-grade APs, it uses the Routing Information Protocol (RIP). Routing features aren't applicable in environments where your AP is the only router on the network. Corporate or campus networks include many routers, all of which must coordinate to move data from origin to destination, often over a number of routers. Each trip to a router is called a *hop.* Dynamic and static routing features can improve efficiency by minimizing the number of hops data must make.

Dynamic Routing

Dynamic routing works by seeking out the most efficient path for data to travel and broadcasts current routing information to other routers on the network. Linksys Dynamic Routing features appear on the Dynamic Routing screen, as shown in Figure 7.21 (click Advanced, and then click the Dynamic Routing tab).

Figure 7.21
Dynamic routing works by locating the most efficient route for data traveling on a multirouter network.

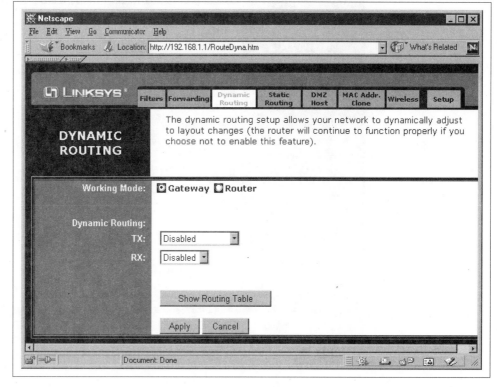

Static Routing

While dynamic routing seeks the fastest data path, *static routing* enforces a fixed path, usually to and from remote networks to which your network needs to connect. Setting static routing options sets the data path. You can set up to 20 static routes, each to a different IP address (Figure 7.22).

Logging and Monitoring

Most APs provide some sort of access logging. Many of these logs have few fields and don't cover a great deal of time, so they aren't much help in monitoring your network for problems or tracking specific problems. Your AP could simply log incoming access attempts by time and whether they were successful. More sophisticated logging covers outbound activity, including

Figure 7.22
Define static routes between your network and up to 20 other IP addresses.

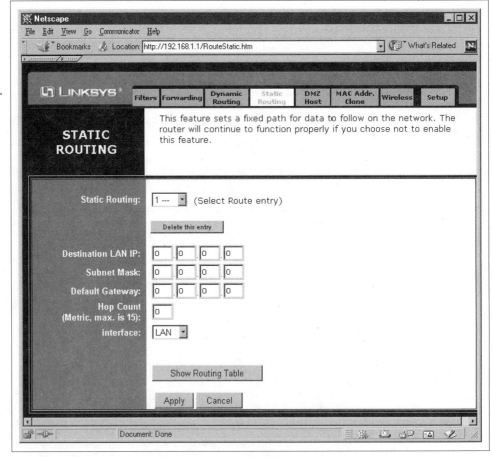

Internet addresses accessed from your network. This sort of logging can be helpful if you need to track suspicious Internet activity of a child or of employees in your business. Good access logging includes the capability to take action, such as alerting the network owner to suspicious activity or at least mailing the log on a regular basis.

Linksys logging is somewhere in the middle. An *incoming access log* shows you the source address of data entering your network and the number of packets received. The *outgoing access log* (Figure 7.23) shows the local address

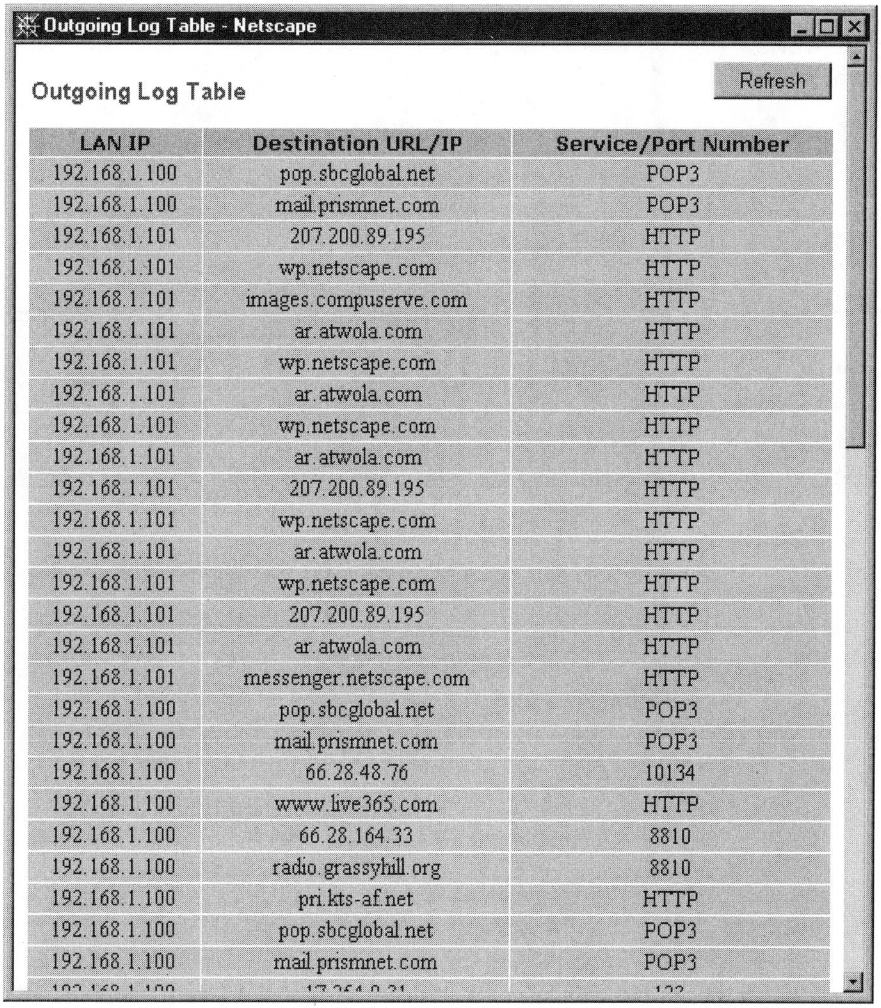

Figure 7.23
The outgoing access log shows the source and destination of Internet traffic originating on your network.

Outgoing Log Table - Netscape

Outgoing Log Table   Refresh

LAN IP	Destination URL/IP	Service/Port Number
192.168.1.100	pop.sbcglobal.net	POP3
192.168.1.100	mail.prismnet.com	POP3
192.168.1.101	207.200.89.195	HTTP
192.168.1.101	wp.netscape.com	HTTP
192.168.1.101	images.compuserve.com	HTTP
192.168.1.101	ar.atwola.com	HTTP
192.168.1.101	wp.netscape.com	HTTP
192.168.1.101	ar.atwola.com	HTTP
192.168.1.101	wp.netscape.com	HTTP
192.168.1.101	ar.atwola.com	HTTP
192.168.1.101	207.200.89.195	HTTP
192.168.1.101	wp.netscape.com	HTTP
192.168.1.101	ar.atwola.com	HTTP
192.168.1.101	wp.netscape.com	HTTP
192.168.1.101	207.200.89.195	HTTP
192.168.1.101	ar.atwola.com	HTTP
192.168.1.101	messenger.netscape.com	HTTP
192.168.1.100	pop.sbcglobal.net	POP3
192.168.1.100	mail.prismnet.com	POP3
192.168.1.100	66.28.48.76	10134
192.168.1.100	www.live365.com	HTTP
192.168.1.100	66.28.164.33	8810
192.168.1.100	radio.grassyhill.org	8810
192.168.1.100	pri.kts-af.net	HTTP
192.168.1.100	pop.sbcglobal.net	POP3
192.168.1.100	mail.prismnet.com	POP3

requesting data, the IP address or Internet domain to which the request was made, and the Internet application involved.

Logging is the strength of NetGear's MR314 product, which keeps logs of incoming and outgoing connections, the IP addresses, and the domains associated with them. You can have the log mailed to you on a schedule you set (Figure 7.24).

Figure 7.24
Do you need to keep close track of connections to and from your network? NetGear's MR314 will send you the log.

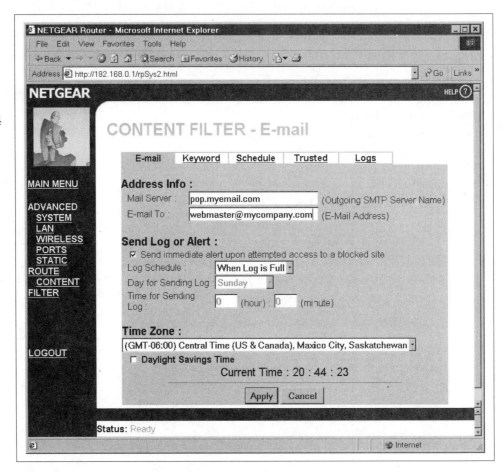

Chapter 8

Setting Up Computers for Wi-Fi

In the previous chapter, you learned to begin a wi-fi network with an access point. Now, you need to set up some computers to connect to the network. This chapter focuses on setting up wi-fi network adapters. To give you a broad range of experiences with these devices, I use several network adapters and operating systems (OSes).

For the most part, installing network adapters and setting up driver software to connect to a wi-fi network is an easy process. Wi-fi hardware and software will look and act in familiar ways to anyone who has installed Ethernet devices. Most inexperienced network installers will get the hang of it. From there, configuration is a matter of identifying an available network, and changing TCP/IP and other protocol settings to match the kind of services available on your network. In this chapter, you learn about some compatibility and OS-related issues, and then you walk through setting up a wi-fi adapter using Windows, Linux, and Mac OS.

The examples chosen are intended to show you a wide range of scenarios, including some in which the ways you use hardware and software together aren't clearly explained or supported by vendors. Since not everyone will use wi-fi with a Windows 2000 laptop containing a PC card, though, and much of the information available in product documentation doesn't directly address the needs of those who use other OSes, and/or those who want to add wi-fi to desktop computers. In this chapter, you learn what hardware and software does and doesn't work together.

Wi-Fi Gear and Operating System Compatibility

Most readers of this book are probably using some version of Microsoft Windows. The rest of you—Macintosh and Linux users—are screaming at the top of your lungs that I'm wrong. And, even if I were correct about the number of Windows users out there, I'd better not ignore those who choose to march to a different OS drummer.

Because not everyone uses the same OS, we need to discuss compatibility between wi-fi equipment and various platforms. Because Macs and PCs use the same I/O connectors these days—USB, PCMCIA, and PCI—finding a network adapter that fits your computer isn't usually the problem. Most network adapters are either PC cards or USB devices (though PCI and ISA adapters sold separately enable you to add a wi-fi adapter to a desktop PC, as described in Chapter 4). The trouble is this: Many wi-fi adapter vendors haven't supported the Mac and Linux with the needed driver software for their products. Resourceful Linux users have written and distributed their own drivers, as have some Mac developers. You learn about third-party options available for Mac and Windows users in the next section, but it's important for you to know whether the network adapter you intend to use works with your OS. Let's look quickly at the w-fi readiness of several OSes.

Windows 2000 and XP

All vendors of wi-fi network adapters provide drivers that work with these OSes. Windows 2000 and XP include drivers for some wi-fi devices, making it possible to get a network adapter up and running with plug-and-play. Wi-fi vendors suggest you install drivers from the CD-ROM that accompanies the adapter, though, or download the latest version from the vendor's web site, rather than relying on plug-and-play. Vendors update their drivers often and some users have reported problems with drivers that came bundled with Windows 2000. Early reports from Windows XP users indicate the bundled drivers might be reliable—more of them exist than in Windows 2000—and Microsoft created a certification program to identify drivers that fully support XP. If you install vendor software that hasn't been certified, Windows warns you, but it lets you install the driver if you choose. At press time, a few vendors provided uncertified XP drivers and indicated that certification from Microsoft was pending.

Windows XP automates the process of associating with a wi-fi network, as you learn later in this chapter. Windows XP also includes support for several security features that are important in corporate wi-fi environments: IEEE 802.1x, built-in VPN capability, and the capability to connect to RADIUS servers (see Chapter 10).

Windows 95, 98, and Me

Microsoft's home-oriented OSes support wi-fi and vendors provide drivers for both 98 and Me. Some wi-fi gear will work with Windows 95 and some won't. If you're a Windows 95 user, check the system requirements of any network adapter to be sure it's compatible with your OS. You should know, as time passes, some vendors will withdraw support for Windows 95. Windows 95 is the oldest "modern" version of Windows and Microsoft itself has announced it won't issue updates any longer. Your best option for the long term is to upgrade to a later version of Windows.

Linux

Like Windows XP, the latest version of the leading Linux distribution, Red Hat Linux 7.3, provides a new level of built-in wi-fi device support. A driver that supports Lucent chipset-based wi-fi devices is part of the pcmcia.cs package that installs along with the OS. This is a significant improvement over older Linux versions, which can support wi-fi, but require you to install and compile a number of tools, along with the wi-fi driver itself. In Red Hat 7.3, you still might need to tweak the system by editing a few files. You also could find that some cards aren't fully supported "out of the box," but that's a lot less involved than rebuilding the kernel or compiling the driver, both requirements under previous versions.

The easiest way to get a Lucent-based PC card to work under Red Hat 7.3 is to insert the card before installing 7.3. Linux will identify and begin the configuration of the card. Once installation is complete, you can complete setup in the Network Configuration tool, accessible from the Gnome desktop. You learn about this process in the section "Configure the Adapter."

Support for PRISM-2 Cards and Older Linux Versions

If you're not working in the plug-and-play-like world of the Lucent chipset and Red Hat 7.3, this overview can give you an idea what lies in store as you get started with Linux.

Some wi-fi vendors supply Linux drivers for their products. These drivers are typically "closed-source" meaning, like drivers for other OSes, the Linux tools can't be modified or customized. In a Linux environment, the capability to tweak software is important for ensuring compatibility and an expected benefit for the user. Many alternatives exist. A number of Linux developers have written open-source wi-fi drivers—meaning the software can be modified by anyone with the know-how to do it. Most users won't need or want to modify a driver, but the open-source approach benefits everyone who uses the driver. *Open source* usually means clever programmers can add features or fix bugs in the driver and the driver is usually free for the downloading. The upshot for a wi-fi user is you have a choice: a vendor-provided Linux driver or one of several more current open-source drivers that have more features than the vendor-supplied ones.

The most popular open-source driver for PRISM-2-based wi-fi PC cards is the linux-wlan-ng driver. Linux-wlan-ng is based on the original linux-wlan, from Absolute Value Systems and works with most popular PRISM-2 cards. A number of other PRISM-2 drivers are available, along with options for cards based on the Symbol, TI, and other chipsets. So, the first order of business is to know what chip your card uses and to locate a compatible driver. Jean Tourrilhes has compiled an extensive list of drivers for all chipsets, which is available at http://www.hpl.hp.com/personal/Jean_Tourrilhes/Linux/Linux.Wireless.drivers.html.

Mac OS X

Apple's Unix-based OS—Mac OS X—includes a driver for the company's own AirPort wi-fi card. At press time, AirPort cards are the only ones supported directly by OS X, and only Cisco ships OS X wi-fi drivers. What's worse, there are currently no USB or PCI adapters that work with OS X. If your Mac is AirPort-ready (all current Macs and all of those shipped within the past couple of years are), Apple's own card is by far your best bet, and all the software you need is part of the OS. If the Mac is OS X-capable, but isn't AirPort-ready, you'll need a third-party card because the AirPort card isn't compatible. You have two choices: buy a Cisco card (or any other device that explicitly provides OS X support) or use an open source tool called WirelessDriver that is still in beta at press time. Useful as WirelessDriver is, it lacks two important features: a full-featured management interface and consistent support for WEP-based security. I offer this as a word of warning, but you might find these limitations are gone in the final version. My advice? Check out the WirelessDriver web site for complete compatibility information before you buy a card to use with a non-AirPort-ready Mac running OS X.

Mac OS 8 and 9

The same rules for AirPort compatibility apply to Mac OS 9 as to OS X. The capability to use Apple-brand wi-fi adapters is dependent on the Mac hardware, not the OS. Using non-Apple hardware with non-AirPort-ready Macs is somewhat easier than OS 9, however, because vendors, including Proxim and Agere (now merged), have provided compatible drivers for their products. You can even use the AirPort software included with OS 9 (and available from Apple's web site) to drive Agere/Orinoco PC cards. If you have another kind of card or if you want to use an OS as old as Mac OS 8.6, an option is available. IO Xperts is developing a driver package that lets you install many wi-fi PC cards into OS 8 or 9 PowerBooks.

Installing Adapters and Drivers

Installation procedures for wi-fi adapters vary by manufacturer. Some instruct you to install the hardware first, while others use drivers you installed to recognize the adapter. The software package for most wi-fi adapters includes both the drivers needed to make the adapter work with your computer and one or more utility applications used to configure the computer to connect to wireless networks.

In this section, you walk through software installation for wi-fi network adapters under Windows XP and 2000, one card under Linux (as well as some general guidance for Linux users) and two under Mac OS. I chose several popular network adapters to demonstrate the installation process under Windows: D-Link's DWL-500 PCI card holder/PC card (DWL-650) and Agere's Orinoco USB adapter. Under all Windows versions, you connect the hardware, and then install the software. I add a wrinkle by installing both the D-Link PC card into a desktop PC, along with a PCI adapter from D-Link. In the Linux section, you learn to install an Orinoco PC card on a laptop running Red Hat Linux 7.3. Finally, I use non-Apple drivers to install a PC card from Linksys under Mac OS X and OS 9, using a pre-AirPort Apple laptop. The devices and OSes chosen for these illustrations are intended to represent a range of experiences that users encounter when trying to match hardware in the real world. All are popular products and a few present challenges that make them great examples.

A Brief Terminology Reminder

Chapters 1 and 2 introduced you to a number of commonly used wi-fi terms. You see more of these terms in the glossary in Appendix A. But because so many abstract terms take concrete form in this chapter, you should look at a few of the most important ones.

❑ **Ad-hoc mode**   When a wi-fi network doesn't include an access point, this is referred to as an *ad-hoc* network. You might also see this referred to as a *peer-to-peer* network. Chapter 9 deals exclusively with setting up and using ad-hoc networks.

❑ **Channel**   The frequency band in which a wi-fi network operates is divided into a number of channels. In 802.11b, all communication among computers connected to a particular access point takes place on a single channel.

❏ **Infrastructure mode**   A computer on a network managed by an access point is said to be in *infrastructure mode*.

❏ **SSID**   The *Service Set ID* is a string that identifies the network. Ad-hoc and infrastructure networks use SSIDs. Most people think of the SSID as the network name.

❏ **WEP**   *Wired Equivalent Privacy* provides a key to encrypt data as it travels over a wireless network. The key is set on the access-point in infrastructure-mode networks and by the computer that begins an ad-hoc network.

Installing the D-Link Card Holder and Network Adapter Under Windows XP

D-Link's wi-fi network adapter ships with drivers for Windows 98, Me, 2000, and XP. The D-Link adapter is a PC card, suitable for use with most laptops. To install the card into a desktop PC, you need a PCI or an ISA card from D-Link. Insert the D-Link card holder into an available PCI or ISA slot in the PC, and then slide the wi-fi adapter into the slot on the card holder. In this section, you install a D-Link wi-fi adapter into a desktop PC, using the PCI card holder. Figure 8.1 shows the card and card holder. To begin, you install driver software for the card holder and the wi-fi adapter, and then you install the hardware.

Install Drivers

To get started, you need to install software drivers for the card holder and the network adapter.

1. Insert the D-Link Driver CD into your CD-ROM drive.

2. When the D-Link splash screen appears (Figure 8.2), click Install Drivers, and then choose to install the PCI Holder Driver. The installer will launch and begin taking you through the installation process.

Figure 8.1
D-Link's PCI card holder contains a slot for a PC card wi-fi adapter. You need to purchase both to add wi-fi to a desktop PC.

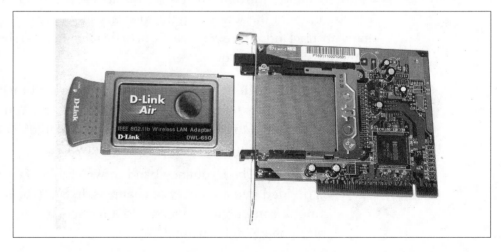

Figure 8.2
Install the PCI
Holder Driver
first, as instructed.

3. Click Next when the wizard appears, and then click Yes when you're asked to read and accept the license agreement.

4. To continue the installation process after the card holder driver is installed, choose not to restart your computer now, and then click Finish.

5. When the D-Link CD screen appears again, click the Install DWL-650 Drivers link. The Installation Wizard opens (Figure 8.3).

6. Click Next to view the license agreement, and then click Yes to accept it.

Figure 8.3
The Installation
Wizard reminds
you to quit other
programs before
installing drivers.

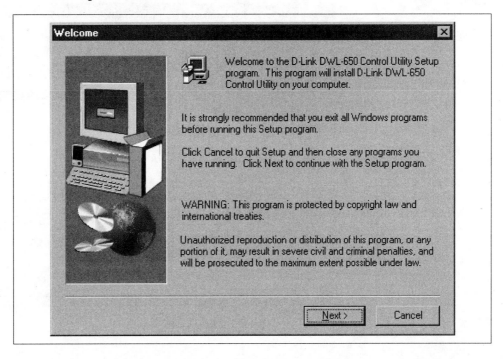

Figure 8.4
Enter your
network's SSID
or leave it
unchanged if
you haven't yet
created a network.

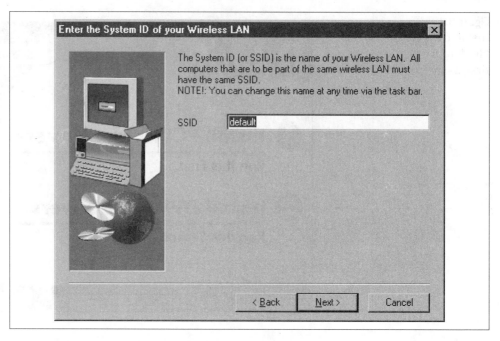

7. If a wireless LAN is already set up, type its SSID (the name by which the network is known to its users) in the box provided (Figure 8.4). If you haven't yet set up a network, leave the SSID set to default or name the network you plan to set up later. You can update the SSID later. Click Next.

8. If your wi-fi network is or will be controlled by an access point, choose Infrastructure, as shown in Figure 8.5. If the network will connect the computer without an access point, click Ad-Hoc. Click Next.

Figure 8.5
Choose
Infrastructure
if your network
will use an
access point.

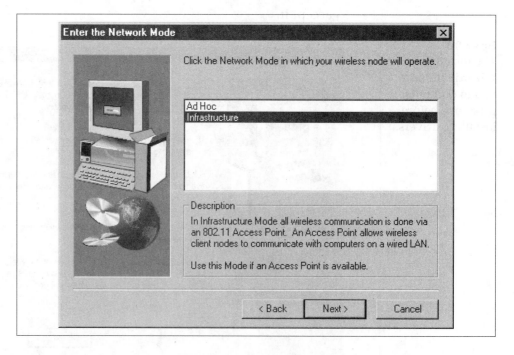

9. Accept or change the default location of the D-Link configuration application, click Next, and then choose how you want D-Link shortcuts to appear on your Start menu. Finally, click Next to finish the installation.

Install Hardware

Follow these steps to install the D-Link hardware:

1. Shut down the computer and unplug the power cable and peripherals.

2. Open the computer according to the directions provided with it. Manufacturers typically provide instructions for opening the box, as well as protecting yourself and the computer from dirt and electrical shock.

3. Install the PCI card holder into an available PCI slot (Figure 8.6). You might need to unscrew and punch out the protective metal cover on the rear of the PCI slot. You can identify the PCI slots in your computer by their size. Most PCs contain several PCI and ISA slots. The PCI slots are significantly shorter than the ISA slots. PCI cards are also considerably smaller than ISA adapter cards. Figure 8.7 shows an ISA card.

4. Slide the D-Link PC card into the PCI card holder's slot (Figure 8.8). The antenna will protrude from the rear of the computer.

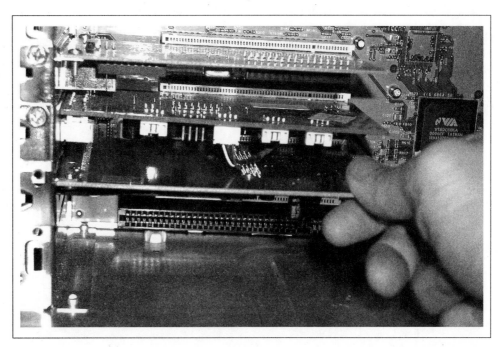

Figure 8.6
Install the card holder into an available PCI slot.

Figure 8.7
Like the PCI card holder, D-Link's ISA card holder supports a PC card network adapter.

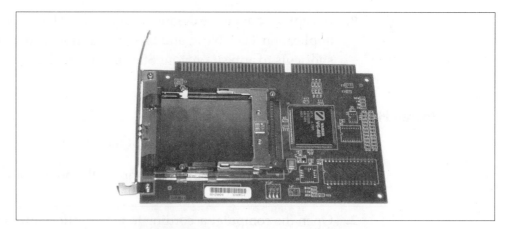

Figure 8.8
Slide the D-Link network adapter into the PCI card holder. Its antenna is visible from the rear of the computer.

5. Make sure the card holder and the network adapter are securely seated in the PC, and then close and restart the computer. Be sure you have the D-Link driver CD handy.

6. When Windows finishes starting up, it will acknowledge the presence of the PCI adapter with the Found New Hardware Wizard (Figure 8.9).

Figure 8.9
The Found New Hardware Wizard identifies the new hardware.

Figure 8.10
The taskbar icon on the left represents the network.

7. Choose to install from a specific list and click Install.

8. Tell Windows to look for drivers in specific locations, and then click the CD-ROM check box. Now browse the CD (insert the CD if it isn't already in the drive) to locate the folder containing the driver you need. Click Next once you select the correct path.

9. When Windows recognizes the D-Link device, click Finish.

Join a Network

Now you're ready to connect the computer to a wireless network. A taskbar icon, as shown in Figure 8.10, now indicates the D-Link network adapter is installed and can join a network. Figure 8.11 shows the network connection's status.

1. Right-click the taskbar icon.

2. From the Taskbar menu, choose View Available Wireless Networks (Figure 8.12).

3. In the Connect to Wireless Network window (Figure 8.13), choose the network you want to join. If the network requires a WEP security key, enter it in the Network Key field. If you don't see entries in the window, then no networks are currently available.

Figure 8.11
If you move the mouse over the icon representing your wireless network, you can see the name and condition of the connection.

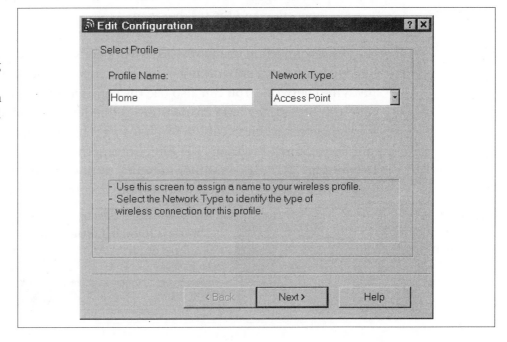

Figure 8.12
Use the Taskbar
menu to open
the configuration
application.

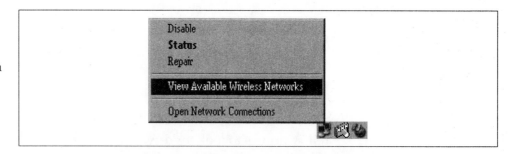

Figure 8.13
Choose the
network you
want to join. All
networks within
range will appear
on the list.

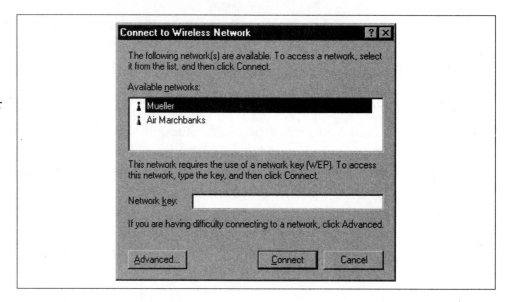

4. Click Connect.

5. The taskbar now has a new icon representing the network you joined (Figure 8.14). A text balloon will briefly indicate your new connection and the taskbar icon.

With a connection to a wireless network active, you can make changes to standard Windows networking properties in the same way you would for any wired network. You can also use the configuration utility to change advanced wi-fi settings or to create profiles that let you quickly join other networks. You can reach the utility by choosing it from the taskbar menu or you can choose Start | Programs | D-Link Control Utility | Configuration Utility. To configure TCP/IP and other network settings, double-click the taskbar icon for the wireless network connection, and then click Properties.

Figure 8.14
An active network
connection is
displayed on
the taskbar.

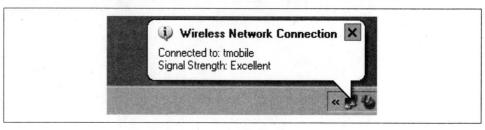

Figure 8.15
Inside the
Agere/Orinoco
USB network
adapter is a
standard PC
card. The vertical
orientation of
the USB device
improves network
range.

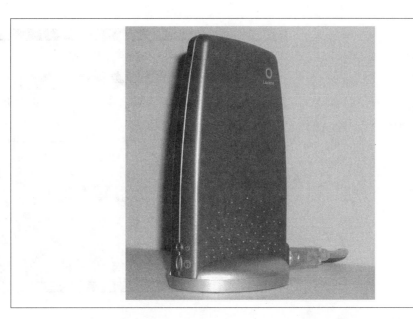

Installing the Agere/Orinoco USB Adapter Under Windows 2000

You can use Agere's Orinoco USB network adapter (Figure 8.15) with all versions of Windows since Windows 95. We'll set up the adapter on a desktop PC running Windows 2000. Like XP, Windows 2000 includes drivers for a variety of devices, including the Agere's PCI product. The USB driver isn't included with Windows 2000, however, although it is provided with Windows XP. This is just as well. You can get an up-to-date driver from the CD that shipped with the adapter and that's what we'll do.

Connecting the Network Adapter and Installing the Driver

1. Plug the Agere USB adapter into an open USB port on your computer. Windows will activate the Found New Hardware Wizard. Click Next.

2. The Found New Hardware Wizard identifies the ORINOCO USB Client. To locate a driver on your CD, click Search for a suitable driver for my device…, and then click Next.

3. Be sure the CD-ROM drives' check box is checked, and uncheck all the other boxes, unless you're installing a driver you downloaded. In that case, click Specify a location instead, and then click Next. Windows will search for the driver it needs. When Windows finds a driver, the path will appear onscreen. Click Next to proceed with installation of this driver.

When Windows has installed the driver, the Add/Edit Configuration Profile window (Figure 8.16) opens. This is where you begin the process of joining a wireless network.

Figure 8.16
The profile
configuration
process begins
in the Add/Edit
Configuration
Profile dialog box.

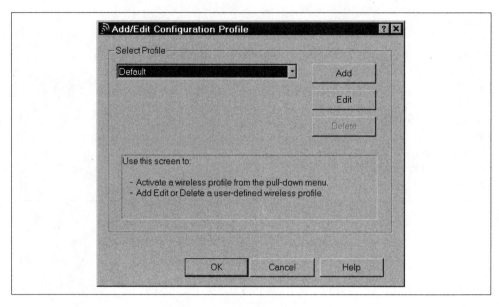

Join a Network

You can create profiles for as many wireless networks as you like, using the Orinoco configuration utility. Once profiles have been set up, laptop users can quickly switch between networks as they travel. Each profile contains the network's SSID, WEP key. Now you'll create a profile and join a wireless network.

1. In the Add/Edit Configuration Profile window, click Add.

2. Type a name for the profile (Figure 8.17).

3. From the menu (Figure 8.18), tell Windows whether the network is controlled by an access point, an Orinoco residential gateway, or is made up of computers that are connected in a peer-to-peer network. Click Next.

4. Click Scan. A list of networks within range of your computer appears. Select the one you want to join, and then click OK.

5. If your network has a WEP key, click the Enable Data Security button. The rest of the fields will become available. If your network doesn't have a WEP key, simply click Next.

6. To enter a WEP key, choose either Alphanumeric or Hexadecimal, and then type the key in the Key 1 field.

7. Click Next.

8. If you connected the USB adapter to a portable computer, consider choosing to turn on power management to reduce the amount of

Figure 8.17
Name the
network profile.

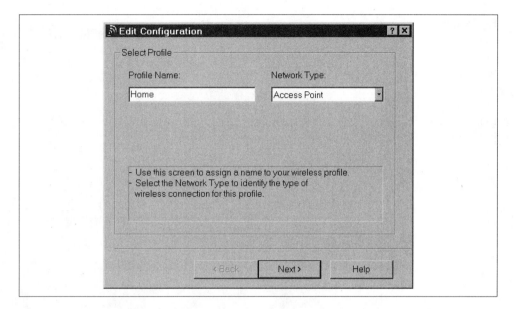

battery power your network adapter draws. Desktop PC users can
leave power management turned off (Figure 8.19). Turning power
management on uses less power, but diminishes the adapter's
performance. Click Next.

9. Click Renew IP Address when selecting this profile. If you use
multiple wireless networks, you'll use a different IP address with
each. Selecting this option instructs the network adapter either to
obtain an IP address from the wireless access point or to use one
associated with this network. Click Finish.

Figure 8.18
If your network
includes an access
point, choose
this option.
If not, choose
Peer-to-Peer
Group.

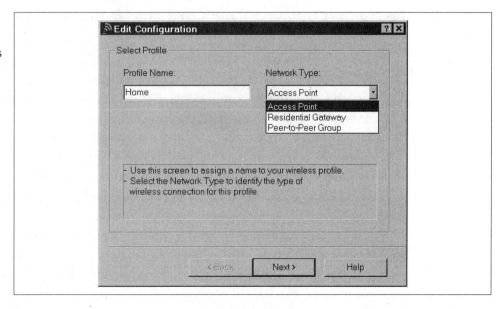

Figure 8.19
Turn power
management
on to conserve
battery power.
Leave it off
to maximize
performance.

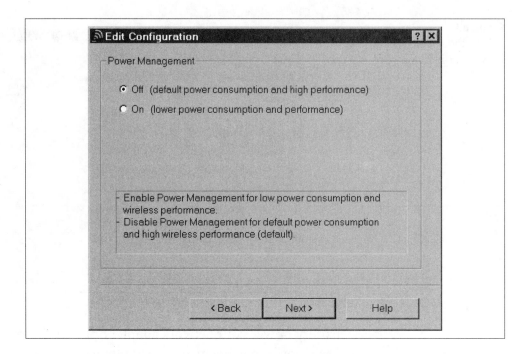

10. If you need to configure Windows networking options, including TCP/IP, double-click the taskbar icon for the wireless network connection, and then click Properties to reach the network protocol options you need. If you obtain a dynamic IP address from your wi-fi access point, you might not need to make any changes to network options.

Installing the Agere Orinoco Silver Card Under Red Hat Linux

The installation example chosen for this section is probably the simplest you'll ever undertake when working with Linux. As described in the OS-compatibility section of this chapter, many Linux distributions and many versions exist of both Linux and its components. Red Hat Linux 7.3, the most recent version at press time, provides good support for Lucent-based wireless devices out of the box. But chances are good you'll need to do some tinkering to get a wi-fi adapter working on your Linux system, especially if you intend to use a PRISM-2-based wi-fi network adapter. In our example, we'll work with an Agere/Orinoco Silver PC card, a device that's well-supported under Red Hat 7.3.

I began this process by installing Red Hat Linux 7.3 on a laptop containing the Orinoco Silver card. The installation process includes a step during which network devices are recognized by the system. In my case, the installer found the laptop's built-in Ethernet adapter and the wi-fi PC card. The installer identifies both as Ethernet devices. Be sure to configure both. The process creates an entry for the new device in /etc/sysconfig/networking/devices.

Configure the Adapter

With Red Hat 7.3 installed and the card recognized, you're ready to configure the network adapter. We'll be working on the Gnome desktop.

1. Open the Network Configuration tool (Programs | System | Network Configuration) to view available network devices (Figure 8.20).

2. Click the item representing the wireless card you configured during installation (en1).

3. Click Apply. This adds a line identifying the Ethernet interface as a wireless one.

4. Close the Network Configuration application.

5. Using the editor of your choice, edit the file /etc/sysconfig/networking/devices/ifcfg-eth1.

6. Change TYPE=Ethernet to TYPE=Wireless (Figure 8.21). Save the file.

Figure 8.20
Once Red Hat Linux recognizes network devices, they appear in the Network Configuration window.

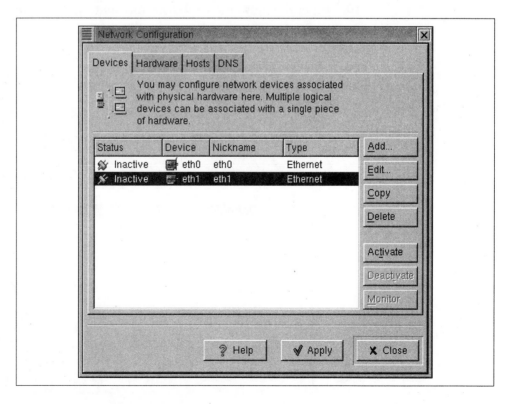

Figure 8.21
Change the TYPE
attribute from
Ethernet to
Wireless.

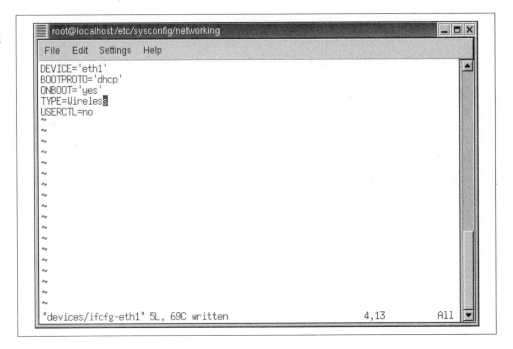

```
root@localhost:/etc/sysconfig/networking                    _ □ ✕

File   Edit   Settings   Help

DEVICE='eth1'
BOOTPROTO='dhcp'
ONBOOT='yes'
TYPE=Wireless
USERCTL=no
~
~
~
~
~
~
~
~
~
~
~
~
~
~
~
~
~
~
"devices/ifcfg-eth1" 5L, 69C written          4,13          All
```

7. Return to the Network Configuration application. The Eth1 device has been updated (Figure 8.22).

8. Select the device, and then click Edit to view Configuration options.

9. Select the Wireless Settings tab (Figure 8.23).

10. Enter the network's SSID. Unfortunately, no scanning feature exists, so you must know the network's exact ID.

Figure 8.22
The PC card now
appears as a
wireless device.

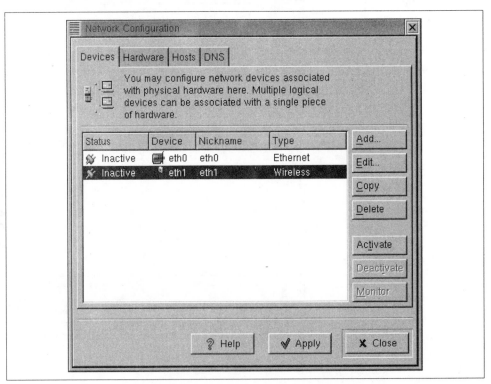

Network Configuration

Devices | Hardware | Hosts | DNS

You may configure network devices associated with physical hardware here. Multiple logical devices can be associated with a single piece of hardware.

Status	Device	Nickname	Type
Inactive	eth0	eth0	Ethernet
Inactive	eth1	eth1	Wireless

Add...
Edit...
Copy
Delete
Activate
Deactivate
Monitor

Help   Apply   Close

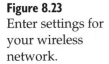

Figure 8.23
Enter settings for
your wireless
network.

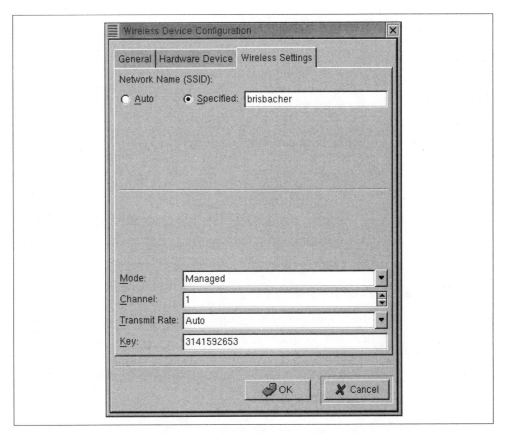

11. Choose a mode from the pull-down menu. Managed is the correct choice for a network that includes an access point. Otherwise, choose Ad-Hoc.

12. Enter a WEP key, if any. There's no need to choose a channel. This information will be supplied to the wi-fi device by the access point.

13. Click OK, and then click Apply.

14. In the main Network Configuration window, press Activate to complete the process.

Enabling Support for a PRISM-2 PC Card Under Linux

Because many variables are associated with providing support for a PRISM-2 card—the distribution and version of Linux, the kernel version, the driver used—I'll review the general steps. You can apply this process to your specific situation. Along the way, I point you toward additional Linux resources.

Our task is to align configurations for the kernel, pcmcia-cs, and the specific wireless driver you intend to use.

Step 1: Prepare the Kernel

To work with a wireless driver, your Linux system needs the kernel headers package, which is part of most Linux distributions, but not necessarily installed. You need the kernel-headers, kernel-source, and kernal-pcmcia packages. To determine whether they're installed, use this command:

```
rpm -ga|grep kernel
```

You'll get a list of items, including the word "kernel."

If the needed kernel files aren't installed, look for them on your Linux distribution CDs. Note it's important that the kernel package versions you install exactly match the version of the kernel and distribution you're using.

Step 2: Prepare pcmcia-cs

Most wireless drivers for Linux are built on information found in pcmcia-cs headers. Chances are good that pcmcia-cs is already installed, especially if you're using a recent version of Red Hat Linux. You'll want to verify this and be sure of the version you have. You can run the following command to verify the packages exist:

```
rpm -ga|grep pcmcia
```

To find out the version of the package, check the /CHANGES directory (usually in /usr/doc or /usr/share/doc). If you need a new version (or want to learn much more about how pcmcia-cs works, visit the Linux PCMCIA Information Page at http://pcmcia-cs.sourceforge.net.

Once you download the software you need, your task is to build the package. *Do not install it, however.* Building the package provides the headers needed by the wireless driver you will install in the next step.

To build the package, unpack it, change to the directory that contains the package, and then type the following:

```
./Configure
```

You'll be asked to locate the Linux source directory (/usr/src/linux-2.4 under Red Hat 7.2). You can accept the default options or make changes to meet you own needs. When the process is complete, type:

```
make all
```

to complete the build.

Install the Driver

Download the linux-wlan-ng driver from http://www.linux-wlan.com/linux-wlan. You'll need to install and configure the driver. You might also need to build it, depending on the Linux distribution you're using. In any case, follow the instructions provided at ftp://ftp.linux-wlan.org/pub/linux-wlan-ng/README. You'll learn much more about options for different Linux setups, troubleshooting than I could possibly tell you in these pages.

Installing the Linksys PC Card Under Mac OS X

As mentioned in the OS compatibility section of this chapter, you can use an open-source driver with network adapters under Mac OS X. WirelessDriver is brought to you by a team of developers led by Rob McKeever. WirelesDriver supports a number of PC card wi-fi adapters, including Orinoco, 3Com, Cabletron, D-Link, Linksys, Farallon, Proxim, and others. No support is available for PCI or USB adapters. I chose a popular card that provides no Mac support out of the box, the Linksys Wireless PC Card (Figure 8.24). I will install it into an Apple PowerBook G3 (Bronze keyboard). This PowerBook is among the last non-AirPort-ready computers Apple produced.

To get started, use Software Update (found in System Preferences) to ensure your OS is current. WirelessDriver requires Mac OS X 10.1.4 or later. Next, download WirelessDriver (available at http://wirelessdriver .sourceforge.net/index.html).

Install the Driver

1. Double-click the wirelessdriver.dmg file. Open the disk image when it mounts on your desktop. The WirelessDriver folder opens (Figure 8.25).

Figure 8.24
I'm going to install a Linksys PC card into a PowerBook G3, running Mac OS X 10.1.5.

Figure 8.25
The WirelessDriver folder contains the installer, readme files, and an uninstaller.

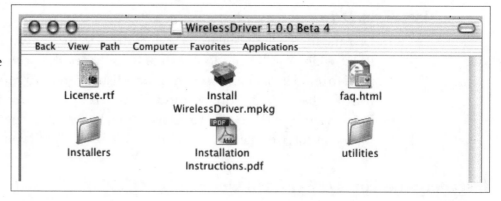

2. Double-click the Install WirelessDriver.mpkg to begin installation.

3. Follow the installer's instructions. You'll need an administrator password to install the software.

4. When the installation is complete, press Restart, and then insert the Linksys PC card.

5. Mac OS X will open System Preferences and the new Wirelessconfig pane. Enter the SSID of your wireless network in the Connect to wireless network named field.

6. If you're using a wi-fi adapter for which WEP is supported by the WirelessDriver, click Use WEP encryption and enter the WEP key (Figure 8.26).

7. Click Apply Now. Wirelessconfig will connect to the network and show the signal strength of the connection (Figure 8.27).

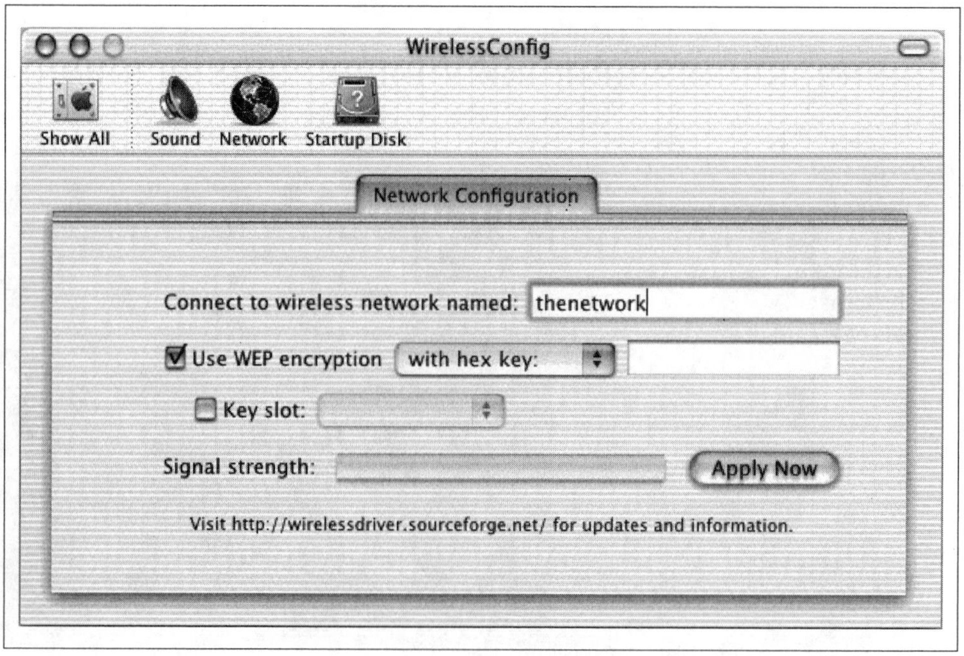

Figure 8.26
Enter the name of the wireless network in the Wirelessconfig.

Figure 8.27
The signal
strength bar
shows the active
network's signal.

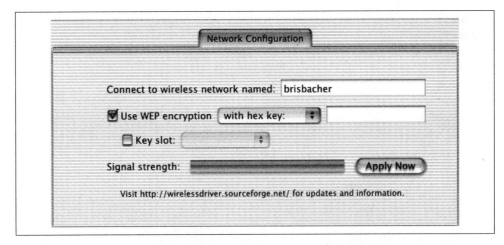

8. OS X tells you a new port has been detected. Activating the wireless driver creates the new port (Figure 8.28). Click OK.

9. The Network pane shows the new port (usually called Ethernet Adapter en1), as shown in Figure 8.29. You can now make changes to the TCP/IP, AppleTalk and/or Proxy settings for the wireless connection. When you're finished, click Apply Now and close the System Preferences application.

You probably noticed that Wirelessconfig doesn't scan for available networks. Instead, you must know the name of the network you want to join. Although this is a little inconvenient, you'll find that when you restart the computer with the wi-fi adapter installed, Wirelessconfig opens automatically, displaying the name of the last network to which it was connected.

Installing the Linksys PC Card Under Mac OS 9

Once again, getting a non-Apple card to work in the Mac environment requires a bit of ingenuity. Agere's Orinoco PC card works nicely with non-AirPort Macs, OS 9, and either Apple's AirPort software or Agere's own driver. To make this interesting, though, and to show you how the IOXperts driver

Figure 8.28
A new network
port is created
when the wireless
driver has been
installed.

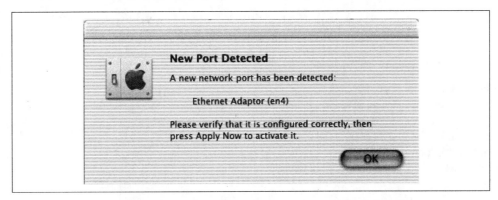

Figure 8.29
Ethernet Adapter
(en) identifies
the wireless card
and driver you
installed.

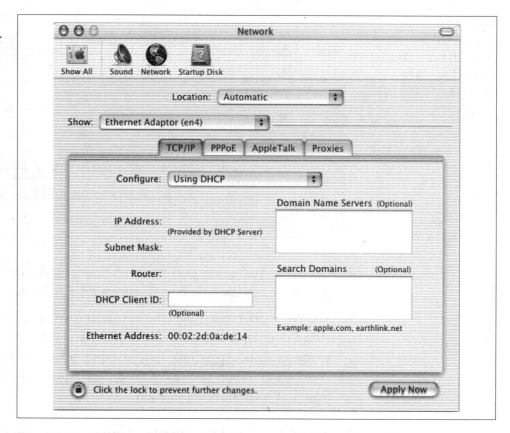

works, I chose to "force" the Linksys adapter used earlier to do its thing in my PowerBook G3 Bronze as a way to illustrate the options available when you must use a third-party driver. If you haven't yet purchased the driver, you will be able to use it for 30 minutes. When you purchase the driver via the IOXperts' Web site, you will be issued a serial number that corresponds to the MAC address of your PC card.

Install and Configure the Driver

1. Download, decompress, and install the IOXperts driver.

2. Insert the Linksys PC card and restart your computer.

3. When the desktop appears, you'll see a new icon labeled Wireless PC Card (Figure 8.30), that the indicating the Mac recognizes the wi-fi adapter.

Figure 8.30
The Wireless
PC Card icon
represents the
active Linksys
PC card.

Figure 8.31
Join a wireless
network.

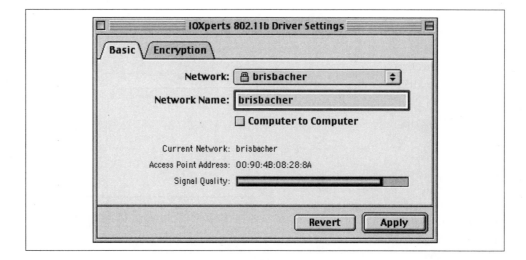

4. Choose Apple menu | Control Panels | IOXperts Network Settings.

5. Choose your wireless network from the menu (Figure 8.31). The status bar will reflect the signal strength of the network.

6. If the network uses WEP, click the Encryption tab (Figure 8.32).

7. Click Apply and close the Network Settings control panel.

8. Double-click the Wireless PC Card icon on the desktop.

9. The TCP/IP control panel opens, showing the IOXperts 802.11b Wireless Driver as the connect method (Figure 8.33). Make any needed changes to your TCP/IP settings and close TCP/IP. In most cases, you'll want TCP/IP to obtain an address from a DHCP server.

You can also reach IOXperts' network settings from the control strip (Figure 8.34).

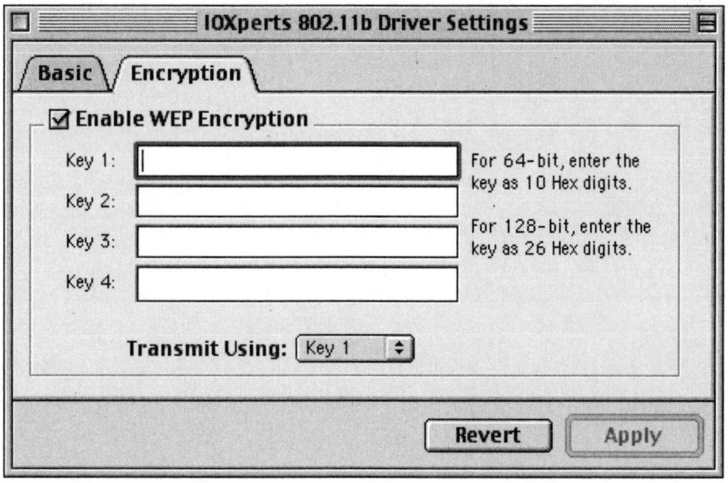

Figure 8.32
Enter the
encryption key
or keys in the
Encryption tab.

Figure 8.33
The Connect via pop-up menu shows the wireless driver is the active network adapter.

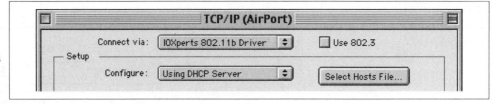

Figure 8.34
The control strip item duplicates the control panel features providing quick access to your wireless connection.

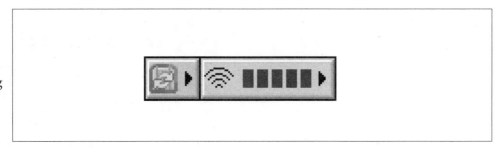

Conclusion

In this chapter, you've learned a lot about getting various network adapters to work with OSes. Your experience will depend on the combination of card and computer you're working with. The good news is that, as wi-fi gains popularity among users of Windows, Linux and Mac OS, the installation and configuration process will continue to grow easier, and you will have a greater choice of compatible wi-fi products.

Chapter 9

Ad-Hoc Wi-Fi

An ad-hoc network, as you learned in Chapter 2, consists of wi-fi-enabled computers only. No access point (AP) manages the wireless network, provides DHCP, a firewall, access to the Internet, or advanced security. On the other hand, an ad-hoc network can be set up anywhere you have two computers with wi-fi adapters: Use one of them to create the network and invite others to join it. Like any local network, an ad-hoc network enables its members to share files, play games, or use any application that supports communication over protocols all devices on the network understand. You can build a network using a software AP, giving you the administration and security features of a typical access point without connecting additional hardware. Both ad-hoc networks and software APs are covered in this chapter.

The Techie Side of Ad-Hoc Wi-Fi

The IEEE 802.11 standard specifies an ad-hoc mode, in which no access point manages the network. The layout of such a network is called an Independent Basic Service Set (IBSS). Recall from Chapter 2, a network that doesn't use multiple access points is called a Basic Service Set (BSS). An IBSS is simply a BSS in ad-hoc mode. Figure 9.1 shows a typical ad-hoc wi-fi network.

The terminology used to describe this kind of network can become a bit confusing, mostly because it isn't used consistently by vendors. The correct name of the mode that enables you to create a network without an access point is independent mode or IBSS. Independent networks are almost always described as being in ad-hoc mode (as opposed to infrastructure mode). In its original version of IEEE 802.11, ad-hoc mode required all computers within an IBSS to use the same channel of the 2.4 GHz wi-fi band. An updated version,

Figure 9.1
An 802.11 IBSS
consists of
wi-fi-equipped
stations.

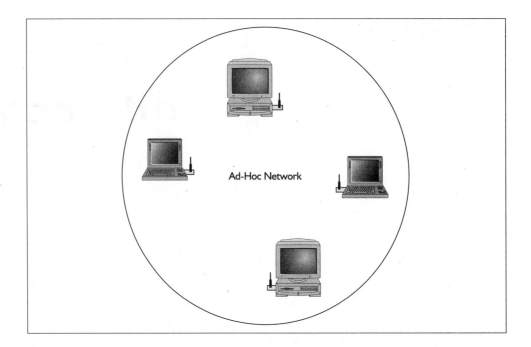

Ad-Hoc Network

called 802.11 ad-hoc mode, adds the requirement that all devices use the same SSID. In this way, 802.11 ad-hoc mode works like infrastructure mode. Most modern wi-fi network adapters use 802.11 ad-hoc mode, but many refer to it simply as ad-hoc or, to make things more interesting, peer-to-peer. The bottom line in all of this is you're using 802.11 ad-hoc mode—regardless of the name—if your network adapter driver asks you to specify both an SSID and the channel on which your network will operate. If you have an old wi-fi card, be sure its firmware and drivers are current. For the remainder of this chapter, IBSS networking is called ad-hoc mode.

All computers on an ad-hoc network are equals. Entering ad-hoc mode and declaring an SSID and channel number begins an ad-hoc network that others can join by duplicating the settings used by the first computer. If a second computer chooses a different SSID, a new network is created. This has an interesting side affect on the network: If the computer that created the network crashes or is turned off, the network remains available to all other users who are still connected to it.

In addition to the SSID, a Basic Service Set Identifier (BSSID) identifies each network. In infrastructure networks, the BSSID is based on the MAC address of the access point. In an ad-hoc network, the code is randomly generated when the network starts. Some wi-fi software hides the BSSID from view, except in advanced settings screens, while others display it. You only need to worry about the BSSID when you're troubleshooting an ad-hoc network, particularly if several are in the same area.

Figure 9.2
The gateway computer connects to a DSL modem via Ethernet and to the wireless network with a USB wi-fi adapter.

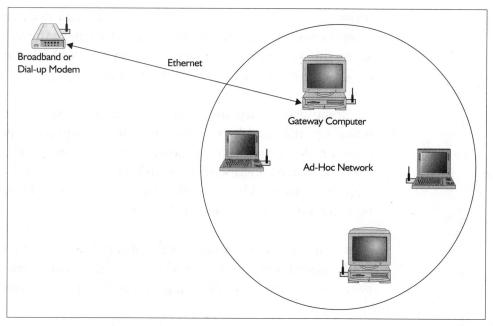

Ad-hoc networks can communicate with the wider world. You can set up one computer on the network as a gateway to the Internet, either with software that's included with the operating system (OS) (in the case of Windows XP and 2000), or with tools you can buy or download. The host computer must have a connection to the Internet, either via a dial-up modem or a connection to a broadband network. A typical arrangement is for a computer to connect to the Internet via an Ethernet connection to a cable or DSL modem, and a wi-fi adapter providing access to the ad-hoc network.

Gateway software acts much like an access point. It routes traffic from the Internet to a local network, and it can include both a DHCP server and a firewall. In most cases, this option won't provide all the features of an access point and will bog down the host computer in large networks, but this is an option for home users on a budget, especially if your OS provides built-in gateway tools. Figure 9.2 shows an ad-hoc wireless network with a gateway to the Internet.

Uses of Ad-Hoc Networks

The best reason to create an ad-hoc network is that it's simple to set up, especially compared to access point setup, and it doesn't require additional equipment. All you need are wi-fi adapters in each computer to be networked. This makes creating a network to exchange files or other information on a temporary basis quick and easy. You can also choose an ad-hoc network if you're on a tight budget. Although access points are typically under $200, an ad-hoc network is still a bargain if you don't need the AP's features. You can share Internet access over an ad-hoc network if one of the computers is also configured to act as an Internet gateway. You learn how to set up this kind of network in the section "Using An Internet Gateway with an Ad-Hoc Network" later in this chapter.

Home users often use ad-hoc networks to play network games, or to move a particular file or folder from one computer to another. When the game or file transfer is over, the network disappears. With the capability to create and save network profiles built into most network adapter utility software, you can quickly reestablish the network the next time you need to connect to another computer in your home.

Ad-hoc networks can also be helpful in business situations where a network doesn't already exist or where you need a network but, for some reason, you don't want to build a permanent wireless network.

Drawbacks to Ad-Hoc Networks

Most of the administration features provided by APs aren't built into an ad-hoc network. Those missing features include DHCP server functions, Internet sharing, firewall protection, NAT, access control, and port forwarding. This means ad-hoc networks are completely self-contained, with no access to resources outside the network. You need access to a wired network and an Internet gateway to bring Internet access to an ad-hoc network.

Ad-hoc networks typically provide less wireless coverage than an access point because they rely exclusively on the low-gain antennas built into wi-fi network adapters. You can boost the range by connecting an external antenna to one or more devices on the network, but even the smallest omni-directional antenna will add $50–$100 to the cost of your "cheap" network. In addition, network adapter antennas usually provide poor coverage because they aren't well located within your building. It's unlikely you would place an ad-hoc computer on a high shelf to maximize its antenna's range as you would an AP.

Ad-Hoc Network Setup

To begin an ad-hoc network, you create it on a host computer and duplicate the initial settings on others you want to add to the network. Once the network is set up, the host computer becomes just another member—it has no special responsibilities. In addition to wi-fi driver settings, you need to set each computer's TCP/IP address so all computers on the network are on the same subnet. In a network where an AP provides IP addresses via DHCP, setting each computer to obtain an IP address automatically ensures that all share the same subnet.

In the following sections, you learn about the ad-hoc network setup process under Windows 2000 and XP, Mac OS X, and Red Hat Linux 7.3. With the network created, you learn how to add computers using the same OS used to create the network. You can add members to the network, regardless of the OS each uses.

Windows XP and Linux make it easy to share an Internet connection via an ad-hoc network. You learn how to enable Internet sharing from the host computer within these OSs and see some suggestions for doing it under Mac OS X and older versions of Windows.

Set Up an Ad-Hoc Network Under Windows XP

Windows XP can, unlike older Windows versions, locate and join wireless networks automatically. The OS provides the functionality to do this, and wi-fi driver software implements it and enables you to customize the feature. You might, for example, want to join only infrastructure networks or limit yourself to a particular wi-fi network. To create and use an ad-hoc network under Windows XP, you need to modify some of the automatic discovery options. In the following steps, I use the Agere/Orinoco USB network adapter.

When you install wi-fi drivers for the first time with a new network adapter, you can choose to start the ad-hoc network during the installation process. Here's how to create a network on a computer that already has a network adapter installed.

1. Right-click the network connection icon for your wireless network from the taskbar, as shown in Figure 9.3, and choose View Available Wireless Networks.

2. The wireless networks listed in the window are those within range of your wi-fi network adapter. Click Advanced.

3. In the Preferred Networks area, select each listed network and remove it by clicking the Remove button. This prevents an accidental connection to one of these networks from being made while you create the ad-hoc network.

4. Click the Advanced button near the bottom of the dialog box.

5. Click the Computer-to-computer (ad-hoc) networks only and uncheck Automatically connect to nonpreferred networks if it's checked (Figure 9.4). Click OK.

6. Click the Add button under Preferred Networks.

Figure 9.3
Begin configuring
an ad-hoc network
from the taskbar.

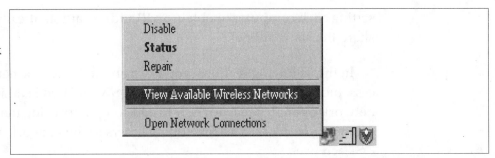

7. Type a network name (SSID) for the ad-hoc network (see Figure 9.5). The name is case-sensitive. Because the SSID won't automatically appear when other computers scan for it, write it down exactly as you type it, so you can share it with others.

8. Don't enable WEP at this time. Test the network first and return to set up WEP later. Click OK. The new network appears in the Preferred Networks portion of the window, with a PC card icon (see Figure 9.6).

9. Click OK to close the Wireless Network Connection Properties dialog box.

Add to the Network

To add a new member to the network, make sure a wi-fi network adapter is installed and configured. Follow these steps:

1. Right-click the network connection icon for your wireless network from the taskbar and choose Available Networks.

2. Choose the ad-hoc network from the list in the Available Networks area of the dialog box, as shown in Figure 9.7. If you don't see the network you just created, click Refresh.

3. Click Configure, and then click OK. The network appears in the list of Preferred Networks, and you've joined the network.

Figure 9.4
These are the
correct settings
for beginning an
ad-hoc network
and disabling
automatic
connections to
other networks.

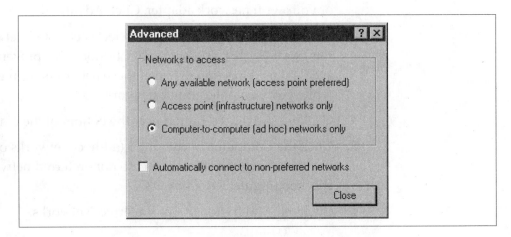

Figure 9.5
Choose a
network SSID
in the Wireless
Network
Properties
dialog box.

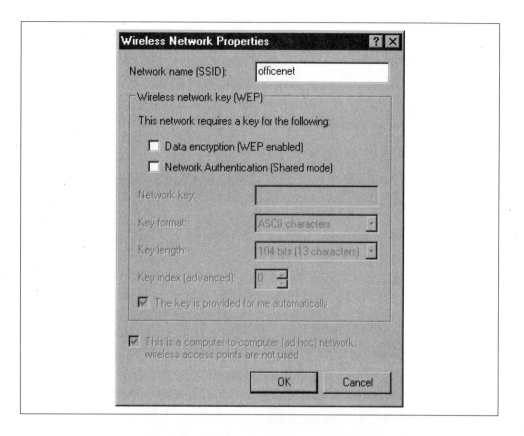

Figure 9.6
Your new ad-hoc
network appears
as a preferred
network.

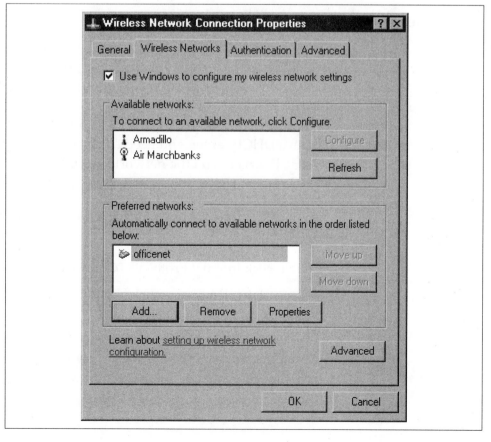

Figure 9.7
The ad-hoc
network appears,
along with
other available
wireless networks.

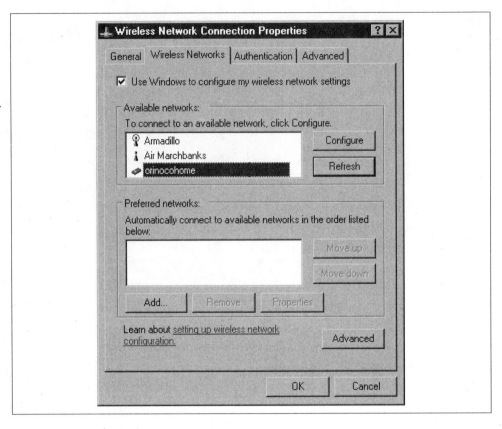

Set IP Addresses

The network I'm building now won't have Internet access. In the section "Windows XP Gateway Setup," you learn how to create an Internet gateway. For now, let's move all the networked computers on to the same IP subnet by changing their IP addresses to static ones. If a computer on the network was previously connected to a network, there's a good chance it gets a dynamic IP address from a DHCP server. You need to use a static IP address instead because no DHCP server is on the network. To change the IP address in Windows XP or Windows 2000, follow these steps:

1. Double-click the network connection on the taskbar.

2. Click Properties.

3. Double-click Internet Protocol (TCP/IP).

4. To use a static IP address, click Use the following IP address. The fields below become active.

5. Type **192.168.0.1** in the IP address field. The exact IP address doesn't matter, as long as all IP addresses are within the same subnet (they have the same first three sets of digits, with the final digit between 0 and 255).

6. Type **255.255.255.0** in the Subnet Mask field. This assumes you used the IP address range suggested in Step 5. Different IP ranges require different subnet masks.

7. If the Default gateway field isn't empty, clear it. If a gateway is set, the computer will try to use it to connect to the Internet. Your dialog box should look like Figure 9.8.

8. Leave the DNS fields blank because you won't need to use a DNS server to resolve IP addresses.

9. Click OK to save the IP address.

10. Repeat Steps 1–8 for all computers on your ad-hoc network. No two machines should have the same IP address.

Set Up an Ad-Hoc Network Under Windows 2000

The Agere/Orinoco wi-fi interface looks different in Windows 2000 than in Windows XP. The configuration steps are a bit different, too, because Windows 2000 lacks the network discovery features of XP. To begin a network under Windows 2000, follow these steps:

1. Open Orinoco Client Manager

2. Choose Actions | Add/Edit Configuration Profile.

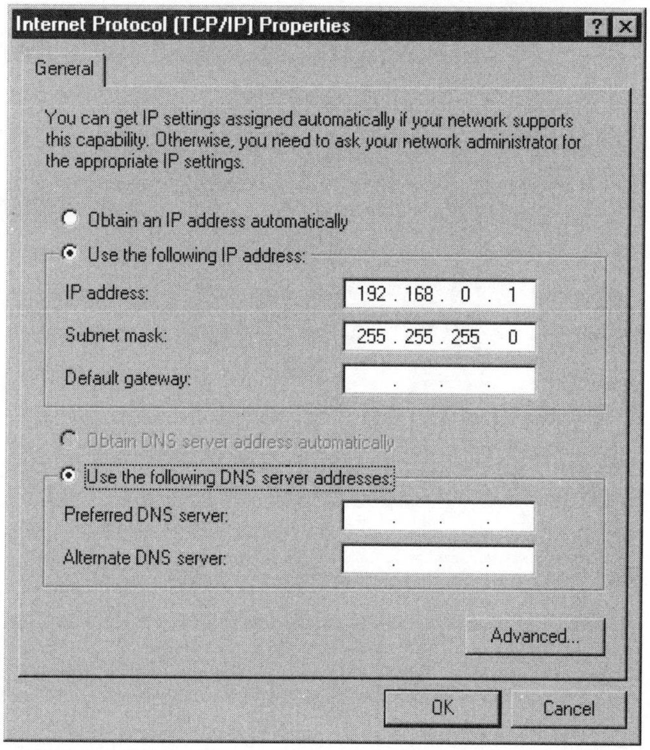

Figure 9.8
Fill out the IP address fields this way to connect to an ad-hoc network.

3. Click Add.

4. Give the new profile a name. This isn't the SSID used to connect to the network, but the name associated with the network profile on this computer.

5. Choose Peer-to-Peer Group from the Network Type menu, as shown in Figure 9.9, and click Next.

6. In the Network Name field, enter the SSID you want to use to identify the network to its users.

7. Choose a channel for the network to use. All users will need to use this channel. In the United States, channels range from 1–11. Click Next.

8. Leave Enable Client Security unchecked. Click Next.

9. If you switch between network profiles on this computer, click the Renew IP Address when selecting this profile check box. Doing this updates your IP address when you return to this configuration.

10. Click Finish, and then click OK to return to the first Client Manager screen. You see icons indicating your network's status, as shown in Figure 9.10. If you followed Step 9, you'll see a dialog box telling you your IP address is being updated to match the profile you created.

Figure 9.9
Name the network and choose Peer-to-Peer Group.

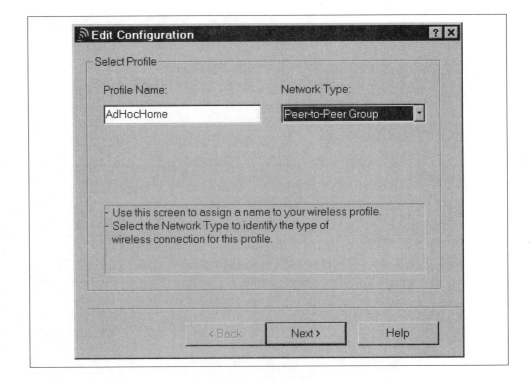

Figure 9.10
The two laptops with wireless signals traveling between them indicate your network was created successfully.

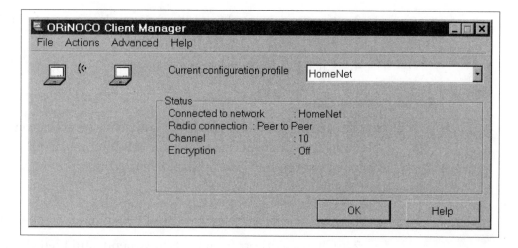

Adding a New User

You add users to the network by following the same steps you used to create the network. Be careful the network name (SSID) and channel are entered exactly as they were when you created the network.

Set Up an Ad-Hoc Network Under Mac OS X

Mac OS X includes all the software you need to use an AirPort card to create or join a network. As you learned in Chapter 8, you need a third-party driver to get a non-AirPort card working under OS X. In this section, you learn how to create an ad-hoc network using an AirPort-equipped Mac and OS X.

1. From the AirPort menu in the upper-right corner of the screen, choose Create Network, as shown in Figure 9.11.

2. Type a name (SSID) for the network. Leave the password fields blank for the moment.

Figure 9.11
The quickest way to create an AirPort network is from the AirPort Status menu in the Finder.

3. Choose a channel from the menu or leave it set to 11. Figure 9.12 shows the completed dialog box.

4. Click OK to complete the network.

Adding a New User

You can use the AirPort menu to join and leave networks once you establish a relationship with them but, to join for the first time, use the Network pane in System Preferences. This is also where you can change your AirPort IP address to join the network.

1. Open System Preferences, and then open the Network pane.

2. Choose AirPort from the Show menu, and then click the AirPort tab.

3. Choose the network you created from the Preferred Networks pull-down menu, as shown in Figure 9.13.

4. If the network has a password (WEP key), the field will be activated and you can enter it. The next step is to set an IP address.

Set IP Addresses

1. While still in the Network pane, with AirPort selected, click the TCP/IP tab.

2. Choose Manually from the Configure menu.

3. Type **192.168.0.1** in the IP Address field and **255.255.255.0** in the Subnet Mack fields. See this set of steps in the Windows XP section for further explanation of your addressing options. Leave the remaining fields blank.

4. Click Apply when you finish entering IP information.

Figure 9.12
Enter the network's SSID, channel, and password (if any) to create it.

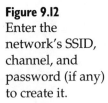

Computer to Computer

Please enter the following information to create a Computer to Computer Network:

Name: HomeNet

Password:

Confirm:

Channel: 4

Cancel   OK

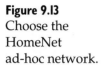
Figure 9.13
Choose the
HomeNet
ad-hoc network.

Set Up an Ad-Hoc Network Under Red Hat Linux 7.3

As you learned in Chapter 8, many Linux drivers are available for wi-fi adapters. Support for ad-hoc networking must be in both the network adapter (a fairly safe bet) and the driver (a reasonably safe bet). If you're not certain, check the driver's documentation and be sure you have the latest release. If your driver doesn't support ad-hoc mode, you might be able to install one that does. Consult the Linux Wireless HowTo (http://www.hpl.hp.com/personal/ Jean_Tourrilhes/Linux/Wireless.html#howto) for a list of drivers that matches your Linux distribution and your wi-fi adapter.

Red Hat 7.3 supports ad-hoc mode and there's a Gnome interface for setting it up.

Test Your Connection

You can verify that a computer has a wireless connection to an ad-hoc network by checking the status area in the client manager or configuration utility for your wi-fi network adapter. To verify that you also have an IP connection, either ping other computers on your network or, if you already set up shared access to networked computers, try to connect to a resource, such as the Network Neighborhood or a shared printer.

To use ping to test the connection from a Windows computer, follow these steps:

1. Choose Start | Run.

2. Type **command,** and then click OK.

3. At the command prompt, type **ping 192.168.0.1**, if this is an address you assigned to a computer on your ad-hoc network, other than the computer on which you're working. If the ping successfully finds the computer with this address, you'll see a screen like Figure 9.14.

4. Type other addresses (excluding the address of the computer you are using) until you've pinged all computers on your network. An unsuccessful ping generates Request timed out errors.

To ping in Linux or Mac OS X, open the terminal application, and then repeat Steps 3 and 4 to ping your network's members.

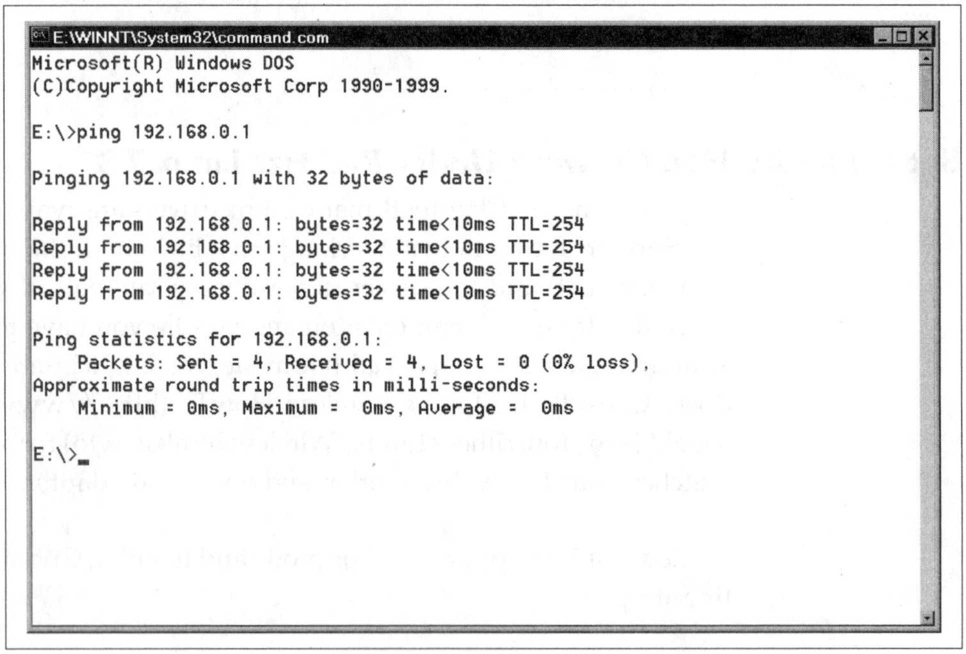

Figure 9.14
A successful ping looks like this.

```
E:\WINNT\System32\command.com                                    _ □ ×
Microsoft(R) Windows DOS
(C)Copyright Microsoft Corp 1990-1999.

E:\>ping 192.168.0.1

Pinging 192.168.0.1 with 32 bytes of data:

Reply from 192.168.0.1: bytes=32 time<10ms TTL=254
Reply from 192.168.0.1: bytes=32 time<10ms TTL=254
Reply from 192.168.0.1: bytes=32 time<10ms TTL=254
Reply from 192.168.0.1: bytes=32 time<10ms TTL=254

Ping statistics for 192.168.0.1:
    Packets: Sent = 4, Received = 4, Lost = 0 (0% loss),
Approximate round trip times in milli-seconds:
    Minimum = 0ms, Maximum =  0ms, Average =  0ms

E:\>_
```

Using an Internet Gateway with an Ad-Hoc Network

You can share an Internet connection over an ad-hoc network. To do this, one of the computers on the network must have an Internet connection from a network interface or a dial-up modem (separate from the wireless network). One of the computers must also be running gateway software that can share the connection with the other members of the network.

Like a wi-fi access point/router, gateway software routes traffic to the local network and serves IP addresses via DHCP. Unlike an access point, typically no built-in firewall—or all the bells and whistles related to access control, NAT, and enhanced security—exists. If you implement a gateway on an ad-hoc network without also adding a firewall, your network is at greater risk from Internet-based attacks that could destroy your files or compromise personal information on networked computers.

Windows XP and Windows 2000 include built-in gateway software. Tools for building a Linux gateway are readily available, although a good knowledge of Linux and some configuration is required. Mac OS X doesn't include a gateway feature, but Mac OS 9 provides what it calls a *Software Base Station*, which is a gateway feature built around Apple's AirPort software. If you're using an older version of Windows, or Mac OS X, you need to add some software to create both a gateway and a firewall.

Gateways Step-by-Step

The procedure for setting up a gateway and getting all member of the network connected to it is similar in all OSs. You learn about the process and specific gateway settings in the next few sections.

First, build the ad-hoc network as previously described. If you intend to add a gateway immediately, you needn't create static IP addresses for each computer on the network. The gateway acts as a DHCP server. Until you have the gateway set up, however, you won't be able to test your network's local connection unless you've given each device an IP address in the chosen subnet. This can help you troubleshoot any problems related to the distance between computers on your network, or improperly entered SSIDs or channel numbers. Even though this is an extra step, I recommend you get the local network connected and tested first, and then proceed to the gateway.

When you're satisfied the ad-hoc network is working properly, choose a host computer for the gateway. The host must have an Internet connection (broadband or dial-up) and it must support gateway software. If you intend to use an ad-hoc network and gateway as a permanent wireless network, this computer's connection to the Internet should be stable. Be prepared to leave this machine on at all times when you want shared Internet access. Test the host's Internet connection to make sure everything is running smoothly before you set up the gateway.

This process of setting up the gateway is the subject of the next few sections. You'll be enabling a DHCP server and Internet routing. Now is the time to add or enable a firewall for security.

Finally, give your networked computers access to the gateway. Change the IP addressing method for each computer to dynamic, so it can obtain an IP address from the DHCP server. A good idea is to restart the computer after changing its IP settings. Test the gateway connection by opening a web browser.

Windows XP Gateway Setup

Both a gateway and a firewall are included with Windows XP. You can choose a different firewall if you want. To set up the Windows XP Internet gateway, follow these steps:

1. Choose Start | Control Panel.

2. Switch to Classic View, choose Network Connections, and then choose the connection (Ethernet or dial-up) you want to share.

3. Click Properties.

4. Click the Advanced tab and select the Allow other network users to connect through this computer's Internet connection check box.

5. Uncheck Allow other network users to control or disable the shared Internet connection.

6. To enable the Internet Connection Firewall (ICF), select the check box. Figure 9.15 shows the gateway and firewall settings. Click OK.

Figure 9.15
Set up the gateway and firewall in the Connection Properties window.

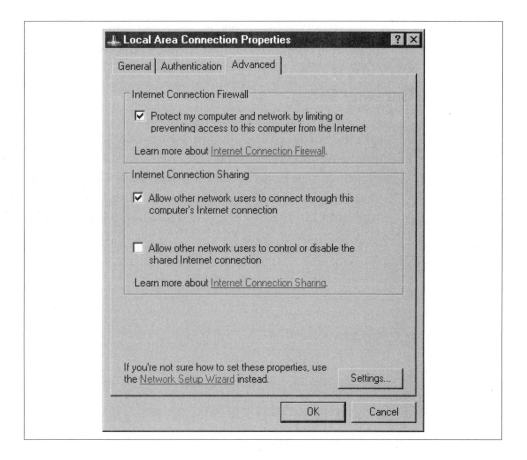

Windows 2000 Gateway Setup

To enable a gateway in Windows 2000, follow these steps:

1. Double-click the connection you want to share from the Taskbar, or choose Start | Settings | Control Panel | Network and Dial-Up Connections, and then choose the connection to be shared.

2. Click Properties, and then click the Advanced tab.

3. Click Enable Internet Connection Sharing on this computer. You'll see a warning that your IP address will be changed to 192.168.0.1. Click OK to make the change.

4. Click OK to close the Properties tab, and then click Close for the network connection.

Because Windows 2000 doesn't provide a firewall, you should acquire and enable one if you intend to share this connection permanently.

Mac OS X Gateway Setup

As previously mentioned, Mac OS X provides no gateway tools. Mac OS X lacks the Software Base Station feature of OS 9, much to the chagrin of many upgrading Mac users. You can create a gateway in OS X with a software router such as Brian R. Hill's BrickHouse (http://personalpages.tds.net/~brian_hill) or geeRoute (http://geeroute.zero.com.hk). BrickHouse provides both Internet sharing and a full-fledged firewall. geeRoute is a simple software router.

Chapter 10

Security

Wireless networks are even more vulnerable to hackers than wired networks. They present special challenges because passers-by could theoretically tap into a network with a laptop and a wireless network card. This chapter introduces you to different ways in which you can secure your network. It also describes security features included with many APs and wireless network adapters, and it suggests ways to enhance security on a wireless network.

The best security plan isn't a single tool or strategy. Instead, the best approach to security is to build multiple barriers that protect network resource and frustrate would-be hackers. For instance, take a bank. Even though the money might be safely stashed in a vault, and all the sensitive documents locked away in drawers and filing cabinets, the manager takes the extra steps of locking the front door and arming the security alarm. He might also go so far as to hire security guards and guard dogs. All these measures serve to add layers of security to thwart the potential wrongdoer. No single system is infallible but putting up multiple barriers improves the odds of defeating potential hackers. This chapter explores a number tools and approaches that could be used together to help protect your network.

Why Security Is Crucial for All Networks

The more organizations and consumers depend on networks to conduct business, the greater the need is to protect the network from unwanted intruders. The networks, servers, applications, and computers that make online commerce work are inherently vulnerable to attack and misuse. This is the case in every industry that's grown to rely on networks. The risk of business interruption, negative publicity, theft of information, liability, and other costly business losses are real if the network isn't protected.

Without proper precautions and security barriers, corporations could experience major security breaches, resulting in serious damages or loss. These risks aren't limited to corporations. Your own home or small office network could be the subject of malicious attack. Regardless of the type—wired or wireless—or the size—small or large—much can be learned from the way corporations secure their networks.

Network security requires continuous review to ensure that current measures are adequate to guard against new threats. Administrators of large corporate networks generally approach security in three phases which follow:

❏ **Creating a security policy**   In this phase, the security goals of the network are documented. The security goals are developed based on many current factors, including a list of resources and applications that need to be protected and the types of access a given individual might need to different areas of the network. This is also relevant to small networks because certain files and content might need to be restricted to only a few users. As a result, even a small network could have multiple security requirements.

❏ **Implementing network security technologies**   This is the execution phase. Multiple tools and layered approaches should be applied to ensure that the enterprise doesn't rely on only one type of technology to solve all security issues. Remember the basic principle of good security is to build layers of barriers that thwart and frustrate attempts to harm the network and its resources. In a home or a small office network, a layered approach could include the implementation of encryption, passwords, and a firewall. A layered approach also includes, as simple as this might seem, being careful to change the default settings that come with the wireless equipment and network applications.

❏ **Auditing the network**   New types of threats frequently appear. To ensure the integrity of the network, the policies, tools, and applications that implement security should be reviewed frequently to ensure that the network isn't subject to these new threats. The results of the audits are used to refine the policies and implement new security measures. Figure 10.1 shows three recurring processes that can help ensure your network remains safe.

Figure 10.1
To ensure a secure network, three processes must be followed: Detect, Prevent, and Respond.

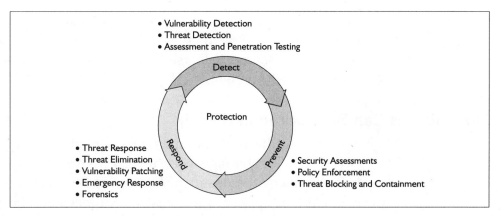

Understanding Wireless Security Issues

Wireless networks are much more vulnerable to intrusion than their wired counterparts. Some of the risks are similar to those of wired networks, some are magnified by wireless connectivity, and some affect wireless networks exclusively. In most cases, gaining access to a wired network requires access to a building, which can be secured. As long as a reasonable measure of security exists for the building, a measure of protection exists for your network. This isn't the case for a wireless network, however. Wireless networks use the air as their medium and the air can't be secured in the same way you can secure a building. The accessibility of the medium is the element that makes wireless networks more vulnerable than wired ones.

The ready availability and the difficulty of securing the medium—the air—magnifies the risks of attack on a wireless network beyond those faced by a wired network. However, once a wired network has been breached—access has been gained to the physical wire—the risk to the network is no greater or less than it would be if the network were wireless. At this point, the risks are the same. The new risk wireless presents is one of containment. Containing your transmission to a specific boundary becomes difficult, if not impossible. The reality is this: If you could contain the signals behind specific boundaries, you could implement measures to protect those boundaries.

The typical threats associated with wireless networks are the breach of confidentiality, the loss of integrity, and denial of service (DoS). Breaches of confidentiality and loss of integrity occur when a transmission can be captured and read, and it contents compromised or used to steal the identity of the source of the transmission. DoS can occur when an intruder gains the ability to block or jam transmitted signals. In this section you see some of the security challenges wireless networks present.

How Signals Can Be Tracked in the Air

Just like a signal that broadcasts pictures or sound through space to a receiving television or radio, the signals emanating from an AP or wireless-equipped computer traverse the air and can be received by any antenna equipped to receive them. Quite possibly, and most likely, the signals of your home wireless network will travel far beyond the walls of your home to your street and your neighbors' property. Anyone with a wireless-equipped computer has the potential to join your network if adequate measures aren't in place to prevent such an occurrence.

Even if you think that the signals transmitted by your wireless network are too distant to be intercepted, you could be mistaken. Distant signals can be enhanced in two ways: boost the signal from the AP or use a better antenna to receive it. Unfortunately, potential hackers, commonly called *war drivers* in the wireless world, also know this. Antennas—installed by you, the network owner, to enhance the signal or used by a war driver going by—can provide access to wireless signals beyond the normal limits of wi-fi.

The war driver can park close to your house, mount an antenna on the roof of his car, and tap into your network. Now, you might never suspect anything because, being the careful person you are, you checked the signal strength around the perimeter of your home using a laptop equipped with a wireless adapter. The signal at that time was barely strong enough to register. Along comes the hacker who uses a much better antenna and can see your network. In this situation, your best defense is a strong, layered security policy.

Without the appropriate security measures, the risk to your network is real. Many large corporate network managers realize the risk of the parking-lot-based attack on their networks and have taken measures to lessen this exposure. Owners of small networks should be just as concerned about the vulnerability of their networks. Figure 10.2 shows the risk you face from war drivers near your home or office.

What Is at Risk?

Many people don't see the benefit of securing a network. For this reason, many wireless networks are installed using the default access point (AP) set-

Figure 10.2
The parking-lot attack is a real potential threat to both large and small wireless networks.

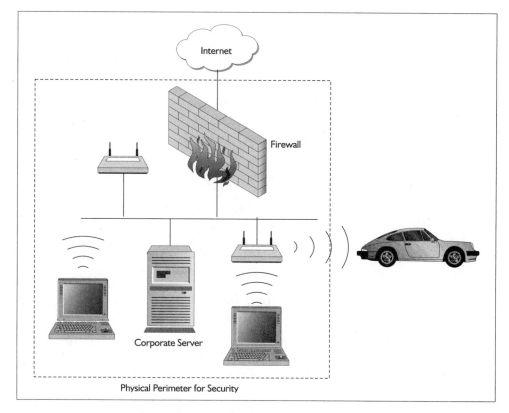

tings, the first and most obvious parameters an attacker would try. The same goes for resources on your network, such as shared folders or applications. Without security, your passwords and data are at risk. These same people would never knowingly allow a stranger to look through their important documents, see their bank balance, or look at the content of a personal e-mail to friends and family. By operating a wireless network without consideration for privacy and security, these people are, in effect, creating the potential for strangers to do the same things they wouldn't allow them to do under normal circumstances.

Your most valuable network asset is information. A hacker who gains access to a network has the potential to cause damage or launch attacks, but the greatest damage is done when you lose sensitive information, such as a Social Security number, a bank account number, credit card numbers, payroll data, or a password. Stealing a Social Security number, for instance, can have a far-reaching and disruptive effect because your identity can be used to secure loans and conduct transactions without your knowledge. By the time you find out, usually so much damage has already been done, you're left to pick up the pieces.

But I don't store my Social Security number on my computer, you might be thinking. If you thought this, then you're overlooking the potential risks to your wireless network, and you're falling into the trap common to many small business and home network users. You needn't consciously store information for it to become vulnerable. All this takes is for you to type the information and send it across the network. Remember when you applied for that credit card or loan, or when you opened an online account and you were prompted for all your personal information? Without adequate security, everything you typed was at risk.

Information security falls into three generic categories:

❏ **Confidentiality**   Information should only be available to those who need to access it.

❏ **Integrity**   Information should be modified only by those who are authorized to do so.

❏ **Availability**   Information should be accessible to those who need it when they need it.

By being aware of these three principles, adequate security policies can be developed to ensure each is addressed.

In addition to information loss, a security breach can result in the misuse of a networked resource. A computer, for example, can be used to create problems for, or be used to access, other more high-profile systems. In this scenario, the network resource is used as a weapon against other systems. This risk is discussed in greater detail in the section "Access to Your Network."

Access to Your Network

Once intruders gain access to your network, they could disable your network, use it to attack other systems or steal information from you. Intruders can see network resources, "borrow" your Internet connection, sniff packets, and then proceed to acquire passwords and data, as described in the following sections. Not all network breaches result in the intruder making a direct connection to the computers on the network. In some cases, a *sniffer* can be used to capture packets on their way to and from your computer. Intruders can install and run sniffer software on a wireless-enabled laptop.

Once a packet is captured, the intruder can drill deep into the structure packet and decode its content. This is especially dangerous in networks where the data isn't encrypted. Without encryption, the intruder could potentially see all you're transmitting—including passwords, Social Security numbers, and even the content of an e-mail or file as it is transferred over your network or to the Internet. If packets are encrypted, however, it becomes significantly more difficult for the intruder to decode its content.

If the intruder manages to progress beyond the network to the point where he gains access to a computer on the network, the scope of mischief he can accomplish multiplies significantly. By gaining access to your computer he has the ability to read confidential information, to make changes to your system, and to erase or modify files. But all these are fairly obvious consequences. Other activities that aren't so obvious can be equally as disruptive or damaging. In many cases, your computer can be used as an intermediary for another attack. In this scenario, your computer becomes the launching pad of attacks to other computers on your own network or to the Internet, if your network has such a connection.

Note that only one successful access is necessary to plant the seed for your machine to be used in subsequent attacks. While you might have beefed up security to the point where the intruder no longer has access, an agent, frequently called a Trojan horse, might have been installed on the compromised computer.

This *agent*—a small application—lies dormant until it receives instructions from a remote machine. These instructions could arrive via the Internet connection and, once received, the agent awakens and begins its dastardly deeds, which usually include participating in a DoS attack on a remote high-profile computer.

The target of the attack in this case is someone else, not your own computer. Your computer is just a means to commit the crime. A DoS attack is one where a device is bombarded with many redundant and useless requests launched from agents on multiple computers, so it becomes bogged down servicing these requests to the point where it can't service legitimate requests. Ultimately, the target device can become so overwhelmed, it crashes. Participating in a DoS unwittingly can bog down your network and also point the finger of suspicion at you when the owner of the target computer begins to take corrective measures.

Many other risks are associated with a breach of your network and your network resources, which won't be covered here. The intent is to highlight risks, so you can appreciate the importance of implementing layers of security.

Password or Other Private Information

As discussed in the previous section, the medium used to transmit your information is freely accessible to everyone. When you stop to consider this, it's akin to performing a private act, such as having a shower at night in the display window of a store. Passers-by might never know what you're doing because you're protected by darkness. But, if a curious person decides to shine a flashlight into the display window, nothing is between you and the eyes of that person. All it took was one curious person with an inexpensive tool. If, however, a curtain was hanging in the window, you would be shielded from the curious, regardless of whether he has a flashlight.

Wireless networking is much like that: All it takes is a curious individual with a laptop that's equipped with a wireless card to intercept your signals. If your network doesn't have the appropriate curtains, such as encryption, the possibility exists that your data will be exposed for all to see. There go your passwords and other private information.

Using a sniffer, a would-be attacker has the potential to capture information, such as passwords, about you if it's transmitted as cleartext. You might not be sharing folders and files across the network, but compromised passwords give access to e-mail, your Internet account, and so on. If someone acquires enough information about your Internet account, he might be able to steal access, as well as your identity.

Your Computer's Files

All versions of Windows since Windows 95 and all Mac operating systems (OSes) since System 7 have included file-sharing capabilities. Sharing is convenient, but it also exposes a shared folder and its contents to the network. Unfortunately, in a wireless world anything that's visible to the network is vulnerable to unauthorized access or accidental damage, if file sharing isn't managed carefully.

In a wireless environment, the capability to intercept signals or to join the network remotely without the need to gain access to a network port makes the challenge of protecting these shared folders and content even more challenging. In many small networks, passwords might not even be in place to protect files because everyone on the premises can be trusted. Wireless opens these resources. Steps must be taken to ensure that only those who should see the content see it and prevent those who shouldn't see it from doing so.

Assessing Your Risk

Risk assessment is a critical part of risk management and *risk management* is an evaluation of the cost of action versus the risk of inaction. This definition of risk management sums up the dilemma faced by most network administrators when they deploy a new network. Somehow, they must evaluate the cost of employing a solution versus the risk of not doing so, especially when resources are scarce.

This is the predicament of many small networks where the resources required to deploy a solid security strategy are somewhat limited. You may, for example, rely exclusively on your access point's firewall, WEP encryption, and your computer and access point's passwords to provide security. Large organizations have the money and expertise to implement more powerful firewalls and conduct sophisticated security audits. It is also probable that these large organizations face much greater security risks from hackers than do most home users. Matching your resources to your true risk of attack and subsequent damage is the key to successful risk assessment and security implementation.

Conducting a risk assessment helps prioritize the things that need to be done now to meet a minimum set of security requirements versus those things that can wait until resources are available. The management of risk is an ongoing process that includes phases for:

❑ Assessing risk
❑ Implementing controls
❑ Promoting awareness
❑ Monitoring effectiveness

Risk assessment ties together information gathered about assets, their value, and their vulnerabilities to attack. For a small business, an asset is anything that gives you a competitive edge or anything that helps you achieve your business objectives, such as software, data, computers, and so on. The value of the asset isn't limited to the actual cost of the asset, it also includes the strategic and productivity value associated with the asset. Here are some practical approaches to risk assessment:

❑ **Analysis of failure and its effect**   Examine the impact that a failed component, application, system, or device would have on meeting a core objective. Say, for instance, one of the core objectives of your wireless LAN is to share access to the Internet. The impact of a failed AP would be more critical than the failure of one of the computers that share the connection. Without an AP, Internet access could not be shared with the members of the network so it would make a lot of sense to guard against failure of this component or its configuration.

❏ **Analysis of historical data**   Review the frequency of past events to determine the probability of a specific problem happening again. As an example, ten attack attempts made on a server in the last month would potentially raise the priority of installing a firewall. If, however, only one such event has occurred in a year, you might choose to do nothing for now and focus on other, more critical areas.

❏ **Analysis of user error**   Understanding the possible impact of user error helps dictate the policies that need to be implemented. If, for instance, giving a novice user access to a certain area of a server could potentially create problems with the operation of the server, you might implement a policy that allows only users with a certain skill level to have access to that area.

❏ **Analysis of probabilities**   Examine the probability of a combination of events and its effect on the operation of the system. In the case of a wireless network, probabilistic analysis includes analyzing the probability of an attack or attempted intrusion because of the accessibility of the medium. The accessibility of the medium increases the probability of someone attempting to snoop or intrude. The answer, therefore, is simple: Appropriate measures must be implemented to guard against this possibility.

The next sections examine other aspects that should be considered when doing a risk assessment.

How Are You Connected to the Internet?

Remember, an attack can originate from any source. Because you installed a wireless network doesn't mean the only source of attacks could come from a drive-by hacker. Attacks could originate from within your own network from a disgruntled employee for example. The attack could even come from your own twelve-year old kid who's trying to gain access to off-limits portions of your computer.

The Internet is another source of potential attacks. Every day individuals seek computers on the Net that can be exploited. Without proper precautions, your machine could be a target. The way you're connected to the Internet must be considered in conjunction with the way in which you plan to use the Net. If you intend to host a server that's accessible from the Internet, you must consider the impact of assigning a static address to this server and relaxing some of your security policies.

If you intend to host a public web server in conjunction with local computers that need to be shielded from potential Internet attacks, a policy must be employed that allows only the web server to be accessible from the Net. Many of these features and techniques were discussed in Chapter 7 in the section "Advanced Access Point Configuration."

The Internet connection itself can be used by an intruder if you don't control access via DHCP and/or MAC addresses.

What Information Is Unsecured?

Knowing what information is unsecured is important because of the way in which layered security works. The best way to explain this is to use an example. Say you intend to share a folder across the network. To do so without a password creates the risk that the folder and its contents could be damaged or lost to an intruder. Because you understand the risk, you implement a policy that requires passwords for all shared folders. The password must be known before it can be shared, so anyone attempting to access the folder will be unable to do so without the password. At this point, the folder and its content are secure, right?

Maybe not, if your network is operating without encryption and the password is being transmitted in cleartext, the folders and their content aren't secure. Anyone who succeeds in capturing the packets containing passwords as they're transmitted could see the password. And, with the password visible, anyone could access the folder.

To ensure that the folder and its content are secured, the network must employ a measure of security that shields the password, the folders, and their content during transmission from any nosey intruder. Knowing what information is unsecured, therefore, requires knowledge of the network and how all the components are operating.

Who Has Access?

Knowing who has access to the network is an important aspect in securing its content. Without knowledge of who will be accessing the network, adequate security policies can't be developed to ensure that only those who need to see certain information are allowed access.

In large corporate networks where security is paramount, security policies go so far as to enforce access privileges. Certain groups of users are permitted to perform certain functions, issue certain commands, and view certain files, depending on their need for access to these resources.

In a network support organization, for instance, the first-level help desk technician might be responsible for taking the problem calls and characterizing the problem before engaging the appropriate technician. To do this particular function, this technician might be required to log on to a router to determine if the problem is circuit or router related. To make this determination, the technician must issue a series of router show commands that his user ID profile allows him to do. However, the technician is never allowed to make any changes to the router, so his user ID prevents him from making changes. The technician is limited to commands that allow him to view the network configuration.

Later, the technician might be promoted to a router technician position, acquiring more responsibility. In his new capacity, the technician is allowed to make changes, so his user ID is moved into a group of users that is authorized to make changes.

This example can be applied to networks of any size. Knowledge of who uses your home or small office network helps you decide who should be able to make changes to the configuration of the network and who should be limited to only accessing files or Internet surfing.

What Security Measures Are in Place?

Knowing the security measures that are in place is critical to performing the appropriate network audits. As new threats appear, security policies and measures must frequently be reviewed to ensure that the network is adequately protected from these new threats. You should look at and write down the existing security measures, from passwords, to disabling access, to resources that shouldn't be shared, to AP security. Making the list forms the basis of the real-world risk assessment.

Wi-Fi Security Methods

Wi-fi security services are provided largely by the Wired Equivalent Privacy (WEP) protocol. WEP, which is part of the IEEE 802.11 spec, was designed to protect communication between a wi-fi device and an AP, as shown in Figure 10.3. As a reminder, 802.11 operates at the PHY and MAC layers, and, therefore, doesn't specify security for applications above these layers. Security above these layers operates in the same way on wired or wireless networks.

Figure 10.3
Wi-fi security services only provide security between the wireless client and the AP.

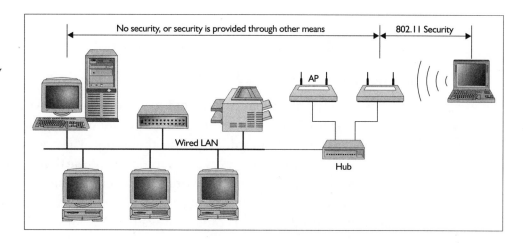

The IEEE defined three basic security services that are provided by WEP, which are

- ❏ Authentication
- ❏ Confidentiality
- ❏ Integrity

The details of these three services are discussed in the next section on WEP.

WEP

Wired Equivalence Privacy was never designed to be an all-inclusive and robust security protocol but, instead, to provide the same level of privacy available on a wired network. The WEP algorithm is used to protect wireless communication from eavesdropping by encrypting data as it travels across the network. And, although this isn't an explicit goal of the protocol, it also aids in authorizing access to the wireless network.

WEP relies on a secret key shared between the wireless client and an AP. The key is used to encrypt packets before they're transmitted. An integrity check is used to ensure the packet wasn't modified during transmission. The actual process of how the key is shared between client and AP isn't defined by the 802.aa standard. Instead, the specific implementation is left up to wi-fi vendors. Most wi-fi products use a single key that's shared among all devices on the wireless LAN.

WEP supports cryptographic key sizes that range from 40 to 104 bits. The larger the key size, the greater the level of encryption. Many vendors refer to 40-bit and 104-bit encryption as 64- and 128-bit encryption, respectively. The additional 24-bits represent the initialization vector (IV) required to manage WEP transmissions.

Authentication

The wi-fi specification for WEP defines two general ways in which a user attempting to join the wireless LAN can be authenticated. One method is based on the use of cryptography and the other is not. The cryptography approach is based on a rudimentary cryptographic technique that doesn't provide mutual authentication. In other words, the client doesn't authenticate the AP and, therefore, has no way of ensuring it's communicating with an AP. The algorithm used in the cryptography is the *RC4 stream cipher*.

The basic way in which the client is authenticated is depicted in Figure 10.4 and is based on a unilateral challenge-response scheme. In essence, the AP sends a random challenge to the client. The client responds by encrypting the challenge with a cryptographic key (WEP key), which is shared with the AP. On receipt, the AP decrypts the response and allows access if the decrypted value matches the random challenge sent.

The second method of authentication doesn't use cryptography. If you disable WEP on the AP, you're using this method of authentication. The Linksys AP we have used as an example in this book, for example, the WEP options provided are mandatory or disable. Using this approach, a wireless client can be authenticated through one of two methods called Open System and Closed System Authentication: Both are based on identity-based verification schemes and both are vulnerable to attacks. A client who wants to join the network using the Open System Authentication method simply sends an

Figure 10.4
Authentication
flow using a
shared WEP key

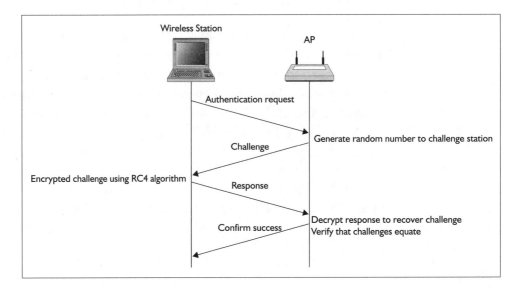

empty string for the Service Set Identifier (SSID). This approach is also sometimes called *NULL authentication*.

A client who wants to join the network using the Closed Authentication Authorization method simply sends the SSID of the wireless network. No real authentication is performed, as is evident from the description of these two techniques. As a result, neither of these methods offers robust security against unauthorized access. Networks configured to operate in this fashion are extremely vulnerable to hackers.

Privacy

The privacy or confidentiality of WEP is also accomplished through the use of cryptographic techniques that use the RC4 symmetric-key, stream cipher algorithm. The *keystream* is added to the data and encrypts the entire packet with the exception of the link layer information, which facilitates communication between the wireless client and the AP. In other words, IP address, TCP ports, and all other layers above those are encrypted, but MAC addresses aren't encrypted.

I strongly recommend using the 128-bit WEP option, which must be supported by all wi-fi devices, when configuring your wireless network.

Integrity

The intent of the integrity security service is to identify and reject any messages that could have been tampered with in transit. This service uses an encrypted cyclic redundancy check (CRC) or frame check sequence. Before the message is transmitted, a CRC is computed and added. Next, the entire message is encrypted using the privacy service, and then it's transmitted. The receiver decrypts the messages, calculates its own CRC, and matches the result to that sent. If they match, the message is accepted. If not, the message is rejected.

Note, the standard didn't attempt to address other security services such as audit, authorization, and nonrepudiation, which is a fancy way of saying the sender and receiver can't deny having sent or received a message. This is the assurance that both parties to a transaction remain honest about their actions and don't dispute their agreement.

These additional security services are equally as important as the three incorporated in WEP. You can see, for example, the importance of non-repudiation in a wireless transaction. In the wired world, if two parties are connected to a single wire and they are the only parties on the wire, it becomes more difficult to deny sending a message that agrees to a transaction. In the wireless world, this could be a problem. Because of the nature of the medium, proving a specific device sent a specific transaction is more difficult because of the potential for another device to masquerade as something it isn't. Nonrepudiation, therefore, becomes relevant in the wireless world.

Weaknesses of WEP

So far in this chapter, you learned about the need to implement encryption to add a degree of privacy to your wireless network. You may assume that implementing WEP is all you need to get adequate protection, After all, WEP is the protocol the IEEE chose to deliver the security services defined for the standard. This isn't the case, however. Depending on WEP alone is a bad idea.

WEP is woefully lacking and leaves many gaps to fill. The remainder of this section highlights some weaknesses of WEP. After reviewing them, you might wonder why the protocol is so weak, considering its target market. This question can't be addressed here, but I hope the information provided here will be enough to convince you to consider deploying additional technologies to help protect your network and its data.

Knowing that WEP is flawed will be enough to convince you that additional security measures are needed. If you fall in this category, you can safely skip the remainder of this section. But even if you don't read the details about WEP, don't give up on wi-fi networking. Fortunately, security help is on its way from the IEEE. Many of the weaknesses of WEP will be addressed in 802.11i and, when this is published, it will be an alternative to WEP and applicable to 802.11a, b, and g. For those of you who are curious and want to know more about the technology, please read on.

Much research has been done in the area of WEP weaknesses. Inexpensive, off-the-shelf equipment has been used by security experts to expose its weaknesses. Before reviewing some of the attacks, you should know about some key principles of how WEP encrypts data. This knowledge will help you later to understand how WEP can be compromised. WEP ensures the integrity of a packet in transit by adding an Integrity Check (IC) field in the packet. As stated earlier, this check consists of a computed CRC value. As each message is transmitted, it's encrypted using pseudorandom keystreams.

The term *ciphertext* is used to describe a message or text encrypted with the keystream, as shown in Figure 10.5. So, obviously, the security of the system is based, in part, on the randomness of the keystream. How then is the keystream made random? To ensure that no two ciphertext messages are encrypted using the same keystream, an IV, which is 24-bits long, is added to the shared secret key to produce a different RC4 key for each packet. The probability of having two ciphertexts encrypted with the same keystream is always there, however. This happens when two stations generate the same IV and, when this happens, an IV collision is said to have occurred. This protocol has more to it, but this bit of information should be all you need to understand some of the protocol's weaknesses.

The following types of attacks were launched and were successful in undermining the security claims of the WEP system:

❏ Passive attacks to decrypt traffic based on statistical analysis. In this type of attack, the intruder passively intercepts all wireless traffic. When an IV collision occurs, the intruder can use the common elements to make inferences about the content of the two messages. When the analysis is inconclusive based on only two messages, the intruder waits for more collisions. Over time, with the knowledge collected, the intruder eventually learns enough to decrypt traffic.

❏ Active attacks to inject new traffic from unauthorized clients based on the knowledge of the cleartext, which might have been learned using the passive attack technique. With knowledge of the cleartext for one encrypted message, the intruder can construct correct encrypted packets. The consequences of this attack are far-reaching. With this knowledge, the intruder can selectively manipulate the message (change a command to erase all files, for instance), recalculate the CRC, reencrypt the new message, and send it on its way. The receiving AP has no way of telling that the message was changed because the CRC is a correct value.

❏ Active attacks to decrypt messages based on tricking the AP.

❏ Attacks based on the analysis of about one day's worth of traffic. The data gathered was then used to allow real-time automated decryption of traffic. This type of attack is sometimes called *dictionary building.*

Figure 10.5
This is how WEP creates the ciphertext from cleartext.

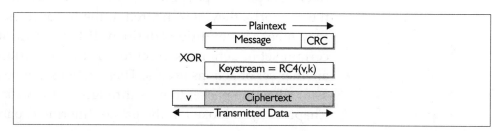

Finally, WEP is also weak in its authentication capabilities. If the cryptographic approach is used, the weakness of the algorithm makes it vulnerable and if the noncryptographic approach is used, authentication is nearly nonexistent.

Firewalls

A firewall is an important tool for your security arsenal. *Firewalls* can be implemented as a dedicated hardware/software solution or totally in software, as is the case in an AP. Most APs provide a number of firewall features, though units sold to home and small business users do not provide the same degree of protection that an enterprise-level AP, or a dedicated firewall system can.

A home or small office network has many of the same security issues as a large corporate network. A firewall, therefore, is as applicable to your network as to a company working on top-secret projects for the Department of Defense. The difference is in scope. In many small offices and home networks, the firewall built into the AP is all you need. The firewall is used as a barrier to keep destructive attacks away from your property or it might be used to protect your children from surfing to places where they shouldn't.

An entire book could be dedicated to the subject of the multifaceted capabilities of a firewall. Because of limited space for this topic, though, you'll learn only some of the features that could prove most relevant for your particular application. If you are interested in a more complete discussion of firewalls, check out Osborne/McGraw-Hill's *Firewalls: The Complete Reference* by Keith Strassberg, Gary Rollie, and Richard Gondek, or *Anti-Hacker Toolkit* by Keith Jones, Mike Shema, and Bradley Johnson.

Firewalls are typically placed at the point of entry to the network or between the segments of the networks that need protection (see Figure 10.6). In general, firewalls use one or more of the following three methods to control the flow of traffic in and out of a network.

❑ **Packet Filtering**   This approach uses a predefined list of rules or filters. As packets pass through the firewall (as they enter and exit the network), they're compared to the list of rules to see whether they meet the conditions defined. If the conditions are met, a certain set of actions is executed. If the conditions aren't met, another set of actions occurs. These actions can be as simple as to allow the packet to pass through, or to be discarded. In Chapter 7, you looked at the packet-filtering capabilities of

Figure 10.6
Firewalls are generally placed at the entry/exit point of the network. In this case, the AP also acts as a firewall; all packets entering and leaving the network pass through it.

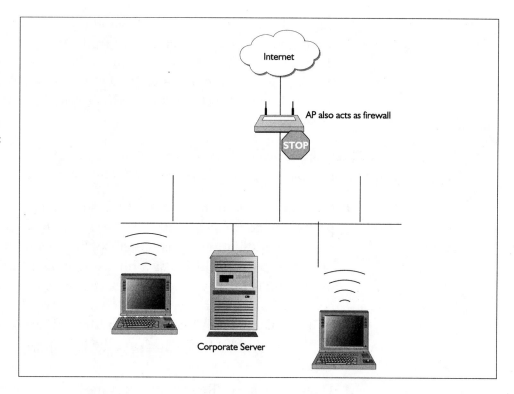

a few access point models. *Packet filtering* is available in most APs. You might not know that this is what was being discussed because consumer-grad APs typically specify this function more in terms of blocking ports, protocols, MAC addresses, and so on. All of these features are made possible by packet filtering.

❏ **Proxy Service**   This service allows the firewall to pretend to be the end point of the connection. A host on the Internet communicates with the firewall, which acts as a proxy for the clients on the local network. The Internet host never knows it isn't communicating directly with the client. However, the IP address the Internet host sees is typically that of the firewall, not the actual client. The client thinks it's communicating directly with the target Internet host. In fact, the client addresses the host using the host's real IP address or URL. The client doesn't necessarily realize that all traffic is, in fact, being passed through the firewall. Behind the firewall, additional rules can be set to control the type of information allowed to pass between the secured and unsecured domains.

❏ **Stateful Inspection**   This is a newer method of traffic control that doesn't examine the content of each packet. Instead, a key part of the packets is compared to a database of trusted information. The characteristics of traffic travelling from inside the network to the outside are compared to the characteristics of the information coming back. If there is a reasonable match, the information is allowed through. Otherwise, the information is discarded.

Filtering rules can be based on many different factors, conditions, and elements of the packets. Common elements for filtering include the following:

❑ **IP Address**   Both the source and destination address of the packet can be used to control packet flow. The use of filtering based on destination is easy to grasp, but seeing the applicability of using a source address as a filter might be difficult. This type of filtering is usually used to block certain computers from communicating with hosts outside your network. In APs such as the Linksys BEFW11S4, source address filtering is described as preventing PCs from accessing the Internet and is found on the filtering screen.

❑ **Domain Names**   Remembering names instead of numbers is much easier for people. For instance, remembering Yahoo.com instead of an IP address of 64.58.79.230 is easier. Domain names can also be used to define firewall rules in some APs.

❑ **Protocols**   Protocols are also a means of controlling what passes through a firewall. You might, for instance, allow Hypertext Transfer Protocol (HTTP) through in order to provide access to web pages, but disallow Telnet, which is used to perform commands on a remote computer. When using protocols as a means of filtering, remember, a hierarchical relationship exists among many protocols. As an example, blocking the IP protocol will block all protocols that rely on it, such as HTTP, Telnet, Simple Mail Transport Protocol (SMTP) used for e-mail, and so forth. Blocking Telnet, however, doesn't impact IP or the other protocols, such as HTTP.

❑ **Ports**   Much has been mentioned about ports in previous chapters. The example cited in Chapter 7 was how to use port forwarding to accommodate hosting web servers without compromising the other computers on the local network. Servers make their services available through the use of numbered ports. HTTP, for example, uses port number 80. Remote users who want to use the web services of the server would attempt a connection to port 80. The relevance of this is in the potential to run many services on a single computer. By allowing access to certain ports you are, in effect, limiting access to only certain services on the server. Using the example of the web server and Telnet, it would be possible to make a single machine totally accessible to people browsing web pages, but inaccessible to anyone wanting to Telnet to it.

❏ **Content Filtering**   Firewalls can also filter based on specific words or phrases. In this case, the firewall acts like a sniffer and examines the packet for the specific words or phrase.

In addition to hardware-based and AP firewalls you can purchase firewall software and install it on a specific computer. With this approach, the computer can act as a gateway to the Internet and provide protection to your local network or, optionally, every computer on your network could have its own personal firewall software. Adding firewall software to a server that's behind your AP firewall, but accessible as a DMZ host gives you a great deal of flexibility in customizing firewall options.

If the AP serves as your only firewall protection, where you place it is important. As mentioned previously, a firewall should be placed at the entry and exit points of your network (unless you're using personal firewalls for your computers). The good news is this: By following the installation instructions for your consumer-grade AP, you naturally optimize its placement. Because of the way the instruction manual suggests you connect the AP to your broadband modem and your network, as described in Chapter 7, the AP is naturally placed at the entry and exit of your network.

Access Control

Access control and authentication are important aspects of a wireless network. As reviewed earlier, the access control and authentication capabilities of WEP are lacking. In fact, if the noncryptographic approach to authentication is used, no real authentication takes place. If the cryptographic method is used instead, the algorithm used is fairly rudimentary and probably won't stand the test of a good hacker.

Therefore, it is foolhardy to develop a security policy that relies exclusively on WEP for authentication and access control. Other measures must be used to beef up this area of security. Later, in the section on 802.1x, I will describe an alternative to WEP that is on its way.

Service Set ID

The *Service Set ID*, (SSID), a 32-character-long identifier, is similar in function to a network identifier and is used to differentiate between wireless LANs.

All devices within a wireless network must reference a common SSID. In addition, the SSID functions as a password when a mobile device attempts to connect to a BSS. The SSID in itself doesn't supply any security to the network. You argue that WEP attempts to use the SSID to offer a level of security by requiring the client to supply a correct SSID when using the Closed Authentication Authorization scheme. This approach is limited, however, because the SSID is transmitted in the clear. Devices within range of this AP can scan and detect its SSID.

Access Control List

Most APs come equipped with access control list (ACL) features. An *ACL* is the technical term for the list of rules to be used for packet filtering. The actual scope of what you can or can't do varies by manufacturers, but all APs do have at least a minimum set of packet-filtering features. Many of the capabilities of ACLs are discussed in the previous section on firewalls. ACLs and their configuration were also discussed in Chapter 7.

Common Sense Hacker-Proofing Techniques

Protecting your network, its components, and your information is also a matter of using good judgement and common sense. Not all security measures require expensive hardware and software solutions. Simple measures, such as implementing passwords, can be an effective tool to help frustrate a would-be hacker. This section is intended to provide an insight into some of the more simple measures you can implement.

❏ *Change default parameters, such as the SSID and password for administration, when implementing your networks.* The excitement of installing a new system often creates a sense of urgency to see the system work. To get the network up and running, you might be tempted to accept default options. This is a dangerous shortcut, however, because default access point parameters are easy to guess, and many vendors make their AP documentation available online, too. In fact, lists of parameters used by vendors are available on the Internet, making the potential intruder's task that much easier. Using a freely available tool such as NetStumbler, the intruder can learn the maker of your access point, check the list or online documentation and connect to the device as its administrator, or join your unprotected network. Change the IP address of the AP. Instead of using the default 192.168.1.1 (the address used by the Linksys BEFW11S4, and many other APs)—the natural choice of any hacker—choose another address, such as 192.168.1.97.

❏ *Enable WEP!* Okay, so you now know WEP isn't as reliable as you might wish. The reality is, however, many small wireless networks will continue to rely on the protocol for its authentication, privacy, and integrity features. Even with its inherent weaknesses, WEP is still a good first line of defense, which can be made more robust if a few simple measures are implemented. An intruder will have to invest several hours of sitting around and waiting in his attempt to compromise the network. For some intruders, this is enough of a deterrent, but for the persistent ones, you can make their job much more difficult by simply changing WEP keys occasionally. You should also make sure your WEP key isn't the same as your SSID. Also, try to use long keys or pass phrases.

❏ *Antenna choice also assists in securing wireless networks.* Using a highly directional antenna helps focus the signal in a specific direction. This strategy can be used to your advantage by limiting the signal strength in the direction of traffic—the street or parking lot, for instance. The direction in which you choose to focus the signal, however, will probably have a much more powerful signal, which extends beyond the perimeter of your home or business, so consider the direction carefully.

❏ *Most wireless APs can be instructed to drop packets that aren't encrypted using the right WEP key.* By taking this approach, your network becomes invisible to scanning software because the AP won't react to unencrypted requests. A spectral analyzer can still be used to detect radio activity in the 2.4 GHz range, however.

❏ *Use the filtering capabilities of your AP.* Define filters that only accept packets from the MAC addresses of devices you know. The flaw in this approach is this: MAC addresses are transmitted in the clear and it's possible to override a wireless card MAC address with a locally assigned one. The intruder would only have to capture the MAC address and override his address with the captured one. If the intruder isn't aware that MAC filtering is in place, however, he might not automatically arrive at the conclusion that this is the reason his attempts at hacking are failing. Remember, good security requires a layered approach. Anything that serves to frustrate or delay success is a valid security option.

❏ *Disable remote AP administration if possible.* As you learned in Chapter 7, some APs don't allow remote administration (from computers outside your network's subnet) unless you specifically enable this option. Others restrict administration to the computer that initially configured the AP, though you can add administrators if you need them. The latter approach is the best one, since a hacker who is able to join your network is no longer remote. He or she can enter your AP's local IP address into a browser and connect to the administration tool unless you have both password-protected the tool and disabled administrative access for most local devices.

❏ *Implement strict password policies for the administration of the AP configuration.* This password should be changed frequently.

In addition to methods for securing your wireless access and administration, other general security measures should be considered.

❏ Plan carefully when you share folders. Share only those folders on local computers that need to be shared.

❏ Implement a password for shared resources. As simple as this seems, having to guess a password can be enough to frustrate an intrusion attempt. Implementing a password is a fairly simple task.

❏ Require the use of passwords on screen savers and on startup of your computers.

❏ Change all passwords on a regular basis.

❏ Implement password rules that require a mix of letters, numbers, and special characters whenever possible.

❏ Create users and groups, and implement a policy that enables members of specific groups access only to those resources they need to access.

❏ Implement access privileges and permissions. By doing so, you gain the additional benefit of controlling the different types of accesses allowed for each person or group.

Security Tools

The case for using additional security tools in conjunction to WEP and other common-sense approaches has been made. You have an appreciation now of the different security options for your wireless LAN, their strengths and weaknesses, and an understanding of the dangers of operating without adequate security. Now, let's look at additional security tools that can be used to beef up the security of your network.

SSH Tunneling

Secure Shell (SSH) tunneling can be used as an additional layer of security for your wireless LAN. SSH is much more secure than WEP and it's fairly easy to set up.

The idea behind a tunneling protocol, as the name implies, is to create a tunnel between the client machine and its server. By using a tunnel, you no longer care about the environment across which the packets move, as long as the packets themselves have a strong security scheme protecting them. Even if the packets are intercepted along the way, the content will be meaningless to the hijacker.

Tunneling is similar to a country in civil unrest: The locals are fighting among themselves with much bloodshed. Things have progressed to the point where no one is safe on the roads, but as long you remain in your home with iron bars over your windows, you'll be relatively safe. In this environment, visiting a grocery store across the street would be difficult. You could be at great risk during the time it takes you to cross the street. If you had the capability to build a tunnel under the street, however, you wouldn't care how bad conditions became on the street. SSH is the tunnel under the street. SSH provides a trusted path through an untrustworthy network.

Let's use a real-world example. If a wireless client needs access to a database that resides on a trusted wired network—one with all the appropriate security measures in place—the client could establish an SSH connection to the target server or a device on the secure LAN.

The SSH client on your laptop sets up a port-forwarding mechanism, which takes the packets intended for the target server, and then forwards them via the encrypted tunnel. Behind the scenes, the SSH client intercepts packets destined to the port of the target application and routes them through the encrypted tunnel. Your local application never knows what's taking place. As far as your local application is concerned, it's speaking directly with the target database.

To set up SSH, you need client software, such as SecureCRT for Windows. The target computer also needs software that allows it to accept SSH connections. Several sites on the Web specialize in free and commercial SSH software. One such site is http://www.freessh.org, which has many useful web links on the topic.

Adding SSH to your wireless network significantly enhances the security of the network. SSH isn't specific to wi-fi networks; it's merely a secure way to traverse an unsecured wired or wireless environment. For wi-fi users, tunneling provides a way for you to get around the weakness of WEP. SSH is also a great way to access your network remotely from a network you don't believe is secure. For example, check your e-mail wirelessly from a coffee shop if SSH is implemented on your home network.

IPsec VPNs

IP security protocol (IPsec) is a set of protocols developed to support secure exchange of packets at the IP layer. A virtual private network (VPN) is a network constructed using a public network, such as the Internet. IPsec is used to implement VPNs. In this case, IPsec can be used to create a secured VPN using the wireless LAN, with all its potential security hazards as the medium. Again, IPsec is simply another layer of security, but a beefy one.

IPsec supports two encryption modes: Transport and Tunnel. *Transport* mode encrypts only the data portion of the packet, but leaves the header of the packet unencrypted. This mode is more efficient, but the endpoints are obvious, so traffic analysis is made easier.

The *Tunnel* mode is a more secure approach and, like the features of tunneling discussed in the previous section on SSH, IPsec provide the full benefits of a tunneling protocol. The tunnel mode is comparatively less efficient, but it hides the nature of the networks behind a security gateway. The traffic of several networks can be concealed in one tunnel, making traffic analysis much more difficult.

The IPsec suite of protocols provide multiple security services, which are more robust than those provided by WEP. The services offered by IPsec include the following:

❑ **Confidentiality**   Makes it difficult for anyone but the receiver to understand the data.

❑ **Integrity**   Guarantees the data doesn't get changed en route.

❑ **Authenticity**   Signs the data, so others can see it originated from the source that sent it.

❑ **Replay Protection**   Ensures a transaction is carried out once, and only once, if it isn't meant to be repeated. If the transaction is meant to be repeated, replay protection allows the transaction to be repeated.

Of course, WEP is also supposed to offer confidentiality, authenticity, and integrity, but it falls short on delivering a robust solution.

Security Analysis and Cracking Tools

Many tools can be used to aid in the assessment of wireless networks. The number of these tools has increased dramatically since wireless LANs were first deployed. These tools cover a wide array of devices and applications performing a wide array of functions—from AP scanners and sniffers to user-account auditing systems. It's impossible to list all the tools that aid in security analysis of wireless networks or all the tools that hackers use to crack networks. Instead, a few are mentioned, but the focus is mainly on what you should look for and the way you approach your security analysis.

Remember, any tools that help you do security analysis or vulnerability assessment are also tools that can aid the would-be intruder in identifying the weaknesses of your network. Once these vulnerabilities are exposed, the intruder turns his full attention to exploiting those weaknesses until they're cracked. You can use this knowledge to your advantage. When assessing the weaknesses of your network, think like a hacker and use some of the tools a hacker uses. Some questions to ask yourself include the following:

❏ What does my network look like from the perspective of an attacker?

❏ What are my most important systems or applications and what would be the consequence if they were taken out of service?

❏ How easy would it be to tell if my data or systems have been changed and what would be the impact of those changes?

❏ What other wireless LANs are operating around me? Can I see them? If I can see them, they might also be able to see me.

❏ How easy would it be for a hacker to get confidential data? Can a hacker get user names and passwords? If so, what's at risk?

❏ What tools do I have that can detect attempts at intrusion? How do I validate that my firewall is doing what it's meant to do?

❏ What's the best way to test the security of a home-grown application?

Now that you've thought through the questions, you have information that can help with the task of locating the holes. Scanning tools can help you in this task. Internet Security Systems' InternetScanner (http://www.internetscanner.com) is an example of such a tool. InternetScanner provides comprehensive network vulnerability assessment for measuring online security risks. It can be used to probe communication services, OSes, applications, and routers to uncover and report systems' vulnerabilities that might leave them open to attack. The following is a list of scan categories, which is here to give you an idea of the extensive range of what can be scanned using some of these scanning tools. They are

❏ Brute Force Password guessing

❏ Critical NT issues

❏ Daemons

- ❏ DCOM
- ❏ Denial of Service
- ❏ DNS
- ❏ E-mail
- ❏ Firewalls
- ❏ FTP
- ❏ IP Spoofing
- ❏ NetBIOS
- ❏ Network
- ❏ NFS
- ❏ NetBIOS Shares
- ❏ NT Users, Groups, and Passwords
- ❏ NT Networking
- ❏ NT Registry
- ❏ NT Services
- ❏ Port Scans
- ❏ RPC
- ❏ Web Browser Vulnerabilities and Security Zones
- ❏ Web Server Scan, Proxy, and CGI-BIN
- ❏ X Windows

This list is a good example of the scope and power of some of the tools available for analyzing your network. You might not have the budget or the need for a tool as powerful as this, though. For the small business and home network, you probably only need a subset of the features. Other products, such as Black Ice also manufactured by Internet Security Systems, are aimed at the small business and home network market, and are priced accordingly. The specific features you'll require are unique to your own specific configuration.

Shareware tools are also an option. Some shareware programs are quite robust and feature-rich. You'll have to try a few to see if they have the particular features you require. Web sites, such as WebAttack (http://www.webattack.com/Shareware/security/swantihack.shtml) have many security analysis tools available for download. Some of these tools include the following:

❏ **NetWatcher 2000** Logs the date, time, IP address, port number, and host used by anyone trying to get into your network.

❏ **NetSpyHunter** A port listener and a registry/hard-drive scanner that listens to ports for Trojans or other attacks.

The following list is provided to give you a general appreciation of what to consider during the security analysis process. This is by no means a comprehensive list, but it's a good starting point. Use this list as a guideline when you select a product.

❏ Scan for network vulnerabilities.

❏ Scan for OS vulnerabilities. (Are all the security patches applied?)

❏ Scan for vulnerable code (CGI, sample scripts).

❏ Note the number of user accounts (remove those no longer needed).

❏ Attempt to obtain account password via brute-force scanning.

Security and Emerging Wireless Standards

Much work is being done to overcome the security weaknesses of the existing wi-fi networks. In addition to using complementary tools to beef up security, the IEEE has also been busy developing new protocols and approaches. Eventually, these new protocols will find their way into existing 802.11a, b, and g networks. In the final section on wi-fi security, you'll learn about a few of these protocols.

802.1X

WEP has never provided much more than a basic and primitive form of access control to your wireless nodes by today's standards. With a shared private key, everyone participating in your network has the potential to eavesdrop on everyone else. Passwords, private e-mails, and web traffic could potentially be logged and reviewed later by anyone who can associate with your AP. IEEE 802.1X provides a method by which clients requesting to be authenticated (to join the network) do so via a central authority. The protocol uses an existing protocol called Extensible Authentication Protocol (EAP) for message exchange during the authentication process. EAP has been around for some time and is typically used to secure Point-to-Point Protocol (PPP) (pronounced *triple P*) payload, as in the case of Microsoft's PPP encryption protocol, MPPE. 802.1X extends the use of EAP to Ethernet and wireless LANs.

802.1X doesn't provide the actual authentication mechanisms. Instead, it uses EAP to do so. Because of this, when you set up the environment, you must choose an EAP type, such as Transport Layer Security (EAP-TLS) or

EAP Tunneled Transport Layer Security (EAP-TTLS), which defines how the authentication takes place. EAP isn't limited to these two types. In fact, you can choose from many EAP types. Another common type is EAP-MD5 CHAP.

In a wireless network equipped with 802.1X, a client requesting access to an AP is placed in an unauthorized state. This causes the client to send an EAP start message. The AP, using EAP, then requests the client's identity. The client responds with its identity to the AP, which responds by enabling a port for passing only EAP packets from the client to an authentication server located on the wired side of the AP. The AP forwards the response with the client's identity, which it received from the client to the authentication server and blocks all other traffic, such as HTTP, DHCP, and POP3 packets, until the AP can verify the client's identity using the authentication server (for example, RADIUS). Once authenticated, the AP opens the client's port for other types of traffic (Figure 10.7).

The 802.1X protocol addresses one of the weak points of wi-fi, specifically, access control and authentication. This protocol provides an effective means to authenticate a client requesting to join the network, regardless of whether you implement 802.11 WEP keys, or no encryption at all. Additional features are necessary to provide all the key management functionality wireless networks require, however. These additional features are being addressed by Task Group I of the IEEE, for ratification in IEEE 802.11i.

802.1X is well on its way to becoming an industry standard. Windows XP implements 802.1X natively and some vendors now support 802.1X in their 802.11 APs. Currently, the implementation of 802.1X in wireless LANs falls outside the scope of the 802.11 standard, but the 802.11i committee is specifying the use of 802.1X to become part of the 802.11 standard eventually.

Figure 10.7
IEEE 802.1X provides a method by which clients requesting authentication gain it by an authentication server.

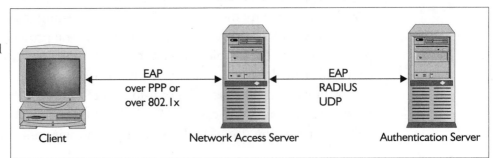

802.11i

In an attempt to address the security vulnerabilities of WEP, Cisco Systems introduced a solution called Lightweight Extensible Authentication Protocol (LEAP), which subsequently became the framework for 802.11i. Ultimately, 802.11i is intended to be deployed to all wireless systems to address a long list of problems. Some of the enhanced features of 802.11i include the following:

❑ A better encryption methodology than WEP.

❑ Modifications to the way networks create and use the IV and key, which lies at the heart of how WEP encrypts traffic.

❑ Protection against replay attacks, forged packets, and IV collision attacks.

❑ Improved authentication and access control.

A draft of the proposed IEEE 802.11i spec was finalized in January 2002, and is being reviewed for eventual approval.

Summary

Implementing a wireless network without taking security precautions is risky business. The technology is already extremely vulnerable because of the medium it uses. Buildings can be secured giving a measure of protection to the wired LAN installed within it. Wireless LANs have no such luxury. The medium they use is air—free space—which is much more difficult to secure.

Instead of accepting the defaults presented when you install your wireless LAN, make changes and give considerable thought to these changes. Think like a hacker, so you can protect against them. Enable WEP. Even though WEP is lacking, it's better than no security at all. Finally, complement WEP by installing additional security features. Remember, security isn't a single solution but, rather, a process of erecting multiple barriers to frustrate and thwart attacks.

Chapter 11

Wi-Fi Applications

With a wireless network up and running, chances are your thoughts will turn
to how you'll use the network. Although the basic applications for a wireless
network are the same as in the wired world—file sharing, printing, and game
playing—you might find wireless access gives you greater flexibility in communicating and presents challenges, especially in an environment where
wired and wireless devices coexist. This chapter is about problems and solutions, and helping you think creatively about the ways you can use your new
wireless network.

File Sharing

Moving files from one computer to another is probably the most ubiquitous
use of a local network. Wireless gives you the capability to add a laptop to a
network quickly and to grab or deliver a file. But the act of sharing files is no
different without wires. You won't learn how to set up file sharing on your
computer here because you can find many resources to help you with this process. Instead, I'll point out some strategies for providing the file access you
want without compromising security. Then, you learn about sharing files in
mixed PC and Mac environments because the use of an access point (or any device that acts as a router) on a network can present difficulties when multiple
operating systems (OSes) and protocols other than TCP/IP are involved.

Think Before You Share

All versions of Windows since Windows 95 and all Mac OSes since System 7
have included file-sharing capabilities. Shared folders are, naturally, exposed
to the network and vulnerable to unauthorized access or accidental damage if

file sharing isn't managed carefully. In a wireless environment, the capability of new members to join the network without plugging in makes file-sharing management even more critical, both to protect those areas of the computer that shouldn't be accessible and to make sure those you do want to share are available to the right people.

Ideally, your access point's WEP security key, plus other security measures you implement, will prevent unwanted visitors from joining your network. If WEP isn't enabled or if it's compromised, anyone who can connect wirelessly to your network and obtain an IP address can see all network resources you shared. So, like any good sports team or military force, you need a second line of defense—one that hides or protects your files, even if an intruder gets in. Prudent file sharing also enables you to share files with some, but not all, people on the network, if you choose. Here are some guidelines for designing an accessible, but secure, file-sharing system on your network:

❑ *Share only what needs to be shared.* Windows XP Professional and Mac OS X each guide you toward a file-sharing arrangement that only provides network access to selected parts of your computer. Each user has a designated set of folders on his or her computer where data files are stored, including public folders into which files to be shared should go. The rest of the folders that contain system files and applications are hidden from view. Adhering to the shared folder setups in these OSes or creating similar ones in older versions of Windows and Mac OS can help reduce unintended sharing.

❑ *Password-protect all shared resources.* Even in a home or small office network, password protection for shared folders is crucial to protecting your computers from intruders or from unintended damage. By default, most OSes don't enforce passwords for computers or for access to shared resources. Setting up a password for your own computer and for the folders you intend to share is easy.

❑ *Create users and groups.* Many families and businesses need to establish several layers of file sharing. You might want to give your spouse access to family financial records, as well as make folders of family photos available to both your spouse and kids. Businesses often create sharing groups for each department within the company, giving only members of that department (along with a senior executive) access. The department might also have a public folder where everyone in the company can go to find forms or news of the department's projects. Users who each have their own password can be given membership in a group. Logging on gives the user access to the shared files he or she has permission to view.

❏ *Use access privileges and permissions.* To follow the business example one step further, assume the marketing staff shares a folder containing their client presentation files. Everyone in the department can see and change the files in the shared folder while the presentation is being developed. When the presentation is complete, it's copied to a public folder to which everyone in the company has access. But now the presentation is read-only. Anyone in the company can open the presentation, but no changes are permitted. Access privileges and permissions ensure data can only be altered by those authorized to make changes.

Cross-Platform File Sharing

Despite the warnings in the previous section about making file sharing secure, most people, especially those in businesses, want and need to share. Now, let's look at situations in which sharing requires some work. Mixed-platform environments, where both Windows and Mac machines are used, can be a challenge to file sharing, but not an insurmountable one. Most of the issues associated with exchanging files between Windows machines and Macs are the same whether your network is wired or wireless. If your network includes Macs running an OS older than OS 9, listen up. Not all access points provide a way for you to share files between wired and wireless users.

A Quick Overview of File-Sharing Protocols

TCP/IP is the indispensable network protocol. To connect to the Internet or to join a local wireless network, your computer must support TCP/IP. Along with TCP/IP for transporting data, however, OSes use different protocols to recognize information and to mount shared volumes. Windows, for example, uses cifs/smb protocols. The native file-sharing protocol in Mac OS is afp. Mac OS X can mount cifs/smb volumes, but Mac OS 9 can't. To mount an afp volume under Windows or a cifs/smb volume under Mac OS 9, you need to add software on one side of the equation. Thorsby Systems' Dave for Mac (Figure 11.1) and PC MacLAN from Miramar are the leaders in this field. Even if you use OS X, Dave makes sharing with Windows machines easier.

So far, so good. All OSes and filing protocols work with TCP/IP, and communication between wired and wireless computers works fine. If you have older Macs, though, or if you want to print to a Mac printer, you need to understand AppleTalk and how it affects wireless networks. AppleTalk is a suite of protocols used by Macs before Apple provided full support for

Figure 11.1
With Dave installed on a Mac running OS X, PCs on the network become visible in the Connect to Server window, and can be mounted on the desktop.

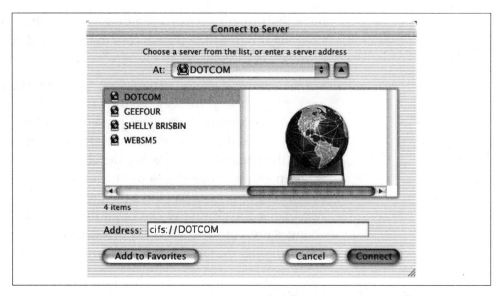

TCP/IP. It's still built into all versions of Mac OS. To share files with a Mac running Mac OS 8 or earlier, you must use AppleTalk because even though TCP/IP was supported for Internet access, you couldn't share files that way.

Wireless access points, which act as bridges for the wired and wireless segments of networks, don't all support AppleTalk. This means a wireless Mac couldn't share files with a wired one that uses AppleTalk exclusively. As you see in the following section, "Printing," the absence of AppleTalk is even more crucial if you need to print to a Mac printer. The bottom line? Choose an access point that supports AppleTalk if you need to use it to share files or printers across the network bridge. Otherwise, confine AppleTalk traffic to one side of the bridge.

Printing

Printing is easy, right? Simply connect your printer to the network and send jobs from wired or wireless computers What if you don't have a networkable printer? Most inkjet printers are intended for use with a single PC and even though you can add Ethernet to some low-cost laser printers, the cost is usually high. Here are your printer-sharing options:

❑ **Locally shared printer** Windows includes printer-sharing software. With this software, you can share any printer that's physically connected to a PC on the network. Wireless and wired computers can share a printer in this way, although the host PC must always be on and printer sharing will become a drain on its processing capability. Even though Macs can't access Windows printer sharing, you can use Dave or PC MacLAN to give them access to a Windows printer, just as you can provide Windows access to a Mac (AppleTalk) printer. For sharing purposes, AppleTalk printers are shared, even though they're network devices. Because AppleTalk printers don't use TCP/IP, they need a print server like Dave of PC MacLAN to work with Windows machines. If you want to print to an AppleTalk printer from wireless devices, you need an access point with AppleTalk support.

❏ **Pocket print server** These devices connect directly to a printer's parallel port and have an Ethernet port for connecting to the network. Some models have multiple printer ports, enabling you to connect several printers (assuming they're quite close to one another). If your network includes Macs and PCs, look for one that supports both TCP/IP and AppleTalk. Again, AppleTalk access from the wireless side of the network requires an AP that supports it.

❏ **Wireless print server (AP based)** Some wi-fi access points include print server capability. Connect a printer directly to the access point to give wired and wireless users of the network access to the printer. This method supports Windows users who simply activate access to the printer over the network.

❏ **Dedicated wireless print server** A wireless print server combines the features of a pocket print server with wireless access. With the printer connected to the server, wireless users can print. Connecting the print server to the network via Ethernet also enables wired clients to print. Some wireless print servers support AppleTalk printing, allowing Macs to print without additional software or configuration.

Setting Up an Access Point Print Server

Zoom's ZoomAir IG-4165 Wireless Internet Gateway contains a print-server feature. The access point/router can be connected to any printer with a parallel port. After installing configuration software on a PC, you can set up the shared printer on each networked machine. You can set up the printer on the first PC, either at the time you install the print server or by configuring the printer first, and then using the settings you already entered to get the print server working. The latter method worked best for me. Here's how to set up the print server under Windows 2000. The order of the steps varies with different Windows versions:

1. Set up and configure the access point for your network. Place the access point near a printer you want to share.

2. Turn off the access point and connect the printer to it before restarting both devices.

Figure 11.2
The Ports tab shows available ports on your computer.

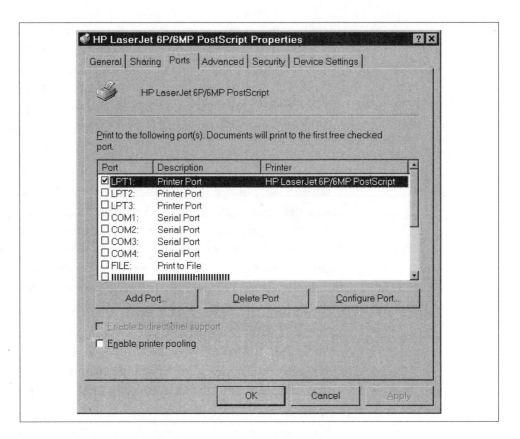

3. Insert the access point CD-ROM into the drive of a computer on the network.

4. Click ZoomAir Software, and then click Install Print Server.

5. Follow the wizard until the server software is installed, and then restart the computer.

6. You can either use a printer that's already been configured or you can set up a new printer to work with the access point. To use a preconfigured printer with the print server, choose Start | Settings | Printers, and then select the name of the printer you set up already.

7. Choose File | Properties.

8. Click the Ports tab. You see a list of available ports (Figure 11.2), including the LPT port the printer currently uses.

9. Choose PRTmate (All-in-1 IP-Sharer). If you don't see this option, click Add Port and choose PRTmate from the list, as shown in Figure 11.3.

10. Select PRTmate port, and then click New Port.

11. The Printer Position dialog box shows the access point's IP address (Figure 11.4). If not, type it and click OK.

Figure 11.3
Because the PRTmate port didn't appear, I added it manually.

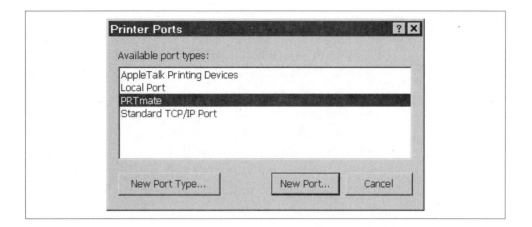

12. Close the Printer Ports dialog box, and then click Close to finish setup.

13. To use the print server with other computers on the network, add a new printer and set it up as a network printer, using the name and IP address for the device you just configured.

Wireless Print Servers

Several vendors sell wireless print servers. These aren't access points, but independent devices that connect to the printer and to the wired and/or wireless network. Some wireless print servers, include the Linksys WPS11, support TCP/IP and AppleTalk, Internet Printing Protocol (IPP), and bidirectional printing.

IPP allows a PC to print to any printer on the Internet that's available through IPP. In order to accept IPP, a printer must have a public Internet address and can't be blocked by a local firewall. To use IPP, a client application must be installed.

Configuring wireless print servers is much like the setup procedure described for the Zoom print server. After installing print-server software and configuring a printer to use it, you need to add a printer port driver to each device to be connected to the wireless print server.

Figure 11.4
The access point's IP address appears.

Printer Position

Enter the Product's IP :

192.168.123.254

OK

Cancel

Network Gaming

Like other network applications, online games rely on access to TCP/IP and to specific Internet ports. For this reason, gaming over the Internet, or even with users on your local network, requires support from your wireless network. The good news is this: playing an online game with another user of your local wi-fi network presents no problem, unless local access has been restricted in some way by a network administrator. In general, wired and wireless users on the same network can also play games over the network. The exception is if a game requires a protocol, such as NetWare IPX, that your access point doesn't support.

To play games over the Internet, you need to punch a hole in your local firewall so the ports used by the game are available. You can do this either by forwarding specific ports (some access points provide preconfigured settings for Battle.net, MSN Gaming Zone, and others) or by setting your gaming computer as the DMZ, exposing all its ports to the Internet. Both procedures are described in Chapter 7.

The DMZ approach is the simplest because you don't have to know the ports that correspond to your game. To set it up, you only need to know the IP address of the gaming computer. On the other hand, the DMZ machine has no protection from port scans and other Internet-based intrusions. If you game infrequently, you might reconfigure DMZ access each time you play or leave the computer off when you're not gaming.

Streaming Video

Like network games, streaming video format such as QuickTime 4 and later, requires access to Internet ports. To protect the largest portion of your network, confine streaming video to a single machine and expose only the needed ports.

Chapter 12

Building a Better Network

Wi-fi networks, like all networks, can be as simple or complicated as necessary to provide the coverage and network access you need for your home or business. Most home users need only set up an access point (AP) and wi-fi devices, as described in earlier chapters. Many small offices can also function well with this sort of network. If your needs are greater, though—if your facility is large or unusually prone to interference, or if you must support a large number of users—the basic wi-fi setup might not meet your needs. In this chapter, you learn how to build a bigger, better network.

The first step to building an advanced wi-fi network is planning. That's true of any complex network, but wi-fi introduces a number of variables not present in wired networks, including radio interference, mobility, and security. With sufficient planning before you install wi-fi equipment, you can save time and money, and you can increase the chances that you provided wi-fi coverage for all areas in need of it. Once the planning process is complete, you can begin building the network, remembering the goals you established during the planning process as you light up the network. Finally, maintaining a wi-fi network requires attention to the changing landscape in your facility: relocation of people and equipment, and expanding coverage needs and network failures when they occur. You learn about all these stages of network building and management in this chapter.

If you're building a home wi-fi network, the information in this chapter could seem like overkill. After all, you don't need to develop a comprehensive network plan or produce facility maps or budgets to get wireless coverage on your patio. However, the information provided about network coverage problems and performance could also apply to you. Issues related to high levels of interference in your environment, problems you'll encounter when covering a large house or yard, and issues related to sharing wi-fi access with your neighbors are all covered.

Planning Your Network

The need for network planning was briefly discussed in Chapter 7. Also mentioned was the theoretical process used by professional network planners when they build or add to a large network. Now it's time to take a detailed look at the planning process; that detailed look begins with requirements' gathering. To build a network effectively, you must know what you want the network to do. Next, you need to conduct a site survey to assess your existing facility, available resources, and any weaknesses that you might need to resolve. Using the information gained in the survey, you can proceed to design a network topology that matches your goals.

Requirements' Gathering

The "home version" of requirements' gathering, described in Chapter 7, says you boil your network plan down to a simple statement of your objective in starting the network. The process is a bit more involved in the business world and, because budgets and management approvals could be involved, it's a good idea to go through a thorough requirements' gathering process. The information you gather can help you build a network now, as well as plan for the future.

Requirements' gathering might seem like a statement of the obvious—a reiteration of what you already know about your needs and goals. In most cases, though, you'll learn something from the process of asking questions. You'll also gain a useful paper trail as you match the network you think you want with the resources and problems you find when you try to build that network. Gather requirements in these categories:

❏ **Facilities**   Start by determining the area to be covered by your network. Does this area incorporate a floor of offices, a warehouse, a store, and a condominium development? Also note if the facility has network resources already, such as an Ethernet LAN, broadband access to the Internet or even phone jacks for dial-up modems. If you need to cover multiple buildings or to add an outdoor space to the coverage area, you'll want to include information about these spaces. Note areas within the facility that might require especially high coverage, such as computer labs or cubicle farms where many users need constant, high-speed network access.

❑ **Mobility**   The beauty of wi-fi is the capability to move around with a laptop or PDA without reestablishing a network connection. If you serve your small facility with a single AP, mobility planning could simply be proper AP positioning to maximize coverage, or the addition of an antenna to the AP or to your laptop. To serve a larger area, you need to understand the role mobility will play. Will users wander at will throughout the building expecting continuous wi-fi access or will users be relatively stationary? Your answer determines not only the placement of equipment, but also the TCP/IP infrastructure required to support wi-fi roaming.

❑ **Application**   Why do you need a wi-fi network? What kinds of uses will people make of it? Are you solving an existing connectivity problem, such as the inability to access e-mail or corporate data from the warehouse, or is the network intended to provide a completely new application, such as collaboration during meetings? Write down the uses you and your colleagues intend for the network, and then anticipate the affect having access to wireless communication will have on the way people work. Understanding a network's application affects more than the coverage area,. It also impacts interconnection to your existing network, throughput requirements for wireless segments, and security.

❑ **Interfaces to network resources**   This category is related to the previous one. Understanding how the network will be used should lead you to a delineation of specific resources and tools wi-fi users will need. This could include access to databases, the Internet, file servers, and printers.

❑ **Users**   Who in your organization needs access to the wi-fi network? How will they use the wi-fi network? And how often will they use the network? Aside from the obvious issue of purchasing equipment for each user, a large number of folks connecting simultaneously could be an indicator that you need to provide redundant APs and to bring them closer together in your building, especially if your network will be predominantly wi-fi. In mixed environments, the number of users and the duration of their use might determine how much of the network infrastructure should be wireless and how much should be wired. The number of people on the network also impacts security planning. If you anticipate guests, such as traveling salespeople or customers, on your network, the actual number of users might be high, but the time they spend on the network could be low. Their location in the building might necessitate the need to concentrate APs in areas with high-network traffic, even if this need arises on an irregular basis.

❑ **Coverage area**   The easiest answer to the question of where you want to provide wi-fi coverage is "I want it everywhere." But, do you really want it everywhere? And do you need it everywhere? Do areas exist that you want to leave inaccessible by wireless, either for security reasons or to achieve some administrative or business goal? Does the cost of providing complete wi-fi coverage make sense? Do you need to ensure that the entire property is covered or can you stick with work areas and save considerable money? Even if you decide universal coverage is the goal, requirements' gathering should include a list of the actual places to serve. You can use the site survey step in the planning process to develop a list of areas to cover, those to be left alone, and those, if any, where you want to prevent wireless access.

❑ **Throughput requirements**   Wi-fi's 11 Mbps top speed matches nicely with Ethernet, which operates at a theoretical 10 Mbps. You won't achieve these speeds, of course, but when a small number of users are connected to a wi-fi network, Ethernet and wi-fi speeds remain somewhat comparable. On the other hand, many organizations have shifted their wired networks to 100 Mbps Fast Ethernet, opening up a potential difference between the speed of wired and wireless users. More significantly, the performance of a wireless network diminishes as the number of users contending for access to network resources, such as an AP, increases. In the wired world, using switches gives each user a dedicated pipe. This isn't the case with wi-fi. You can provide wi-fi speeds that are comparable with a wired network by increasing redundancy. If you need truly high-speed access, though, consider creating an 802.11a network or waiting for 802.11g products to become available. Both provide rated speeds of up to 54 Mbps. At the requirement-gathering stage, your goal is to determine the likelihood that speed will be an issue. You can make the choice of technology later.

❑ **Integration with existing networks**   If one or more networks already exist in your environment, you need to plan for integration between them and the wi-fi network. If the goal is to build one large network, you need to determine what, if any, new equipment, configuration, and network services will be needed to link the networks. If an existing network uses technology other than 10/100 BASE-T Ethernet, you need to determine if it's possible or desirable to integrate the network with wi-fi. Most wi-fi equipment connects to wired network devices via the same kind of RJ-45 jacks used in 10/10 BASE-T Ethernet. The same holds true for networks that use transport protocols other than TCP/IP. Wi-fi networks require TCP/IP. And, although some APs also support other protocols, such as AppleTalk and IPX, other protocols probably won't be directly compatible with wi-fi. If a wireless network already exists, you also need to determine if the current network will cause interference with the new one or if it will be replaced by wi-fi.

❑ **Scalability** Don't assume your network will stay the same size. Every business wants to grow and the mere presence of a technology that enables users to do new things has a tendency to expand its use. The better job you can do evaluating the number of users your network will have in the future, the more able you'll be to add to it before the need becomes critical.

❑ **Security requirements** As you learned in Chapter 10, wireless networks present a variety of security issues and you have many choices for dealing with them. You could also have security issues related to the kind of work you do, the way users interact with the network, and the risks you face from crackers who might have targeted you. Other security issues crop up when you establish point-to-point links or the need to provide remote access to your network.

❑ **Budget** Nothing is special about budgeting for a wireless network installation. All the usual costs of network design, equipment, and installation apply. Because wi-fi equipment prices have been dropping lately, you might be tempted to assume that building a network is merely a matter of buying a cheap AP and setting it up. You get what you pay for, though, in terms of hardware, design assistance, and installation. If you hire professional help to build your network, look for experts who have specific wireless experience. If you undertake the project yourself, follow the planning steps described in this chapter and do plenty of research before you choose your products.

❑ **Timeframe** Like most technology-related projects, a wireless installation is subject to premature obsolescence. Just when you get a tech project going, a newer, cooler technology comes out, rendering your equipment out-of-date. New technologies like 802.11a and g have the potential to outpace 802.11b as a business technology within the next year. Home and small office users won't experience this sort of obsolescence as keenly as organizations planning larger installations, so they can safely proceed with building a network. Large installations will be affected more by advancing technology. Aside from understanding the technological issues this presents, such as interoperability and the lack of real-world testing the newer standards have had, consider the potential productivity loss associated with waiting. Also consider the budgetary impact of creating a network now that could become outdated in only a few years. In short, the timing of your project is a balancing act.

The Site Survey

With a list of network requirements in hand, you're ready to conduct a site survey. The level of detail required for your survey can vary a great deal, based on the size and complexity of your facility and other requirements, but the process is an important one. A site survey gives you information about physical constraints on your plans, both obvious and hidden. You can take measurements, spot potential access and antenna locations, and test your facility for coverage patterns and potential interference.

The most basic kind of site survey is a walkthrough of your facility. Take a tape measure and a notepad with you and make a diagram of the building and/or outdoor areas you intend to cover. If you have blueprints for the building, also bring them along. Note building elements that could increase indoor interference, such as metal walls, pipe, window screens, and coated windows. Other sources of environmental interference include cordless phones and microwave ovens. Outdoors, buildings, and even wind, can cause interference and path loss, as do the typically longer distances between antennas. Trees are especially pesky sources of interference because of their water content. Water absorbs radio waves in the 2.4 GHz band, preventing them from reaching their destination.

Add measurements of rooms and other spaces to your diagram. Note the physical characteristics, too, such as extensive open spaces, the presence of large amounts of furniture, and so forth. Next, mark the locations where network users will work—at their desks or in conference rooms, computer labs, customer service areas, and so on. Also note the existing technology infrastructure, including server rooms and phone closets (from which broadband access might be provided). If Internet access comes to users' desktops from dial-up modems or another setup besides a central phone closet, note this information as well.

Live Testing

Diagrams are great, but they don't take the place of a real-world test. Rules of thumb for AP placement say that a single AP can provide coverage from over

100 to 300 feet. As in so many situations, your mileage (coverage, in this case) will vary, especially if considerable interference is present. APs have different range characteristics, depending on the antenna attached to the AP. Vendors often provide range specifications, but they aren't useful in the real world.

Using the guidance provided in Chapter 3, you can select an AP that meets your networking needs, and then test it in your environment. As discussed in that chapter, buying all your equipment from the same vendor to maximize compatibility and ease of management is a good idea. If you can, obtain an AP and wi-fi network adapters from the vendor you intend to use and place the equipment where you think it will perform best. Next, add a wi-fi network adapter to your laptop and open the administration software, so you can see the strength of your network signal. Carry the laptop around the facility, noting the signal strength characteristics of various locations on your diagram. Try moving the test AP around and note the impact on signal as you travel through the office.

The High-End Site Survey

This section concentrates on a relatively simply site survey that you can do yourself. If your budget allows, you can hire a professional network planner to survey your site and/or install the network based on the survey. If you can't afford a professional and your site presents complex problems, consider using a spectral analyzer. This device can be particularly helpful in tracking down radio interference in the 2.4 GHz spectrum, which you might be unable to spot otherwise.

Analyzing Site Survey Results

By now, you should have a lot of paper in hand. A list of requirements and diagrams from your site survey won't do you any good unless you can analyze them and build your network based on the information you've collected. Begin by creating a coverage map that identifies proposed locations for APs and antennas, based on what you know about your facility, your users, and their needs for wireless connectivity. (If you need management approval for your project, you might also have to complete a report or a budget.) Be sure to describe the locations where wireless devices will be placed, including interference characteristics and the reasons the locations you chose are desirable. You might or might not yet know what specific network topology you need to use, so your coverage map will probably undergo another revision after you analyze potential problem areas or adjust your needs to the available budget. Consider this map a preliminary plan for your network.

Network Topology and Design

Choosing a network design represents the marriage of the requirements' gathering and site survey process. Using the information you have about what your network must do and its relationship to any existing network, a network design provides a solution to problems that have been discovered in the site survey.

Wireless networking topology, as you learned in Chapter 2, provides three ways to build a wireless network: ad-hoc (IBSS), single-access point (BSS), and multiaccess point (ESS). BSS and IBSS networks are the types most commonly found in homes and small offices, as described in detail in Chapters 7 and 9. In this section, you learn more about ESS networks.

Network design, as opposed to topology, defines the process used to construct the network, including the physical and logical organization of its parts, and how they connect to one another. You can design a network using a combination of a wireless and a wired topology. To choose a network design effectively for a larger network, you need to understand the basic structure and limitations of an IBSS, as well as the concept of roaming. Next, you learn about several network designs and the best ways to use them.

ESS Basics

An *ESS* consists of multiple wi-fi APs, configured so they form a single network. Once a user joins the network, that user can move freely as long as he or she is within range of at least one of the APs that form the ESS. This is called *roaming.* In an ESS, APs are configured with the same SSID, but each is tuned to a different frequency, identified by individual channels. In the United States, there are 11 wi-fi channels. To build an ESS, all APs must support roaming. The ESS should be set up so the coverage area of each AP overlaps others, which creates a network with no dead spots. Figure 12.1 shows a typical ESS.

Figure 12.1
Each AP in an ESS uses the same SSID and is tuned to a different channel.

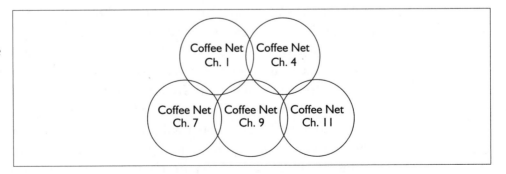

To allow a user to obtain and maintain a single IP address while roaming across the network, the DHCP-server functions of the APs must be disabled. In a wireless-only network, you can use one of the APs as a DHCP server. If your network includes Ethernet segments, the setup issues are more complicated. Because wi-fi devices must be in the same IP subnet to roam and function as peers of wired devices, you either need to use a DHCP server that's accessible to both segments of the network or add a DHCP-relay device to pass IP addresses from a server on the wired side to the wireless clients. A third alternative is to assign static IP addresses to all devices on the network. This requires more configuration and management work than using dynamic addressing.

You can facilitate roaming and wireless links over large areas in other ways, but these are beyond the scope of this book. If you need to build a complex network including large-scale wi-fi roaming, consult a professional network planner.

Wireless-Only Networks

You might choose a wireless-only network if you're building a brand-new network or if your need for communication with the outside world is limited. You can bring the Internet to a wi-fi network, as you learned in previous chapters. In that case, technically, at least one wire is connected to your wireless network. Ease of setup is probably the greatest advantage of a wireless-only network, though ESS installations might require some careful analysis of coverage and network range.

Adding Wireless to an Established Ethernet LAN

Businesses with existing network infrastructure, including broadband Internet access, don't need or want to rearrange it to make a wireless AP/router as the center of their network. And there's no reason to change. Often, the Ethernet LAN, complete with 100 Mbps switched access for all users, works fine. You can add wireless access to the existing network for new users or for travelers returning to the office by adding an AP and leaving the rest of the network unchanged. Plug the AP into an existing Ethernet hub or switch, giving it access to the network (be sure to disable the AP's DHCP server). Wireless clients join the network by associating with the AP, and then they have full access to both wired and wireless resources. Figure 12.2 shows an Ethernet LAN to which wireless access was added.

A variation of this approach is to use a software router, hosted by a wired computer. If you already share an Internet connection, using Windows ICS, winProxy, or some other gateway software, you can add wireless clients to

Figure 12.2
Connect an AP to a switched port on the Ethernet network to give wireless clients access to the network.

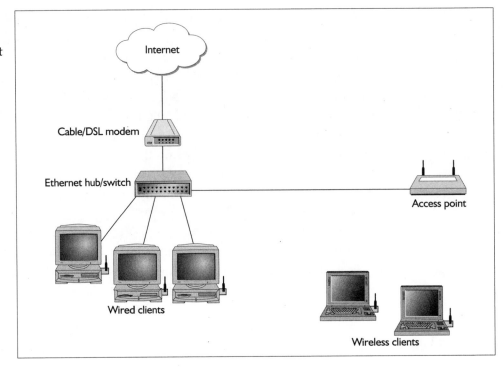

the network by connecting an AP to an Ethernet port or adapter in the gateway computer, or to a wired hub or switch.

Ethernet LANs Bridges and a Wireless Bridge

A pair of wireless bridges (not to be confused with an AP that bridges wired and wireless network segments) can be used to bridge two wired networks, as shown in Figure 12.3. Bridges can be used to link two network segments that otherwise operate separately from one another. You might use *wireless bridging* to join networks in two buildings across the street from one another or even networks separated by a floor within the same building. Wireless bridging is an alternative to cabling the remote networks together. Attaching a high-gain antenna to each wireless bridge significantly extends the distance you can bridge.

Unlike APs, many wireless bridges only communicate with other bridges. Wireless bridges aren't intended to support wireless clients directly. In this sense, a wireless bridge isn't intended to help you build a wi-fi network but, instead, it's intended to extend the usefulness of a couple of wired networks.

Another issue for potential wireless bridge users is the need to coordinate between the remote network segments you're connecting. To communicate locally, all devices must operate on the same IP subnet, just as in a wireless

Figure 12.3
Two Ethernet
networks can
become one
with a pair of
wireless bridges
connecting them.

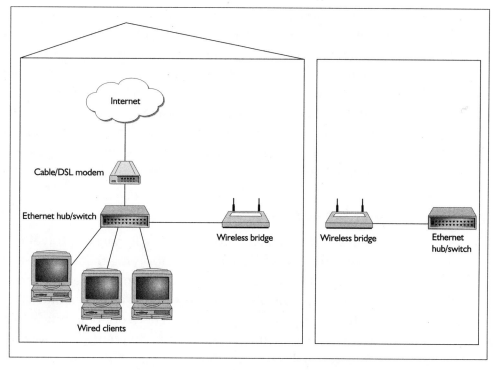

ESS. If you want to join two networks that have operated separately until now (such as a design firm and a print shop that often do business together), bridging might not be the best choice because the two networks must be joined together.

Although you can't support wireless clients using the bridging setup described because bridges don't typically provide AP features, you can do so by adding an AP to one or both bridged network segments. If you take this approach, the two bridges should be set to the same channel and SSID. APs on either side can be set to the same channel and SSID, as long as these settings are different (and preferably on distant channels) from the bridges. Finally, products exist (the name isn't always a good indicator) that can act as both a bridge and an AP. If you want to use such a device, read the specs carefully before buying something you think will work as both an AP and a bridge.

A Bit More About Bridging

Bridging two wired network segments as described is called a *point-to-point link*. Two bridges are configured to communicate exclusively with one another. They identify one another by MAC address. Bridges can also operate in *point-to-multipoint* mode, in which a single network segment, including an access point, communicates with multiple locations, using wired or wireless network segments. The *point* segment is the master bridge, while the others function as slaves. Use a point-to-multipoint setup to provide access from a main building to several remote locations that don't currently use a network. The master bridge connects to a powerful antenna that can be reached brom all of the remote locations, as shown in Figure 12.4. The terminology might vary from vendor to vendor, but the idea is the same. If you want to put one bridge in charge of communications among segments, create a point-to-multipoint link.

A Closer Look at Wi-Fi Range

Rules of thumb about how far wi-fi signals can travel in different environments are somewhat useful, but applying them to real-world environments is difficult. Sources and degrees of signal loss and interference differ based on the unpredictable contents of most environments. The best way to deal with this imprecise aspect of wi-fi network planning is to know what factors contribute to poor coverage and to do plenty of real-world testing to make sure your APs and antennas are optimally located.

Despite a theoretical signal range of several hundred feet, many wi-fi users find indoor reception is much less than predicted. Many people find they need to install more APs and/or antennas than initially planned to compensate

Figure 12.4
Installing a master bridge and a high-gain antenna in the main school building and slave bridges in out buildings (also sporting antennas) creates a point-to-multipoint wireless link between the buildings.

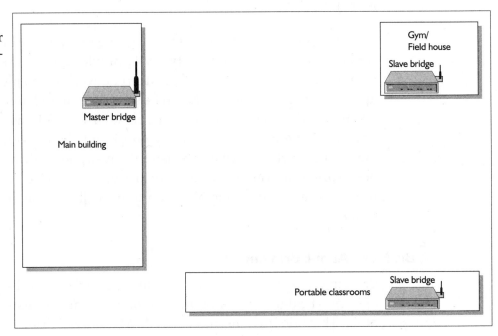

for the lower-than-expected coverage. The reason for the disappointing (if you believe the theoretical estimates) range of wi-fi is this: Radio signals are subject to path loss and interference from a variety of sources, including walls, ceilings, conduit, and radio-based noise.

A more scientific version of this conundrum is explained in a paper entitled "Indoor WLAN Radio Performance Part II: Range Performance in a Dense Office Environment," by John C. Stein of Harris Semiconductor (now Intersil). Stein identifies the three physical modes an indoor signal experiences: reflection, diffraction, and scattering. The degree of signal *reflection* indicates whether the signal bounces off a surface with which it comes in contact or is absorbed by it. Most surfaces do both, allowing some of the signal to continue its journey, while the absorbed portion is lost. Walls, floors, ceilings, and furniture reflect signals. Thicker materials absorb more signal than thinner ones. Figure 12.5 shows a signal that is partially reflected as it passes through an obstacle.

Diffraction occurs when sharp angles or edges are present in the environment. When a signal encounters an obstruction, it bends to get around the obstruction, generating the signal behind or to the side of an obstruction. Figure 12.6 shows a diffracted signal.

Scattering occurs when a signal encounters a large number of objects in its path, especially if those objects are small, relative to the size of the signal wavelength. Scattering sends signals in all directions, generating interference and reducing the signal's strength (Figure 12.7). Metal building material and conduit are important sources of signal scattering.

Figure 12.5
Some of the radio signal is reflected as it reaches the wall, while the rest of the signal passes through the wall.

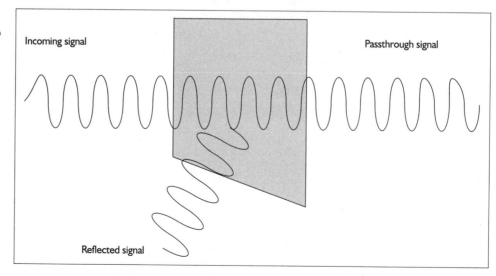

Figure 12.6
When a signal encounters sharp edges or angled objects, it bends to get around the sharp edge.

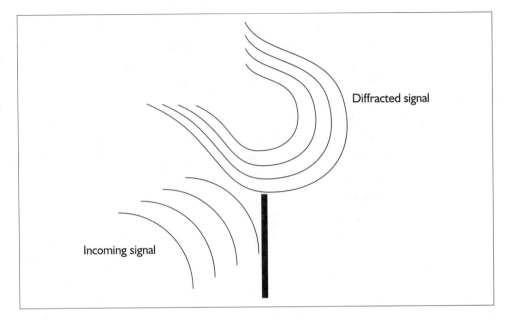

Indoor environments experience three types of indoor path loss, all of which decrease coverage: free space loss, line-of-sight loss, and obstruction path loss. Of the three, *obstruction path loss* is the most significant indoors. *Free space loss* and *line-of-sight loss* occur in relatively small amounts as the distance between two radios increases.

Stein reports some estimates of the amount of signal attenuation caused by various obstructions, which appear in Table 12-1.

Signal loss is also caused by multipath and fading effects. Because signals radiate in all directions from the source (unless they're contained by a highly directional antenna) and because they're subject to reflection, diffraction,

Figure 12.7
Once scattered, a signal breaks up in several directions.

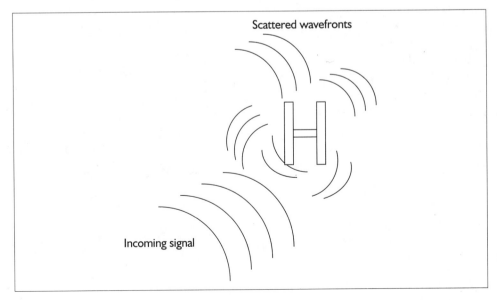

Source of Obstruction Loss	Loss in dB
Window Brick Wall	2
Metal Frame Glass Wall into Building	6
Office Wall	6
Metal Door in Office Wall	6
Cinder Block Wall	4
Metal Door in Brick Wall	12.4
Brick Wall Next to Metal Door	3

Table 12-1
John C. Stein's Estimates of Signal Attenuation in Typical Office Environments

and scattering, signals are subject to multipath loss. Fading effects occur as the signal is obstructed in progress. Fading doesn't occur at a predictable rate: Sometimes a signal fades quickly over a short distance and sometimes it fades slowly. Fading is often accelerated by movement in the environment, such as people walking around or the turning of metal fan blades.

Another factor that affects signal strength and quality, even where good line-of-sight exists between two antennas, is related to refraction and reflection. The Fresnel Effect, named for physicist Augustin Fresnel, says that a signal's strength will increase or decrease in intensity, based on its distance from an object around which the signal is refracted. To maximize a refracted signal, you must keep the area impacted by the Fresnel effect (called the *Fresnel zone*) free of obstructions. The size of the Fresnel zone varies with the kind of objects near the signal's path—trees and plants, which contain water, generate a larger Fresnel zone because their water content absorbs a significant amount of the radio signal.

Stein's study of indoor wi-fi performance found that an AP's dipole antenna (often, two exist), with its omnidirectional, highly horizontal coverage pattern, contributes significantly to improved network coverage. Stein also found that, as most people acknowledge, the antennas integrated into wi-fi network adapter cards are poor. Combining this information with what you learned about antenna selection in Chapter 5, along with a healthy dose of testing in your own environment, is the best way to assess your existing coverage and to find the steps needed to improve your coverage in areas where it's weak.

Putting It All Together

The final step in the planning process is creating an implementation plan that includes detailed maps of your network, including locations of hardware, and the physical and logical design of the network you intend to build. Now is the time to turn those abstract drawings of networks into a roadmap for your own installation project. You'll especially want to consider the logical network layout—how devices and network segments interact with one another, and what role each plays in the larger network. For example, this is the time to decide how each client on all parts of your network will obtain an IP address, connect to the Internet, gain access to the wireless network, and, if you implemented it, interact with advanced security features, such as a VPN or authentication system.

Buying Stuff

Based on your requirements, including future needs and budget, you're now ready to acquire equipment, including APs and network adapters for wireless clients. You might also need new routers (wired or wireless) and bridges if you're building a network consisting of two or more remote segments. Although many vendors sell wi-fi certified products that work well together, buying everything from a single vendor is best. Besides easing your management tasks and reducing the learning curve, a single-vendor solution improves the chances that your calls to tech support will result in an efficient resolution of your problem.

To the extent you can, buy expandable or upgradeable products, especially if you're interested in moving from 802.11b to a future technology. A few vendors sell APs that enable you to replace radios. Most vendors also provide a port for an external antenna—a necessity if you have a highly obstructed environment or you want to create point-to-point or point-to-multipoint links.

Installing the Network

With good plans in place, network installation should be more a matter of rote than heavy thinking. Follow the plan you've made and keep careful track of your progress. This applies to naming and tracking the location of all the equipment you install. Good record keeping can save you considerable trouble later when you need to rearrange the network to accommodate growth or bring it into sync with a larger office reorganization project.

Remember the potential for equipment you install to be moved. If you carefully placed an AP on a high shelf, but you haven't bolted it down, it might be moved by a coworker, causing a breakdown in wi-fi coverage. If you can, mount your equipment to walls or otherwise prevent it from being moved accidentally.

As you install equipment, perform tests to see if you're achieving the coverage you intend. These tests are best performed during the workday, when your space is filled with the people and objects that normally occupy it. Remember, some signal losses occur as a result of movement.

Chapter 13

Advanced Wireless Settings and Network Analysis

Networks rarely remain the same for long. Despite careful planning and testing, problems often develop as people and organizations mold the network to their own needs. This is especially true in the wireless world, where network devices are, by definition, mobile. The network you created and tested a few months ago might begin to experience performance problems as new users join or when someone moves an access point (AP) from its high perch to dust the shelf where it sits, without understanding the consequences this action can have for network performance. If, as is usually the case, problems on your network can't be traced to a single cause, you need the tools to analyze what's happening. The problem could be related to network interference, changed AP configuration, or problems associated with higher-level network protocols. You can begin to address problems, especially performance-related ones, by tweaking advanced wireless settings on your AP. Although many consumer-grade APs do not provide the full range of advanced settings, some of the better ones do give you the capability to adjust timing, power management, and other settings. To dig deeper into what's going on with your network, consider using software tools that can analyze the radio signal, as well as the actual packets that travel between devices on your network. In this chapter, you learn how to tweak network performance, and how to find and choose software that analyzes all aspects of your wi-fi network.

Tuning Access Points

Many radio-related network problems occur because of the split-second timing required to negotiate communication between devices. Recall from Chapter 2 that wi-fi networks use CSMA/CA technology to prevent network collisions from occurring. As a consequence, wi-fi radios don't transmit when a collision is likely and unless the radio is sure its signal will reach its target.

Tuning can also help solve the "hidden node" problem that occurs in networks where wi-fi stations can connect to an AP, but aren't within range of other stations with which they want to communicate. Radios use RTS/CTS packets to mark each transaction between devices. When two stations can't communicate directly with one another, unanswered RTS packets create interference on the network. Several of the tuning settings described in this section help resolve RTS/CTS problems where hidden nodes exist.

Now, let's return to the Linksys BEFW11S4 AP/router used as an example in Chapter 7. The BEFW11S4 has many, but not all, of the available tuning settings discussed in this section. Many consumer products provide less access to these features. To tune the AP, open the administration interface, click Advanced, and then click Wireless. Figure 13.1 shows the available settings.

Figure 13.1
Configure advanced settings on the Wireless screen of the Linksys BEFW11S4 AP/router.

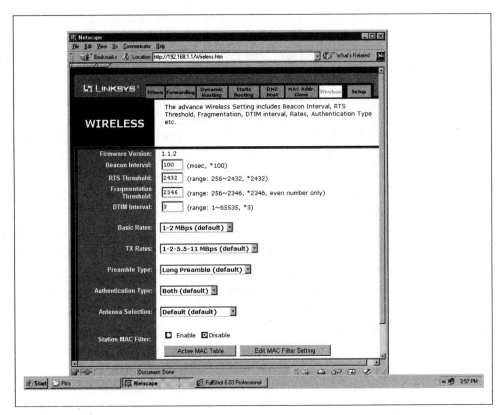

❑ **Beacon Interval** Wi-fi radios broadcast beacons that indicate their service, area, IP address, and other information that identifies and locates them for other radios on the network. Reducing the beacon interval provides more current information on the network, which is helpful to wi-fi devices roaming though large networks. On the other hand, beacons create network overhead. You might reduce the beacon interval to quiet the network, especially if it isn't a complex ESS.

❑ **RTS Threshold** Changing the threshold for RTS packets affects the amount of data included with each. A larger RTS packet that goes unanswered because the network includes a hidden node results in greater interference for all. If you don't experience hidden nodes (if your network is small and not particularly mobile), there's no point in changing the RTS threshold setting. Even in complex networks, you might find altering this setting has little impact on performance.

❑ **Fragmentation Threshold** *Fragmentation* refers to the amount of network overhead found in wireless transmissions. Of course, plenty of overhead reduces the amount and speed of data transfers. The fragmentation threshold regulates the size of MAC layer packets by breaking up oversized packets and transmitting the overage as a new one. A poor fragmentation threshold is characterized by excessive interference on the network. Tweaking the threshold within a small range of the default might reduce interference, but setting the threshold too low or too high can have negative affects on throughput.

❑ **DTIM Interval** When the AP has data to send to clients, it sends a Delivery Traffic Indication Message (DTIM) beacon, telling the client to listen for forthcoming data. A longer DTIM interval conserves power on the client side by decreasing the frequency with which it listens to the AP. On the downside, a longer interval decreases the buffer size available for data on the AP and introduces a delay into the transaction. (A related setting, not found in our example AP, is Listening Interval. The Listening Interval setting specifies the time a station should wait for a new DTIM beacon from the AP. Like the DTIM interval, the Listening Interval setting can be tweaked to provide better power management for wi-fi devices.)

❑ **Preamble Type** The default-long preamble type defines a larger CRC block at the beginning of network transactions between the AP and roaming stations. Shorter preambles might be helpful in larger networks where decreasing network overhead is important.

❑ **Antenna Type** Adding a second antenna near the AP to boost its signal is called *antenna diversity*.

The Basic Rates, TX Rates, Authentication Type, and Station MAC Filter options on the Linksys screen aren't tuning options. Basic and TX Rates settings simply enable you to choose the data rates supported by your AP. You rarely have a reason to use anything other than the default settings, which support all data rates used by 802.11 networks. *Authentication Type* is used in situations when an authentication system is in force on the network. Authentication Type tells the AP how authentication keys are managed. *Station MAC Filter* controls wireless access to the configuration software.

Here are some other advanced configuration settings available on high-end APs:

❑ **Retry Limits** Devices whose packets fail to reach their destination retry a specified number of times before giving up. Changing the number of retries on an AP either reduces errors (if retries are increased) or cuts network overhead (if the limits are lowered). Use this setting if you encountered a large number of dropped packets.

❑ **Scan Timing** Active scan timing controls the speed with which a device searches the network for other devices. To locate the largest number of devices on the network (particularly in an ESS environment), decrease the scan interval (increase scan speed). Passive scan timing controls the amount of time a device listens for other devices on a single channel before moving to a different channel.

Network Analysis

You can gather information about your wi-fi network in several ways and at many levels of detail, depending on your needs. You can use utility software that ships with most wi-fi network adapters to quickly look at the card's condition—its connection to the network, signal strength, and so forth. In most case, you can even use your utility to find available wi-fi networks. Windows XP builds this feature into the operating system (OS). If you're interested in scanning for and capturing data about networks as you move around your facility or the neighborhood, the popular NetStumbler (http://www.netstumbler.com) will oblige, providing each AP's SSID, channel, device type, WEP status (on or off), signal information, and the time the network was spotted. You can even hook up a GPS unit to your laptop and capture an AP's coordinates. NetStumbler is best known as a tool for *war drivers*, people who drive, walk, or bike through an area, searching for wi-fi networks. But NetStumbler can be a useful tool for anyone who needs to manage multiple APs or who wants to keep a record of network signal strength and noise. NetStumbler creates a real-time graph as it scans (Figure 13.2).

MacStumbler (http://homepage.mac.com/macstumbler) is a Macintosh NetStumbler clone. Try Kismet (http://www.kismetwireless.net) if you're a Linux user

Packet Analysis

As you learned in Chapters 1 and 2, wi-fi has many similarities to wired technologies, like Ethernet. Although the physical and data-link layers specified for wi-fi contain different sublayers than Ethernet, the relationship between these low layers and the upper layers, where network protocols like TCP/IP and AppleTalk operate, are the same. Network analysis begins with packet analysis. You can use a network sniffer to capture and analyze packets as they move across the network. Errors in the packets themselves or excessive amounts of a certain kind of traffic can indicate the network isn't working properly. Packet analysis can also be used to investigate potential network attacks or suspicious access attempts. At a higher level, packet analyzers can track the use of transport and other higher-level protocols on the network.

Figure I3.2
NetStumbler can display the strength of a network signal over time.

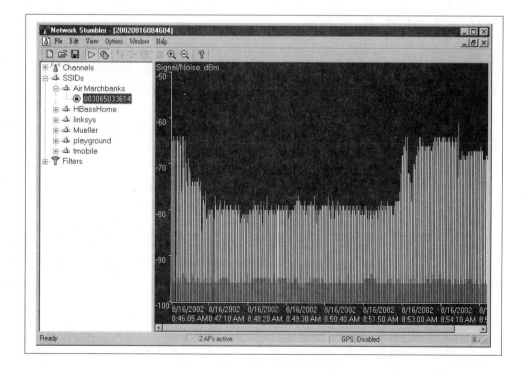

Like Ethernet, wi-fi packets come in three types: data, control, and network management. Wi-fi and Ethernet part company when it comes to the structure of these packets. Wi-fi packets include long PLCP and MAC headers to accommodate RF and mobility-related information.

Analyzing the three kinds of network packets and their headers provides considerable information that can be used to diagnose problems. Control packets, for example, provide a useful window into wireless transmission patterns and quality of transactions. RTS, CTS, and ACK (send, receive, and acknowledge) are all types of control packets transferred as part of every data transaction. Errors in these packets could indicate a problem with communication between wi-fi radios. Management packets negotiate the relationship between devices on a network, including association with APs, authentication, and synchronization. Analyzing these packets might help detect problems in a large ESS where devices are having trouble communicating with APs or other stations. Finally, data packet analysis, which provides access to all the information being transmitted, can be used to identify the source of hacking attempts. Such analysis doesn't detect intruders, but it can be used to flag failed attempts to gain access to the network. Of course, sniffing out data packets can also provide unauthorized access to information. The capability to sniff a network's data packets is among the most important reason for multilayer security measures that encrypt the data and make the network itself inaccessible to unwanted guests.

Packet Analysis Software

Because of the unique packet types found in wi-fi, Ethernet analysis software isn't effective, even if you're primarily interested in higher-level protocols. On the most basic level, the software must be compatible with the wi-fi network adapter (and its chipset) being used in its host computer. The software must also be able to read and interpret wireless packet structure.

Several commercial and open-source analyzers are available. WildPackets, makers of analyzers for Ethernet and other protocols, sells two flavors of AiroPeek. Both are packet analyzers that cost from $2,500 to $3,500. You can download demos from http://www.wildpackets.com. Network Associates' (http://www.sniffer.com) Sniffer Wireless is another option. Ethereal (http://www.ethereal.com) is an open-source packet analyzer. Ethereal works with many UNIX variants and a Windows version is also available.

Appendix A

Glossary

Access Point   An access point (AP) manages communication between wi-fi devices that are connected in infrastructure mode. APs can be used to provide support for a local network and a connection to the Internet.

Ad-Hoc Mode   A wi-fi network that doesn't include an access point is referred to as an ad-hoc network. Devices must be configured to communicate in ad-hoc mode in order to join the network. An ad-hoc network is also sometimes referred to as a *peer-to-peer* network or an Independent Basic Service Set (IBSS).

Antenna Diversity   Adding a second antenna in the vicinity of an access point to boost signals is known as antenna diversity.

Basic Service Set   A wi-fi network containing a single access point and client devices is a Basic Service Set (BSS).

Bluetooth   This is a radio-based wireless standard best suited to short-range communication (less than 50 feet) among a computer, peripherals, and hand-held devices.

Bridge   A network bridge joins two segments of the same network. Access points act as bridges between the wired and wireless segments of a network. Another kind of bridge is the wireless bridge, which is used in pairs to join wired network segments.

Channel   The frequency band in which a wi-fi network operates is divided into a number of channels. In 802.11b, all communication among computers connected to a particular access point takes place on a single channel.

Client   This is a network device that's fully or partially dependent on some sort of server. In a wi-fi network, a client is a computer, PDA, or other device that communicates with the network through an access point. Clients are also referred to as stations.

CSMA/CA   Wi-fi devices use carrier sense multiple access with collision avoidance (CSMA/CA) to negotiate communication between devices. Where Ethernet uses collision detection to "get over" collisions on the network, wi-fi's collision avoidance won't allow transmissions to be completed if a collision occurs.

DHCP   The Dynamic Host Configuration Protocol makes it possible for devices on a network to obtain an IP address when they join the network.

Driver   All devices connected to, or installed in, a computer require driver software to identify the device to the host. Wi-fi driver software for several versions of Microsoft Windows is usually provided by network adapter vendors. Linux and Mac users sometimes obtain drivers from the card vendor or they might need to acquire them from other sources.

DSSS   Direct Sequence Spread Spectrum is the frequency modulation technique specified in the original 802.11 specification and used (in its high-rate version) by 802.11b.

ESS   An Extended Service Set consists of multiple BSS networks joined together to allow roaming among them. Devices that have access to an ESS can remain connected to the network as long as they're within range of at least one of the ESS's access points.

FHSS   Frequency hopping spread spectrum is the second frequency modulation standard provided in the 802.11 specification. FHSS isn't used by any current 802.11 implementations, although Bluetooth does use it.

Firewall   A firewall protects a local network from intruders by preventing access to a computer or network. Firewalls provide different types and levels of protection, including blocking the ports used by Internet applications to connect to other computers, excluding traffic based on its origin, and analyzing and rebuffing intrusion attempts based on suspicious access patterns. Most access points include a firewall. You can configure most firewalls to allow some access to specific portions of your network or to deny all outside access.

HiperLAN/2   HiperLAN/2 is a wireless networking standard operating in the 5 GHz frequency band. It shares many operational similarities with IEEE 802.11 specs. HiperLAN/2 has gained a great deal of momentum in Europe, but isn't widely known in the United States.

HomeRF Promoted by Intel (among others), HomeRF is a 2.4 GHz wireless networking standard originally intended to become the standard for networking in residential environments. IEEE 802.11b overtook HomeRF in the marketplace and Intel has switched its support from HomeRF to 802.11.

IBSS An ad-hoc network is also called an Independent Basic Service Set.

IEEE 802.11 The Institute of Electrical and Electronics Engineers (IEEE) is an organization devoted to creation of a variety of computer standards. The IEEE's standards are designated by numbers. IEEE 802.11 is a group of wireless networking standards characterized by the use of the radio spectrum. 802.11 standards follow rules established by the IEEE that govern a variety of networking standards. This larger group of standards is designated by 802.

IEEE 802.11a This is a high-speed, radio-based standard operating in the 5 GHz frequency band. IEEE 802.11a uses Orthogonal Frequency Division Multiplexing (OFDM) frequency modulation and has a top speed of 54 Mbps.

IEEE 802.11b The current leader among IEEE 802.11-based networking standards, 802.11b operates in the 2.4 GHz radio frequency spectrum at 11 Mbps.

IEEE 802.11e The 802.11e standard provides quality of service to 802.11 networks. QoS, as it's known in the parlance of network management professionals, gives some data packets priority over other packets. QoS is considered critical to make 802.11 a robust standard, suitable for use as a medium for voice and data communication, as well as multimedia.

IEEE802.11g The most recent of the 802.11 standards, 802.11g operates in the same 2.4 GHz band as 802.11b. Like 802.11a, 802.11g provides higher data rates (up to 54 Mbps) than 802.11b and uses OFDM spread spectrum technology. Because it uses the 2.4 GHz spectrum, 802.11g networks will probably be backward-compatible with 802.11b. At press time, 802.11g still awaits final approval from the IEEE and no products are yet available.

IEEE 802.11h The IEEE Task Group h is specifically working on a supplement to 802.11a. Making the 5 GHz standard less noisy will give it access to European Union countries, where HiperLAN/2 (also operating in the 5 GHz band) currently has a market advantage.

IEEE 802.11i   Motivated by the documented weaknesses in Wired Equivalent Privacy (WEP), the encryption scheme built into 802.11, the IEEE is developing a new security method to replace it. Currently called Temporal Key Integrity Protocol (TKIP), the proposal being reviewed by Task Group i will probably boast longer encryption keys that change over time for enhanced security, rather than the permanent, relatively short keys that WEP uses.

IEEE 802.1x   The 802.1x security standard provides a method for authenticating users who want to access a network. This standard isn't specific to wi-fi networks, but has been heralded as a solution to the security flaws in WEP. This is because the 802.1x security standard is both more secure and offers server-based authentication, which WEP doesn't.

Infrastructure Mode   Wi-fi devices that communicate using an access point operate in infrastructure mode. The alternative is ad-hoc mode, in which no access point is part of the network.

IP   Internet Protocol is the protocol used by all Internet applications. IP is also the most commonly used protocol for LANs and WANs. All wi-fi devices support IP.

IPSec   Internet security protocol is among the most common protocols used to build virtual private networks (VPNs). IPSec uses public key encryption to scramble the contents of data and header packets as they're transmitted, and then creates a secure path, using either a tunneling or transport protocol. Many access points support IPSec passthrough, meaning that someone on a wi-fi network can use a VPN to connect to a network also using IPSec.

LAN   A local area network consists of all devices physically connected (whether wired or wireless) in a single location. LAN segments can be used to connect portions of the network within the same local area, but all devices are said to be part of a single LAN.

NAT   Network Address Translation allows a network of computers using private IP addresses to communicate with the Internet and other networks by sharing a single, public IP address. In wi-fi networks, an access point that provides NAT makes it possible to share an Internet connection with all devices that use the AP's DHCP server to obtain addresses. NAT also enables the creation of a firewall for the network and disguises the IP address of client machines on the network.

OFDM   Orthogonal Frequency Division Multiplexing is a spread-spectrum frequency-modulation method used by 802.11a.

OSI Model   The Open Systems Interconnect model of network hierarchy represents the structure of network protocols as a series of vertical layers, from the physical layer at the bottom to the application layer at the top. Wi-fi networks operate at the physical and link layers of the OSI model.

Packets   Information transmitted over a network above layer 2 (the MAC layer) is organized into packets. (Within layers 1 and 2, the units are called frames.) Some packets contain the data being transmitted between devices, while others include information needed to control and manage the transaction.

RF   Radio frequency is any frequency associated with radio wave propagation.

Roaming   Wireless devices can move between access points that are configured as a single network, without losing a connection to the host network. This is known as roaming.

Sniffer   Network administrators or hackers can use a sniffer to view and intercept network packets as they travel over a wire or over the air. Sniffers can be hardware or software based. They can be set to capture some or all network traffic, and to analyze, either for the purpose of diagnosing network problems or violating the security of the network.

Spread Spectrum   A spread spectrum disperses a radio signal across a number of allocated frequencies within a specified band. All wi-fi devices use one of three spread-spectrum methods to communicate.

SSID   The Service Set Identifier is a string that identifies the network. Ad-hoc and infrastructure networks use SSIDs. Many people think of the SSID as the network name.

VPN   A virtual private network provides a secure channel for communication between a user and a remote network, usually a corporate one. Using standard Internet protocols, along with a secure protocol that manages the authentication process, a VPN prevents data from being intercepted or decoded by a user not authorized to use the private network. Many access points support access to VPNs by passing the specific VPN protocol from the user to the secure network.

WECA   The Wireless Ethernet Compatibility Alliance consists of vendors and others interested in promoting IEEE 802.11 standards. WECA is responsible for the Wi-Fi Certification Program.

WEP   Wired Equivalent Privacy is a security mechanism that encrypts data as it travels over a wireless link. WEP is specified within the IEEE 802.11 standard. WEP encryption has been rendered less useful because the algorithm that keeps encryption keys secret has been cracked and keys can easily be acquired by crackers.

Wi-Fi   WECA adapted the term "wireless fidelity" (wi-fi) to refer to products certified compliant not only with the IEEE 802.11 standard, but also with its own testing regime. Wi-fi certification currently applies to 802.11b and 802.11a products. Wi-fi certification is expected to be applied to 802.11g and future implementations as they become available.

Appendix B

Wi-Fi Resources

Ad-Hoc and Mesh Networking

Archipelago Project	http://www.cnds.jhu.edu/research/networks/archipelago
Mobile Ad-Hoc Networking Protocol	http://www.ietf.org/html.charters/manet-charter.html
Mobile IP	http://www.computer.org/internet/v2n1/mobile.htm
WiFind	http://www.wi-find.com/index2.html

Antenna-Related Information

How to Build a Tin Can Waveguide Antenna	http://www.turnpoint.net/wireless/cantennahowto.html
`LMR Cable Chart	http://www.cepainc.com/LMR%20Cables.htm
Outdoor Antenna/Access Point HowTo	http://www.nycwireless.net/articles/enclosure/index.html
Pigtail FAQ (Seattle Wireless)	http://www.seattlewireless.net/index.cgi/PigTail
Yagi Antenna Design	http://www.netscum.com/~clapp/wireless.html

Antenna Equipment

Allcom	http://www.allcompc.com
Antenna Systems	http://www.antennasystems.com/broadband.html
BaProducts (connectors)	http://www.baproducts.com/rf-conn.htm#ntype
Envirocon Antenna Masts	http://www.envirocom.co.za/products.htm
Hyperlink	http://www.hyperlinktech.com/web/antennas_2400.php
Maxrad	http://www.maxrad.com
NetNimble	http://www.netnimble.net
Pacific Wireless	http://www.pacwireless.com/html/ant_quote.htm

Superpass	http://www.superpass.com
Team Electro	http://www.teamelectro-comm.com/shopping/ (search for "2.4 GHz antenna")
Teletronics	http://www.teletronics.com/tii/products/products.html
Telex Wireless	http://www.telexwireless.com

Broadband Connectivity

Broadband Reports	http://www.dslreports.com
CableModemHelp	http://www.cablemodemhelp.com
CableModemInfo	http://www.cablemodeminfo.com/index.html-ssi
CableSense	http://www.cablesense.com
DSL/Cable Web Server	http://www.dslwebserver.com
xDSL Technology	http://www.tuketu.com/dsl/xdsl.htm

Community Wireless Projects and Information

Ashland Unwired	http://www.ashlandunwired.com
Austin Wireless User's Group	http://austinwireless.net
Bay Area Wireless User Group	http://www.bawug.org
Champaign-Urbana Grassroots Wireless Internet Project	http://wireless.ucimc.org
Electronic Frontier Foundation Wireless-Friendly ISP List	http://www.eff.org/Infra/Wireless_cellular_radio/wireless_friendly_isp_list.html
FreeNetworks.Org	http://freenetworks.org
HoustonWireless	http://www.houstonwireless.org/cgi-bin/wiki.pl
NoCatNet (Sonoma County, CA)	http://nocat.net
NYCWireless	http://www.nycwireless.net
PDXWireless (Portland, OR)	http://www.pdxwireless.org
Personal Telco (Portland, OR)	http://www.personaltelco.net/index.cgi/FrontPage
Rooftops	http://rooftops.media.mit.edu
SBay Wireless (Silicon Valley, CA)	http://www.sbay.org/wireless-net.htm
SeattleWireless	http://www.seattlewireless.net

Equipment Retailers (APs and Network Adapters)

Wireless Central	http://www.wirelesscentral.net

Equipment Vendors (APs and Network Adapters)

3Com	http://www.3com.com
Apple Computer	http://www.info.apple.com/usen/airport/Buffalo
Asante	http://www.asante.com
Cisco	http://www.cisco.com
Compaq	http://www.compaq.com/products/wireless/wlan
D-Link	http://www.dlink.com
Enterasys	http://www.enterasys.com/roamabout
Intel	http://www.intel.com/wireless/lan
Linksys	http://www.linksys.com
NetGear	http://www.netgear.com
Nokia	http://www.nokia.com/corporate/wlan
Proxim	http://www.proxim.com
SMC	http://www.smc.com
Symbol	http://www.symbol.com/products/wireless/wireless.html
Zoom	http://www.zoom.com/zoomair/index.html

Linux and Wi-Fi

AbsoluteValue Systems	http://www.linux-wlan.com/linux-wlan
Host AP Driver for the Prism-2 Chipset	http://hostap.epitest.fi
Linux Driver Page	http://www.hpl.hp.com/personal/Jean_Tourrilhes/Linux/Linux.Wireless.drivers.html
Linux PCMCIA Information Page	http://pcmcia-cs.sourceforge.net
Running Linux on the AirPort Base Station	http://www-hft.ee.tu-berlin.de/~strauman/airport/airport.html
Wireless LAN Resources for Linux	http://www.hpl.hp.com/personal/Jean_Tourrilhes/Linux

Macintosh and Wi-Fi

AirPort Utilities	http://gicl.mcs.drexel.edu/people/sevy/airport
IOXperts Wi-Fi Driver	http://www.ioxperts.com/80211b.html
MacWindows Cross-Platform AirPort Wireless Networks	http://www.macwindows.com/airportpc.html
An Unofficial AirPort Site	http://www.vonwentzel.net/ABS/index.html
WirelessDriver for OS X	http://homepage.mac.com/robm

Mailing Lists

BAWUG	http://www.bawug.org/communicate
SecureWLAN	http://groups.yahoo.com/group/SecureWLANs
WirelessLAN	http://groups.yahoo.com/group/wirelesslan/?yguid=72564750

News, Tutorials, and Reviews

802.11 Planet	http://www.80211-planet.com
Alan Reiter's Wireless Data Web Log	http://reiter.weblogger.com
Focus on Wireless Broadband Internet Access	http://www.strohpub.com/focus.htm
Glenn Fleshman's Wireless Web Log	http://80211b.weblogger.com
Mostly Harmless	http://wireless.mostlyharmless.dk
NetworkWorld's Wireless in the Enterprise Newsletter	http://www.nwfusion.com/newsletters/wireless/index.html
Practically Networked	http://www.practicallynetworked.com
Sifry's Alerts	http://www.sifry.com/alerts
Small NetBuilder	http://www.smallnetbuilder.com
Wireless Developer Network	http://www.wirelessdevnet.com
Wireless Week	http://www.wirelessweek.com

Organizations

WECA	http://www.wi-fi.org
WLANA	http://www.wlana.com

Security

SecurityGeeks	http://securitygeeks.shmoo.com
Unofficial 802.11 Security Web Page	http://www.drizzle.com/~aboba/IEEE/
Wireless Security Vulnerabilities	http://www.cs.umd.edu/~waa/wireless.html

Software

AirSnort	http://airsnort.shmoo.com
APScan for Mac OS X	http://www.mxinternet.net/~markw
CKrellm	http://gkrellm.luon.net/gkrellmwireless.phtml
Ethereal Protocol Analyzer	http://www.Ethereal.com
FreeBase AirPort Configuration for Windows	http://freebase.sourceforge.net
Interactive Network Wireless Design Utilities	http://www.ecommwireless.com/calculations.html
Kismet	http://www.kismetwireless.net
MacStumbler	http://homepage.mac.com/macstumbler
NetStumbler	http://www.netstumbler.com
Network Associates (Sniffer Wireless)	http://www.sniffer.com/products/wireless/default.asp?A=5
WildPackets	http://www.wildpackets.com

Standards, Regulations, and Technology

IEEE 802.11 Working Group	http://www.ieee802.org/11
FCC Part 15	http://www.access.gpo.gov/nara/cfr/waisidx_00/47cfr15_00.html
PCC Part 15 Papers	http://www.lns.com/papers/part15

Windows and Wi-Fi

Microsoft Wireless Resources	http://www.microsoft.com/windows2000/technologies/communications/wifi/default.asp

Index

INTERNATIONAL CONTACT INFORMATION

AUSTRALIA
McGraw-Hill Book Company Australia Pty. Ltd.
TEL +61-2-9900-1800
FAX +61-2-9878-8881
http://www.mcgraw-hill.com.au
books-it_sydney@mcgraw-hill.com

CANADA
McGraw-Hill Ryerson Ltd.
TEL +905-430-5000
FAX +905-430-5020
http://www.mcgraw-hill.ca

**GREECE, MIDDLE EAST, & AFRICA
(Excluding South Africa)**
McGraw-Hill Hellas
TEL +30-1-656-0990-3-4
FAX +30-1-654-5525

MEXICO (Also serving Latin America)
McGraw-Hill Interamericana Editores S.A. de C.V.
TEL +525-117-1583
FAX +525-117-1589
http://www.mcgraw-hill.com.mx
fernando_castellanos@mcgraw-hill.com

SINGAPORE (Serving Asia)
McGraw-Hill Book Company
TEL +65-863-1580
FAX +65-862-3354
http://www.mcgraw-hill.com.sg
mghasia@mcgraw-hill.com

SOUTH AFRICA
McGraw-Hill South Africa
TEL +27-11-622-7512
FAX +27-11-622-9045
robyn_swanepoel@mcgraw-hill.com

SPAIN
McGraw-Hill/Interamericana de España, S.A.U.
TEL +34-91-180-3000
FAX +34-91-372-8513
http://www.mcgraw-hill.es
professional@mcgraw-hill.es

**UNITED KINGDOM, NORTHERN,
EASTERN, & CENTRAL EUROPE**
McGraw-Hill Education Europe
TEL +44-1-628-502500
FAX +44-1-628-770224
http://www.mcgraw-hill.co.uk
computing_neurope@mcgraw-hill.com

ALL OTHER INQUIRIES Contact:
Osborne/McGraw-Hill
TEL +1-510-549-6600
FAX +1-510-883-7600
http://www.osborne.com
omg_international@mcgraw-hill.com